Soc Sci £3.00 24/24 RM

British Women's Histories of the First World War

This lively collection of essays showcases recent research into the impact of the conflict on British women during the First World War and since.

Looking outside of the familiar representations of wartime women as nurses, munitionettes, and land girls, it introduces the reader to lesser-known aspects of women's war experience, including female composers' musical responses to the war, changes in the culture of women's mourning dress, and the complex relationships between war, motherhood, and politics. Written during the war's centenary, the chapters also consider the gendered nature of war memory in Britain, exploring the emotional legacies of the conflict today, and the place of women's wartime stories on the contemporary stage.

The collection brings together work by emerging and established scholars contributing to the shared project of rewriting British women's history of the First World War. It is an essential text for anyone researching or studying this history. This book was originally published as a special issue of *Women's History Review*.

Maggie Andrews is Professor of Cultural History at the University of Worcester, UK. Her research and publications explore domesticity and femininity in twentieth century Britain with a particular focus on the Home Front in both the First and Second World Wars, including *The Home Front in Britain: Images, Myths and Forgotten Experiences since 1914* (edited with Janis Lomas, 2014).

Alison Fell is Professor of French Cultural History at the University of Leeds, UK. She has published widely on British and French women's responses to, and experiences in, the First World War, including *Women as Veterans in Britain and France after the First World War* (2018).

Lucy Noakes is the Rab Butler Professor of Modern History at the University of Essex, UK. She researches and publishes in the fields of war, gender, memory, and national identity, with a particular interest in twentieth century Britain.

June Purvis is Professor Emerita of Women's and Gender History at the University of Portsmouth, UK. She has published widely on women's education in nineteenth century Britain, and especially on the suffragette movement in Edwardian Britain, including the acclaimed *Emmeline Pankhurst: a biography* (2002), and *Christabel Pankhurst: a biography* (2018).

British Women's Histories of the First World War

Representing, Remembering, Rewriting

Edited by
Maggie Andrews, Alison Fell, Lucy Noakes and June Purvis

Routledge
Taylor & Francis Group

LONDON AND NEW YORK

First published 2020
by Routledge
2 Park Square, Milton Park, Abingdon, Oxon, OX14 4RN

and by Routledge
52 Vanderbilt Avenue, New York, NY 10017

Routledge is an imprint of the Taylor & Francis Group, an informa business

Chapters 1–5, 7–9 © 2020 Taylor & Francis

Chapter 6 © 2017 Lucie Whitmore. Originally published as Open Access. This work was funded by the Arts and Humanities Research Council and supported by the University of Glasgow.

British Library Cataloguing in Publication Data
A catalogue record for this book is available from the British Library

ISBN13: 978-0-367-33320-1

Typeset in Minion Pro
by Newgen Publishing UK

Publisher's Note
The publisher accepts responsibility for any inconsistencies that may have arisen during the conversion of this book from journal articles to book chapters, namely the inclusion of journal terminology.

Disclaimer
Every effort has been made to contact copyright holders for their permission to reprint material in this book. The publishers would be grateful to hear from any copyright holder who is not here acknowledged and will undertake to rectify any errors or omissions in future editions of this book.

Printed in the United Kingdom
by Henry Ling Limited

Contents

Citation Information

The chapters in this book were originally published in *Women's History Review*, volume 27, issue 4 (July 2018). When citing this material, please use the original page numbering for each article, as follows:

Chapter 1

Representing, Remembering and Rewriting Women's Histories of the First World War
Maggie Andrews, Alison Fell, Lucy Noakes and June Purvis
Women's History Review, volume 27, issue 4 (July 2018) pp. 511–515

Chapter 2

The Carer, the Combatant and the Clandestine: images of women in the First World War in War Illustrated *magazine*
Jonathan Rayner
Women's History Review, volume 27, issue 4 (July 2018) pp. 516–533

Chapter 3

Suffragettes and the Scottish Press during the First World War
Sarah Pedersen
Women's History Review, volume 27, issue 4 (July 2018) pp. 534–550

Chapter 4

Antimilitarism, Citizenship and Motherhood: the formation and early years of the Women's International League (WIL), 1915–1919
Sarah Hellawell
Women's History Review, volume 27, issue 4 (July 2018) pp. 551–564

Chapter 5

'Giddy Girls', 'Scandalous Statements' and a 'Burst Bubble': the war babies panic of 1914–1915
Catherine Lee
Women's History Review, volume 27, issue 4 (July 2018) pp. 565–578

For any permission-related enquiries please visit:
www.tandfonline.com/page/help/permissions

Notes on Contributors

Maggie Andrews is Professor of Cultural History at the University of Worcester, UK. Her research and publications explore domesticity and femininity in twentieth century Britain with a particular focus on the Home Front in both the First and Second World Wars.

Alison Fell is Professor of French Cultural History at the University of Leeds, UK. She has published widely on British and French women's responses to, and experiences in, the First World War.

Sarah Hellawell is a Lecturer in Modern British History at the University of Sunderland, UK. She is currently researching the formation and early years of the British Women's International League.

Catherine Lee is Associate Lecturer and Honorary Associate in History at the Open University, UK. Her recent research interests include the 'war baby' moral panic of 1914/15.

Lucy Noakes is the Rab Butler Professor of Modern History at the University of Essex, UK. She researches and publishes in the fields of war, gender, memory, and national identity, with a particular interest in twentieth century Britain.

Sarah Pedersen is Professor of Communication and Media at the School of Creative and Cultural Business at Robert Gordon University, UK. Her research focuses on women's use of the media in both contemporary and historical contexts.

Amanda Phipps is an Honorary Research Fellow in the History Department at the University of Exeter, UK. Her PhD thesis examined the beginning of the centenary of the First World War with a particular focus on contemporary performances of the conflict and its position in British history education.

June Purvis is Professor Emerita of Women's and Gender History at the University of Portsmouth, UK. She has published widely on women's education in nineteenth century Britain, and especially on the suffragette movement in Edwardian Britain.

Jonathan Rayner is a Professor of Film Studies in the School of English at the University of Sheffield, UK. His research interests include representations of naval and war history in popular culture, the relationships between cinema and landscape, genre films, auteur studies, and Australasian cinema.

Laura Seddon is a Tutor in the School of Languages and Area Studies at the University of Portsmouth, UK, and is Director of Contemporary Connections, an arts production organisation who commission contemporary music by women in response to historical musicological research.

Lucie Whitmore is a Fashion Curator at the Museum of London, UK. She has given papers on mourning dress and other elements of First World War fashion at a number of national and international conferences.

1 Introduction – Representing, Remembering and Rewriting Women's Histories of the First World War

Maggie Andrews, Alison Fell, Lucy Noakes and June Purvis

As Dan Todman has persuasively argued, in the British popular imagination the First World War is associated with mud, barbed wire, the trenches and the Tommy on the Western Front.[1] Perhaps inevitably, therefore, public commemoration of the war has often been dominated by a focus on the men in the armed forces, who risked or lost their lives for causes that at the time may or may not have seemed heroic, noble or simply unavoidable. The visual spectacle of Paul Cummins' 'Blood Swept Lands and Seas of Red', the art installation at the Tower of London in which 888,246 ceramic poppies filled the moat from 17 July to 11 November 2014, was the most visited artistic response to the war in its centenary years, while Jeremy Deller's 'We're Here Because We're Here', commemorating the first day of the Battle of the Somme, provided a widely seen and moving memorial to the victims.[2] This vision of the conflict, focusing exclusively on the combatant dead, should not, however, become the only history of the conflict. There are, as the research brought together here demonstrates, multiple histories of the First World War.

Where women have been included in centenary commemorations, certain women feature more than others. This selectivity in the representation of women occurred during the First World War itself, and since the conflict has been reproduced in museums and by heritage sites. It has provided a lexicon of images, impressions, roles and portrayals of women which still tend to shape the histories of women and the conflict. The Imperial War Museum's project *Lives of the First World War*, for example, has pulled together the life stories of over eight million men and women from across Britain and the Commonwealth who served in uniform and worked on the Home Front during the First World War. However, its narrow definition of service as paid work outside the home has re-enforced the tendency to reproduce iconic images of nurses, munitionettes and landgirls.

The articles in this Special Issue are drawn from papers presented at the 'Women, Gender and the First World War: Home Fronts and War Fronts' conference held at the University of Portsmouth in October 2015.[3] The articles are by both established and newly emerging scholars, but all build upon the work of a number of historians who, in recent years have resisted any simplistic framing of the debates about women and war. They do not, then, stake a claim for women's importance in the histories of the war by presenting them as heroic 'female Tommies', or by seeing war as an agent of positive change for women's position in society, a perspective articulated by Arthur Marwick over fifty years ago.[4] Rather, the articles presented here are in the tradition of historians such as Susan Grayzel,[5] Christine Hallett,[6] Deborah Thom,[7] Joanna Bourke,[8] Susan Pedersen,[9] Karen Hunt,[10] Susan Kingsley Kent,[11] Nicoletta Gullace[12] and Janet Watson,[13] who have sought to stretch, challenge, expand and rework histories of the First World War. Building on this historiography, they place women's histories and questions about gender more centrally in our understanding of the conflict. Gender, class, age, and the social, cultural and economic specificity of the different localities in which British women lived, shaped the impact of the First World War on their lives. The articles in this Special Issue demonstrate that women's involvements in this first industrialized, mechanized total war was experienced, represented and remembered in the minutiae of practices, cultural interactions and emotions of their everyday lives in families or communities. Thus their choice of mourning dress, the music they listened to, the moral panics around their behaviour and the magazines in which they were portrayed are revealed to be an important part of the history of the First World War, complementing the history of soldiers on the battlefield.

The critical approach of Jonathan Rayner's article 'The Carer, the Combatant and the Clandestine', exploring the representation of women in *War Illustrated* magazine, is a welcome contribution to contemporary scholarship. He draws our attention to how central images of female civilians in Europe were to British narratives of German atrocities. Further, he illuminates the complex representation of female nurses, who were portrayed both as vulnerable carers and potential victims whilst paradoxically as active heroines, involved in activities that could be viewed as transgressive in gender terms. Sarah Pedersen's article 'Suffragettes and the Scottish Press during the First World War' also focuses on the representation of women during the conflict in print media. In doing so it unpicks the myth that all suffragettes suspended lobbying and campaigning in order to support the war effort and explores some of their more complex and varied responses. The continuing lobbying of the British section of the Women's International League for the franchise discussed in Sarah Hellawell's article 'Antimilitarism, Citizenship and Motherhood: the formation and early years of the Women's International League (WIL), 1915–1919' re-enforces this point.

Hellawell's article also reveals the extent to which the First World War amplified the growing preoccupation of social welfare and medical reformers with motherhood.[14] She explains how the WIL drew upon social and cultural experiences of motherhood both to challenge and to build bridges between women of enemy nations and to add weight to women's demands for citizenship. Alternatively, Catherine Lee's '"Giddy Girls", "Scandalous Statements" and a "Burst Bubble": the war babies panic of 1914–15' interrogates the moral panic around the babies that it was alleged were likely to be born to unmarried young women and girls in the months that followed men's 'rush to the colours' and subsequent departure to the Western Front in the early months of the war. By demonstrating that it was particularly young working-class women who were believed to be vulnerable to 'khaki fever', Lee shows how existing beliefs and prejudices could be refocused by wartime conditions.

Practices of everyday life and the cultural production of the era also significantly or subtly evolved as the influence and impact of the war rippled out into music, theatre, and fashion. Ideas of appropriate emotional responses, displays of feelings and intimate actions could be stretched and reimagined. Lucie Whitmore, in her article 'A Matter of Individual Opinion and Feeling' addresses the changes that took place within the culture of mourning dress between 1914 and 1918. She considers how attitudes towards death and the rituals associated with bereavement were altered by the conflict. The numbers of younger war widows, for example, changed what was considered appropriate dress, and women's magazines bear witness to the extent to which women's mourning practices were shifting in response to the hundreds of thousands of war deaths. Laura Seddon, in 'Gendered Musical Responses to First World War Experiences' investigates how women composers responded to the conflict in 1915 and 1916. She suggests that this music, largely neglected by critics and historians, contributes to a re-evaluation of how women composers experienced the cultural impacts of the war.

Who is remembered and how they are remembered, whether at a national level or at an individual, family or community level, is the result of a complex interplay of different forces. Lucy Noakes's article 'My husband is interested in war generally' explores the emotional legacies of total war, drawing on a 2014 Mass Observation Directive which asked its panellists to reflect on their feelings about the war. Many of them, men and women, focused on the ways the war had negatively impacted on their families, leaving women widowed, children fatherless and returning men physically and mentally scarred. She points out that older women often had a personal memory of the lived legacies, and felt a responsibility to pass on the 'lessons' of war to a younger generation who, they feared, had little or no sense of the horrors of warfare. Finally, Amanda Phipps also addresses questions around contemporary memories of the war in her article 'What the Women Did: remembering or reducing women of the First World War on the contemporary British stage'. Here, she considers a trio of wartime plays revived by Two's Company at the Southwark Playhouse in 2014. Unlike many recent productions that focused on the soldier's story, these theatrical performances brought a wider range of women's stories to life by revealing their failings, suffering and ambivalence towards men. However, the fact that they were low-budget and small-scale also demonstrates the competitive and commodified nature of remembrance that dictates which stories are kept alive in the twenty-first century.

The articles published here are only a small sample of the papers discussed at the conference but they have been chosen to reflect something of the diversity of topics that were explored. There are of course many gaps in a publication that focuses upon only one country, and within Britain there are many geographical areas which have been omitted. The aim is not to offer a complete or necessarily a representative portrayal of contemporary scholarship on British women's relationship with the First World War, but to make a contribution to what is an ongoing and evolving process of rewriting British women's histories of the conflict. We hope the material here will stimulate debate, discussion and further scholarship.

Notes

1. Dan Todman (2005) *The Great War: myth and memory* (London: Bloomsbury).
2. 'We're here because we're here' marked the centenary of the first day of the Battle of the Somme. Hundreds of volunteers, working with the artist Jeremy Deller, Birmingham

Repertory Theatre, the National Theatre and 1914–18 NOW, commemorated the centenary by re-enacting as soldiers in cities, towns and the countryside around Britain. First World War soldiers were seen at train stations, shopping centres, beaches, car parks and high streets. For further details see: https://becausewearehere.co.uk/
3. The conference was organized by June Purvis with financial support from Women's History Network Southern, the Centre for European and International Studies Research Centre (CEISR) at the University of Portsmouth, and the AHRC funded Gateways to the First World War public engagement centre, based at the University of Kent, of which Brad Beavan, the University of Portsmouth, is a key member.
4. Arthur Marwick (1968) *Britain in the Century of Total War: war, peace, and social change, 1900–1967* (London: Little, Brown) and (1991) *The Deluge: British society and the First World War* (Houndmills: Macmillan).
5. Susan R. Grayzel (1999) *Women's Identities at War: gender, motherhood, and politics in Britain and France during the First World War* (Chapel Hill: University of North Carolina Press).
6. Christine E. Hallett (2009) *Containing Trauma: nursing work in the First World War* (Manchester: Manchester University Press).
7. Deborah Thom (1998) *Nice Girls and Rude Girls: women workers in World War 1* (London: I.B. Tauris).
8. Joanna Bourke (1996) *Dismembering the Male: men's bodies, Britain, and the Great War* (Chicago: University of Chicago Press).
9. Susan Pedersen (1995) *Family, Dependence, and the Origins of the Welfare State: Britain and France, 1914–1945* (Cambridge: Cambridge University Press).
10. Karen Hunt (2010) The Politics of Food and Women's Neighborhood Activism in First World War Britain, *International Labor and Working-Class History*, 77(1), pp. 8–26.
11. Susan Kingsley Kent (1988) The Politics of Sexual Difference: World War I and the demise of British feminism, *The Journal of British Studies*, 27(3), pp. 232–253.
12. Nicoletta Gullace (2002) *The 'Blood of Our Sons': men, women and the renegotiation of British citizenship during the Great War* (Basingstoke: Palgrave).
13. Janet Watson (2004) *Fighting Different Wars: experience, memory and the First World War in Britain* (Cambridge University Press)
14. Grayzel, *Women's Identities at War*; Anna Davin (1978) Imperialism and Motherhood, *History Workshop Journal*, April, pp. 9–65.

Disclosure statement

No potential conflict of interest was reported by the authors.

2 The Carer, the Combatant and the Clandestine

Images of women in the First World War in *War Illustrated* magazine

Jonathan Rayner

ABSTRACT

This essay examines the representation of women in *War Illustrated* magazine. Images of female civilians in Europe are central to narratives of German atrocities, while depictions of British women engaging in new occupations are key to the propagation of concepts of national unity. Women engaged in front-line nursing occupy a fluctuating status as vulnerable, potential victims and valiant pseudo-combatants. Female endeavours are celebrated in certain gender-specific roles (e.g. nursing, recruitment and charity work), while other occupations (spying, uniformed service and engaging in combat), are represented in paradoxical terms as responsible and heroic, or dangerous, transgressive activities. Within the magazine, images of women reinforce specific propagandist discourses, giving prominence to yet also problematising women's contributions to the conflict.

Introduction

> Women's war history was, and often still is, overlaid with myth. They have their own stereo-typical roles to fill. There is scope for them to be seen as victims, villains or heroines [...] The increasing interest over time in 'the woman worker' reflects a general shift towards those who did something *different* as a result of war, and in someway [sic] challenged the existing social order.[1]

This essay examines the reporting and visual representation of women in Britain and throughout Europe during the First World War in the weekly magazine *The War Illustrated*. *War Illustrated* was a popular pictorial record of the conflict, incorporating numerous maps, photographs and illustrations, and the work of war artists alongside weekly reporting and editorials on the conduct, events and consequences of the global conflict. Its articles included regular columns and commissioned contributions from notable figures such as Sidney Low, H.G. Wells, Jerome K. Jerome and Fred T. Jane. *War Illustrated* was published in London by William Berry (owner of the *Daily Telegraph*) and first appeared on 22 August 1914. By the end of the First World War, its circulation had risen to three-quarters of a million copies per week.[2] Through most of the conflict the magazine was sold at a price of two pence (2d.), increasing to three pence in 1918. At a time when daily newspapers sold for a penny (1d.) this cover price, along with the length and vocabulary employed in its articles, implies that its target audience was an adult, middle-class readership. However, its conception as an extensively illustrated, and therefore highly visual and affective, record of the war equally suggests its accessibility to both lower-class and younger readers.

War Illustrated's reporting evolved to incorporate several consistent forms or serials as the war progressed. For example, within the first year weekly columns were added to convey the geographical span and technological change of the conflict, by reporting on the 'War by Land', the 'War by Sea' and eventually the 'War by Air'. The magazine's staples were, nonetheless, concise illustrated reports and summaries accompanying pages of visual representation (either one- or two-page artistic depictions or collections and collages of photographs) used to illuminate and actively interpret recent, important and topical events. In the current study, the magazine's images, captions and reports are analysed in relation to the interconnection of visual representation and verbal articulation of the facts of contemporary events, the influence of political stances, and the imperatives of dominant ideological positions. Interpretative distinctions are drawn between the editor's and writers' choices (aesthetic in terms of the use of photography or art work, linguistic in terms of diction) in the reading of their effects upon the developing representation of the conflict.

Although the frequently evocative and manipulative images permeating the pages of the magazine can be seen to accord consciously with wartime establishment discourses of recruitment, propaganda and commitment to the communal, national purpose, *War Illustrated* is more than simply an unquestioning propaganda organ. Indeed, the magazine's admission of a broad constituency of writers and its incorporation of various categories of visual representation reinforce its palimpsestic and polyphonic form. It can be seen to articulate as much as seek to form public opinion when it expresses concern and criticism for the conduct and leadership of the war (for example in relation to Winston Churchill's responsibility for the disastrous 1915 Gallipoli campaign, and the significance of the inconclusive Battle of Jutland in 1916). In comparison with peer publications (such as the *Illustrated War News* which also appeared throughout the conflict), *War Illustrated* uses similar numbers of photographs but makes significantly greater use of war artists' work and illustrations. While illustrations are often used simply to depict incidents unrecorded in any other fashion, the privileging of vivid and dramatic illustrations is also frequently devoted to propagandist exaggeration or representations of events of doubtful veracity.

While the magazine is certainly capable of demonising the enemy and valorising the successes of Britain and her allies in conventional and predictable fashion, it also admits a spectrum of divergent and controversial opinions. In the case of the treatment of non-combatants such as women and children (whether or not these groups might have constituted or even been recognised as readerships), the magazine's exploration of the conflict as a fundamentally transformative experience both reflects and qualifies contemporary propaganda discourses. Identifying and interpreting the magazine's conscious utilisation or exploitation of female narratives and images (conforming to the pervasive stereotypes of victimhood, villainy and heroism noted by Gail Braybon) must be seen in comparison and contrast to both the recollections and retrospective writing by women exploring their war-time experiences and to the magazine's inclusion of women's personal perspectives and opinions on the conflict, in their own words.[3]

The roles adopted by women during the conflict took many forms in civilian and uniformed contexts, encompassing charitable work, paid employment, volunteer and professional nursing and recruitment to auxiliary military services. Some of the professional and charitable nursing organisations (such as the Queen Alexandra's Imperial Military Nursing Service, the Territorial Force Nursing Service and the First Aid Nursing Yeomanry) which existed before the war had a far lower profile than the Voluntary Aid Detachments (VADs) which included a large proportion of upper- and middle-class female volunteers.[4] By contrast, women occupying forms of employment vacated by men recruited to the armed services, and particularly those women undertaking vital war work in munitions factories, were those from the lower classes who in many cases had already been in paid employment before the war began.[5] Although the female military services (the Women's Auxiliary Army Corps, the Women's Royal Naval Service, and the Women's Royal Air Force) created in 1917 were more varied in their pattern of recruitment from British society, there was widespread criticism of and resistance to the notion and presence of British women in military uniform.[6]

In depicting the roles ascribed to women in wartime propaganda, the tasks impressed upon women by wartime circumstances and the responsibilities shouldered by women under the stimuli of national, political or individual needs, *War Illustrated*'s coverage accommodates the competing if not openly contradictory narratives of female participation in and experience of the war. Within its pages some of the war's overlaying 'myths' (including examples of those surrounding women's involvement) can be seen at their moment of inception. Conversely, the magazine's accommodation of diverse perspectives and its contemporary treatment of still-evolving events mean that unorthodox and oppositional views occasionally occur, in spite of the demands of propaganda. Above all, the magazine's condensation, modification and magnification of contemporary opinion makes it a fertile source for reappraisal and retrospection in the light of the current centenary re-evaluation of the conflict, including reappraisal of the roles and experiences of civilians. As a primary source it is able to reflect the current consciousness (and inform more recent and retrospective revaluation) of the potential 'challenge to social order' represented by women's involvement in and engagement with the conflict. Examining the continuities and developmental changes within *War Illustrated*'s reporting of the roles assumed by women within the conflict, in the representational cross-section considered here, also provides a key contextualisation to understandings of the war's interpretation and narrativisation in other texts and by other commentators.

European War and European Women

Through collating the representation of women (both in images and in print) in *War Illustrated*, the intentions and objectives of propaganda and development of public opinion can be discerned in the publication's reporting. Women appear to be as useful to the achievement of war aims on the basis of their representation in popular culture as they are in uniformed auxiliary service, nursing or war-factory work in actuality. Depictions of women (as spouses and mothers) stoically sending their menfolk off to war, which appear in the magazine in September 1914, epitomise the expected and appropriate sacrificial, supportive attitude to the war inculcated by contemporary propaganda.[7] In these examples the civilian (female) population is shown to be mobilised in terms of sympathy and support rather than in parallel activity alongside the uniformed (male) combatants. Images of women are also used to symbolise civilised, human values understood to be synonymous with the characteristics of national identity. As the victims of war's effects (as the targets of atrocity and sufferers of hardship), European women become a visual justification for British involvement in the continental war in the defence of the putatively universal moral standards and collective humane responsibilities. However, portrayals of women's active involvement in the conflict prove more difficult to accommodate within such prescriptive or pragmatic constructions of gender and nationality. Women's war service, in or out of uniform, their presence in or near the front line, and their participation in actual combat represent difficult and double-edged subjects or images for stable representation and reading. Examples of these categorisations and utilisations of women within *War Illustrated*'s pages reflect the elaboration of their place within the magazine's evolving interpretation of the conflict, balancing propaganda, commentary and acknowledgement of the changing circumstances of British women in its reactive reportage.

The depiction of womanhood as the symbol of a threatened domestic peace, and the image of the vulnerable family standing metaphorically for the beleaguered nation, can be seen in an example from 1915 showing the suffering of civilians in Europe (Figure 1). Juxtaposing the invading German soldiers accused of barbaric behaviour with a scene of destroyed domesticity emblematic of French and Belgian suffering (which the accompanying text describes simply as 'cause and effect'), this page's caption reads:

> What words could tell a more complete story of the tragedy than is depicted by the grass-grown ruins of the little French cottage, the tears of the woman, and the dejection of the peasant who has returned, after months of weary wandering as a refugee, to find his home an empty shell?[8]

Both of these images evince a stilted and posed quality which underlines the problematic nature of the photographic as much as the artistic images employed within the publication. The apparent realism of photographic reproduction belies the artifice with which the images appear to have been produced. The use of illustrations substitutes for the absence of photographic records of many of the events the magazine describes, yet even the photos it does include often appear self-consciously staged, or doctored subsequently for effect. In this instance, the emphasis upon the woman's status as wife and mother, and her observable vulnerability and grief, are mirrored and enhanced by her proximity to the ruined home. A similar example from the same year, describing the 'annihilation of a family' during the flight of refugees in Serbia, uses a war artist's work to illustrate the story of a mother who, after her six children 'fell down one by one to perish by the road side', became 'distracted with grief' and threw rocks at the German lines until she was cut down by a machine gun.[9] Although this story is located specifically in Eastern Europe within one widely reported occurrence of civilian suffering, its exaggerated tone and the vivid, sensationalised full-page illustration exemplify the treatment given to contemporary accounts of German 'frightfulness'.[10] Such stories became associated particularly with the atrocities allegedly committed by German soldiers in the so-called 'Rape of Belgium', which permeated the popular press in the wake of the publication of the Bryce report in 1915.[11]

The plight of vulnerable, feminine Europe was used as one reinforcing justification for British involvement in the conflict, but other depictions from the first half of the war also romanticise the contact between European women and British troops. An illustration from March 1916 (Figure 2) provides a light-hearted representation of an amorous encounter behind the lines between emblematic national figures. The accompanying caption reads:

Figure 1. 22nd May 1915—'The Teutonic Wave and the Wreck it Leaves' (University of Sheffield, Special Collections).

> Not infrequently a fascinating Belgian or French peasant girl will brave the stray shell to bring fodder to the horses, and if Tommy is in the offing a pretty though somewhat incoherent flirtation will ensue. But who cares about neatly-polished phrases when youth, beauty and gallantry are eloquence itself?[12]

Here the distribution of gender and class characteristics between British and European incarnations (the emblematic 'Tommy' and the embodiment of 'fascinating', coy, continental femininity) underlines the affirmed righteousness and perceptible paternalism of Britain's cause. The war artist's romantically imaginative scene echoes a similarly sentimentalised photographic rendering from the previous year, showing European women fraternising with off-duty British soldiers.[13] Elsewhere imperilled European womanhood, as emblematic of domestic ideals and civilised, moral principles, has been an integral part of the imagery supporting propaganda discourses justifying Britain's involvement in the

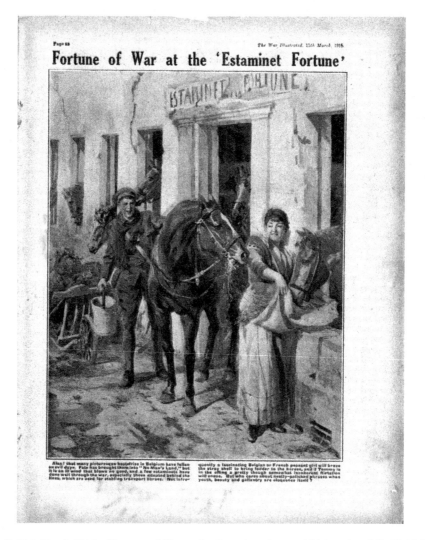

Figure 2. 11th March 1916—'Fortune of War at the Estaminet Fortune' (University of Sheffield Special Collections).

war, but in this instance, the depiction of romantic continental femininity is used to suggest an amorous dividend for, as well as a validation of, Britain's mobilisation. *War Illustrated*'s inclusion of many such examples of war artists' work is crucial to the construction and assertion of concepts of national identity, morality and duty for both sexes, and here couches defended and defending nationalities in strictly conventional, gendered terms.

The Nurse and/as the Combatant

While vulnerable female civilians in Europe are portrayed in *War Illustrated* for propaganda purposes in close contact with combatants, and affected by or actually involved in combat, the reporting of a deliberate transformation of women's circumstances through intentional participation in the conflict gradually gains in importance and frequency as the war continues. An early example of this trend is a page of varied photographs depicting 'War's Diverse Effects on Feminine Temperament'.[14] Of the seven photographs assembled on the page, three are portraits of women of high society whose acts of beneficence inspired by and in support of the war span the charitable to the idiosyncratic. The captions note that Baroness Reitzes 'sold her pearl necklace for £17,000 to buy bread for Vienna's poor'; Countess Manon von Drumreicher 'supplied five thousand cork legs for Austria's maimed soldiers'; and Luise Elrich, the wife of an Austrian millionaire, 'for charity entered a circus lions' den and fed them'. These high-profile, individual or peculiar acts by aristocratic women (notably all representatives of the Central Powers) are contrasted with a photograph of British volunteer 'women gardeners' growing vegetables for military hospitals who remain modestly unnamed. The page's central image is of a wounded soldier tended by a French nurse, whose contribution is described as 'the most noble form of woman's wartime work'. The contrasts between virtuous 'Allied' and eccentric 'enemy' women in these images are apparent in the forms their involvement in the war takes, and the associated foregrounding or obfuscation of class. The activities of selfless, subordinate and class-less Allied women are contrasted with the egotistic and condescending acts of the enemy's aristocracy. However, both sides are juxtaposed with the page's other photographs, which show Italian women 'in militant mood', learning to use rifles and forming a 'Corps of Amazons'. These photographs of women spontaneously arming and training are more remarkable since they precede Italy's entry to the war. The women's actions appear to anticipate Italy's involvement and perhaps implicitly criticise their nation's reluctance to mobilise, yet the caption's tone (perhaps reflecting ambivalence in the British public and media to the active mobilisation of women) seems neither to condemn nor condone them.[15]

In comparison with whimsical or mundane reporting of female contributions to the war, celebratory depictions of nurses at the front appear to justify and require enhancement with heroic endeavour and endangerment. A vivid illustration from late 1914 accompanies the account of an incident alleged to have occurred in Poland, in which a Red Cross nurse is carried away on horseback by a German officer.[16] Although she is 'bruised from her struggle and in despair of her fate', the caption tells how she is rescued by a gallant Cossack. Another Russian nurse, identified as Mira Miksailovich Ivanoff, is portrayed and described as a 'modern Joan of Arc'.[17] In a desperate moment of battle she ceased her caring duties and rallied her countrymen to drive back the attacking Germans, losing her own life in the process. Such captioned pictures, eulogising extraordinary examples of male and female heroism in essentially unverifiable narratives, proliferate in *War Illustrated*, with the hyperbolically described masculine and feminine virtues embodied in representatives of the allied nations throwing into sharper relief the craven inhumanity, barbarity and immorality of the enemy.

These examples foreground the figure of the military or Red Cross nurse, depicted as the perfect amalgam of the female in a nurturing role, sharing male frontline hardships, yet also susceptible to enticingly gender-specific peril. A story from November 1914 (Figure 3) tells of a nurse who defends British wounded soldiers she is tending from German troops trying to take them prisoner. The account and picture again juxtapose the fearless, vulnerable female figure with the threatening, martial Teutonic male, with the nurse appearing almost saintly or chivalric with her white apron bearing a red

Figure 3. 14th November 1914—'Brave Nurse who Protected British Wounded' (University of Sheffield Special Collections).

cross, at which the German aims his revolver.[18] A comparable story from a year later, also accompanying a full-page war rendering by a war artist, recounts what is labelled 'one of the most heroic episodes of the war', when nurses from a transport ship sunk in the Aegean implore sailors in lifeboats to rescue the fighting men shipwrecked with them first. The caption reports that 'ten of these unnamed heroines were drowned'. Here, the elevation of the nurses' maternal duty and sacrifice results, paradoxically, in active gender inversion and reversal of the adage 'women and children first'. These hyperbolic examples from early in the war exemplify the use of illustrations rather than photographs in the crafting of impactful, propagandist narratives.

The figure of the selfless, nurturing and endangered nurse, at the heart of and attuned to the needs of combat and the combatant, perhaps reaches its apotheosis in the coverage of the death of Edith Cavell. *War Illustrated* devotes its inside cover to 'the murder of Nurse Cavell', extracting propaganda value from this episode's converging threads of German brutality and injustice, and feminine courage, integrity and vulnerability. Accompanying an artist's illustration of her death, the caption reads:

> The civilised world, which had become almost apathetic to recurring German outrage, suffered a severe shock on hearing of the execution of Nurse Cavell by the Huns at Brussels. Nurse Cavell was charged with helping to smuggle Belgian men across the frontier, and found guilty by a German court-martial. A summary sentence of death was passed, and though Nurse Cavell had worked consistently to alleviate the suffering of wounded German officers at the hospital in Brussels, the penalty was inflicted under circumstances of peculiar brutality. The ill-fated woman had no strength to face the firing-party, and swooned away, whereupon the officer in charge approached the prostrate form, and, drawing a heavy Service pistol, took his murderous aim.[19]

This account accentuates the shocking application of the death penalty, but glosses over the truth of German allegations against Edith Cavell, and the consequent indefensibility of her conduct from a British as well as international perspective. Edith Cavell's compassion for German officers as much as Belgian civilians and allied soldiers is presented as British, Christian, feminine benevolence which transcends the specificities of nationality and legality in war. Conversely, feminine duplicity, in the guise of the spy or collaborator, precipitates a transformation of the female figure into a violent, unpredictable adversary. A sensational story, also from 1915, describes the discovery of female collaboration and clandestine intelligence-gathering behind the French lines. The caption accompanying the dramatic illustration reads:

> A French officer and private were participants in an exciting adventure which reads more like some romantic French novel than actual fact. Having lost their way, they proceeded at nightfall to a French farmhouse in quest of food. The proprietress tearfully complained that the Germans had ransacked the place, leaving her destitute. The two French soldiers, however, insisted on searching the cellar, to discover a secret German telephone in charge of a German soldier who had hidden himself in a barrel. In the course of the struggle which ensued the woman sprang upon the French private and tried to throttle him. The innocent farmhouse was in communication with the German lines. (Figure 4)[20]

The condemnatory convergence of femininity and espionage in this example of exaggerated early war propaganda resurfaces later in an article (written by novelist and journalist Tighe Hopkins) on the training of spies:

> In time of war many (of both sexes) are cajoled or forced into the ranks whose preparation has been of the rough and ready sort [...] it is now also well known that the Germans have made scandalous use of women of no character attired as war nurses.[21]

While this 'report' might be dismissed as no more than propagandist fiction, the insistence with which it erases any sympathy for these implicitly vulnerable females 'cajoled' into devious service, not only by their being described as 'women of no character' but also by their shameful adoption of disguise as war nurses, underlines the strictly defined parameters of and connections between female war work and female morality. This denunciation of subterfuge is as severe as the censure of unbridled sexuality levelled at 'Mata Hari' in a report of her execution (accompanied by a photograph of her in an exotic dancing costume) describing her as 'one of Germany's most skilful women spies'.[22]

Figure 4. 2nd January 1915—'Woman Spy guards secret German Telephone' (University of Sheffield Special Collections).

Perhaps the most serious challenge to such restrictive constructions of wartime gender identity is occasioned by the depiction of women not only engaged in dangerous, unprecedented war roles but also dressed in military, as opposed to medical, uniforms. The adoption of military uniforms by British women joining volunteer and auxiliary services was subject to severe popular criticism, because of the apparent insult it represented to male uniformed services, its inappropriateness in comparison with proper female activity in nursing and support, and because of the immoral and coarsened conduct it was alleged to encourage.[23] Pointedly, *War Illustrated* includes many more depictions of British women engaged in nursing, voluntary or factory work than it does of women serving in military auxiliaries. (A cover devoted to an illustration of members of the 'Sister Services' the Women's Royal Naval Service and Queen Mary's Army Auxiliary Corps, appears only in 1918, a year after the creation of both services.[24]) An explanation for this may be found in the combination of perplexity and prurience with which examples of foreign women in uniform are described in its pages. The caption accompanying an image of an Austrian woman in army uniform, which describes her as a 'modern Amazon' in the service of the 'Teutonic cause', is peculiarly ambivalent, presenting this example as neither an admirable precedent British women might imitate nor simply an unnatural foreign aberration to be reviled.[25] The only officially organised unit of female combatants during the war which operated on the Eastern Front, the Russian 'Legion of Death', appears in an illustrated report from 1917. The women's masculine attire and hairstyles, and their markedly greater courage than male regiments, are diffidently noted in the accompanying captions. However, given long-established assumptions about acts of sexual violence committed by German soldiers, the article emphasises meaningfully that the only thing the unit's members fear is capture, stressing the particularities of the women's peril entailed by their service. Although a policy to admit women to the armed services was instituted in response to numbers of women volunteering to serve, the creation of Russian female units became a mark of equality, along with the right to vote, celebrated in the country after the 1917 revolution.[26]

The examples highlighted so far exhibit the role and utility within propagandist reporting of female participants and victims of the conflict at the front or in occupied Europe, as embodiments of virtue, service and sacrifice, and as targets for brutality, desire and suspicion. Despite an assumed universal commitment to the needs of the conflict, women's difference is constantly emphasised and utilised within dominant discourses. However, the exploration of the specific experiences of women behind the lines gains in importance and coverage to the relative detriment of these earlier exaggerated and emotive stories as the war progresses. The socio-political and economic effects of women's gathering involvement in the war on the British home front become the subject of frequent articles and commentaries. In June 1915, a typical page of captioned photos, showing female postal workers, underground railway conductors and porters and recruiters, frame an anonymous, celebratory pronouncement on the beneficial, transformative effects of the conflict for the feminist cause (Figure 5):

> Undoubtedly the war has done more to enable Woman to prove her capabilities in wider spheres than all the Suffragettte and feminist propagandas of those days that seem so long ago. Now, indeed, the true Awakening of Woman is come. She has gained much of that freedom for which so many agitated, and she is using it with grand patriotism for the benefit of the state in this great crisis.[27]

Not only are 'Awakened women' now at one with the state, its objectives and needs, but apparently at one with each other across regional and class divides. The same endorsement of women's war work is found in the caption for a full-page photo of female factory workers, dubbed the 'Ministering angels of the Ministry of Munitions', for whom 'Britain's necessity has proved women's opportunity'.[28] Emphasised femininity is nonetheless shown to be consistent with the war aims of the patriarchal establishment at a crucial juncture.

Although it might be assumed that the author of these captions is the male editor of *War Illustrated*, J. A. Hammerton, their tone is echoed in the summary accounts of the war's importance in female experience and feminist politics written for the magazine by prominent campaigners for women's rights. Writing in November 1915, the suffragist Cicely

Figure 5. 4th March 1916—'Some of the Women Behind the Guns' (University of Sheffield Special Collections).

Hamilton anticipates the scale and significance of women's post-war role in what she describes prophetically as the 'Manless Homes of England'. She proposes legal frameworks for female guardianship of a generation of orphaned children and the offspring of widowed mothers, and stresses the influence that women must expect to wield after the war:

> The public opinion of the next few years will be chiefly the opinion of women. It would be well, however, if we realised the position and its meaning, realised that upon the women of Britain will fall much of the work of reconstruction, and that the folly and wisdom of the next few years will have the feminine touch. The responsibility for education will be more and more in their hands—and by education I do not mean only the accepted methods of instruction and school routine; but that newspapers and books will be written for women, and react on the new generation. Then, whether they have direct representation or not, public measures will be taken with a view to the approval of women. If I am right in this, the opportunity we asked for has come, the power we clamoured for so long and so earnestly now lies very close to hand. One can only hope that we shall know how to use it aright—scrupulously, with patience, and with tolerance.[29]

Hamilton's observations temper optimism with caution in the exercise of the sway women will have as members, rather than necessarily leaders, of the post-war populace. Her conviction that women should dedicate themselves to the needs of the country through care (conceived of in very broad but still largely conventional terms) of the future generation even without the assurance or reward of the vote, appears as much as a concession to the good will of a masculine establishment as an exhortation to dutiful British womanhood.

A more forceful essay, written for the magazine in 1917 by the President of the National Union of Women's Suffrage Societies Millicent Garrett Fawcett, vigorously criticises the perceived waste of women's potential in the pre- and early war periods, and proposes reci-procal benefits to women and society at large if the model of war work is maintained. Notably, Garrett Fawcett's article inaugurates a new series of essays for *War Illustrated* entitled 'The Great Issues of the War' (later essays addressed the war's impact on the Empire, labour relations, literature and religion[30]). After censuring the government's failure to act on the advice of the NUWSS in 1914 to find suitable employment for women in order to free up the male labour force, and lamenting the enduring obstacles within the professions and trades-union movement to the equal employment of women in vital occupations, Fawcett goes on to consider the common sense and innate justice of appropriate employment opportunities for all in the post-war world:

> A great many women whose husbands are now in the Army or Navy will, if their men come back at the end of the war, return to ordinary domestic work in their own homes. On the other hand, many women will, unfortunately, not get their husbands back; they will be widows or wives of permanently disabled men. These women will have to remain in industry as the main breadwinners of their families. No decent man could possibly urge the return of a system which excluded them from the possibility of earning good wages. Women have shown their industrial capacity during the war in a way which has shattered many anti-feminist prejudices and preconceptions [...] They have known the sweets of economic independence and the joy of service to a cause they love. They have gained in dignity and self-reliance, and the country has found in their labour an asset which will not be neglected in future as it has been in the past.[31]

Although generally considered to be a liberal and acceptable representative of the cause of British women, Garrett Fawcett's arguments and assertions are nonetheless redolent of the individual and communal losses inflicted by the war, while they avow the need and justi-fication for social change.[32] Here, as the war enters its closing phases, the mobilisation of women representationally for propaganda purposes has given place to (albeit restricted) political representation, in challenges to the very prejudices and stereotypes which have rendered a service to the war effort valued initially at least, it seems, above women's mili-tary and economic participation. *War Illustrated*'s coverage of women's place within the male perspective and pursuit of war, and their iconographic and ideological place inside its justification and momentum, have to a limited degree been replaced by acknowledgement and articulation of their expression and experience of the conflict, and its anticipated con-sequences for them in peace.

Conclusion: 'Manly Heroism' vs. 'Womanly Devotion'

From the consideration of only a limited number of examples, the critically important, pervasive but also constantly evolving depiction of women within *War Illustrated* can be discerned and appreciated. Within the magazine's recording and reading of the influ-ences and effects of the war, women have been accepted and shown as carers, lauded or criticised as combatants, and censured for clandestine, deceitful feminine espionage. Specific aspects of gender definition and representation are crucial to both celebratory and condemnatory examples. Women have been celebrated as workers within specified environments and employments, and rendered romantic, exotic, eccentric or endangering when they have assumed military duties or martial dress. However, their official, predict-able and pragmatic roles in the conduct, iconography and narrativisation of the war have been succeeded by the establishment's topical acceptance and accommodation of women's

desire and deserving of more challenging, fundamental change, signalled by the accommodation of the views of high-profile female commentators and campaigners within its pages.
Here *War Illustrated* appears to diverge (and develop) from its highly visual, exaggerated
and propagandist use of female objectification to become a positive platform for feminist
representation. By contrast, the longstanding weekly feature 'Women and the War' by
Claudine Cleve in the *Illustrated War News* (included from June 1916 onwards), while cel-
ebrating a wide range of women's wartime activities, skirts controversy and eschews commentary on women's rights, as the following excerpt from Part 23 of the series shows:

> This article is not in any sense intended as a plea for Women's Suffrage. Like its predecessors,
> it merely aims at recording a fraction of the part that women are playing in the greatest war
> the world has ever known.[33]

The extent to which representations of women within wartime publications such as *War
Illustrated*, in their manipulation and reinforcement of certain stereotypes and imagery
alongside their accommodation of a spectrum of opinion, might merely comment upon
and record social change, assist and stimulate it or criticise and actively oppose it, is
plainly open to considerable variation. Although depictions and commentary in *War Illustrated* do not appear to replicate the popular objections to women's adoption of military
uniform or recruitment to military auxiliaries, they do not appear to support or celebrate
these developments either, preferring instead to portray women as nurses and factory and
agricultural workers, females replacing males in home-front employment, and female civilian members of volunteer organisations and recruitment campaigners. While it is exalted
as surely 'the noblest and most beautiful sphere of womanly activity', the role and representation of nursing is nonetheless expanded in *War Illustrated* to embrace contact
with the enemy in front-line peril, and literal or metaphorical leadership and protection
of male combatants.[34] By contrast the association of other allegedly innate feminine
traits with covert, duplicitous action in the clandestine world of espionage represents
the polar opposite in gender pigeon-holing and the most drastic distinction from
moral, masculine uniformed service.

What these examples also suggest is a constant juggling of not just arbitrarily applied
moral standards, but also the criteria and anticipations of the extraordinary or the
simply expected in the conduct of women in wartime roles. This is significant to the
debates preceding and running parallel with the conflict itself, in relation to the establishment of gender equality and women's suffrage. Perceptions of women's roles, as much as
the environments, values and details of the roles themselves, required (and underwent)
change during the war.[35] Paradoxes and contradictions inevitably emerge in the recognition afforded to women's exceptional achievement within roles deemed gender specific
and dependent upon innate, natural feminine qualities, while universally applicable
notions of responsible and patriotic citizenship are understood to require all members
of society to commit themselves to national duty:

> After years of struggle, why did feminists accept only partial women's suffrage, not suffrage
> on the same terms as men? In part because they believed, correctly, that once women had
> some form of suffrage further reform would follow. They also proved willing to compromise
> and unwilling to cause a public stink during the war. Some have suggested that it was ironic
> that the franchise failed to extend the vote to those women workers under age of 30 who had
> so valiantly served the nation and proved themselves 'worthy of citizenship'. Suffragist

leaders acknowledged this but suggested, in the words of Millicent Garrett Fawcett, that what British women had obtained was a 'motherhood franchise'.[36]

The paradoxes and prejudices attending the recognition and interpretation of female wartime service can be seen in instances in *War Illustrated*'s reporting where notions of difference and equality, and grounds for celebration and discrimination converge to startling effect (Figure 6). Marking the recent extension of the award of the Military Cross ('for exceptional bravery') to women, a page of photographs representing the presentation of medals for gallantry juxtaposes male and female recipients.[37] Two of the pictures are taken at ceremonies at which General Joffre has conferred decorations on a young colonial soldier and two British Army officers for their service in the recent Battle of the Somme. The other two pictures are individual portraits of British nurses who are 'among the first to

Figure 6. 23rd September 1916—'For Manly Heroism and Womanly Devotion' (University of Sheffield Special Collections).

receive the Military Medal for bravery in the field'. Both women were decorated for their bravery when their casualty-clearing station was shelled, with the male-equivalent award reflecting the comparability of their conduct under fire.[38] However, the women are apparently not honoured for the male quality of heroism, but for the female virtue of devotion, transforming the page's title from a new equation to a persisting segregation.

Irrespective of the national, military or political objectives and opportunities occasioned by the war, on the basis of this outcome from the period of conflict for women's circumstances Susan Grayzel identifies what she considers to be the 'failure of the war to free the majority of women from being held responsible for their households and children'.[39] Inevitably, disputable perceptions of comparability rather than notions of genuine equivalence mark the consideration of distinctive gendered war-time work in contemporary popular debates, in co-existing examples of popular culture, and in retrospective evaluation.

Notes

1. Gail Braybon (2003) Winners or Losers: women's symbolic role in the war story, in Gail Braybon (Ed.) *Evidence, History and the Great War: historians and the impact of 1914–18* (New York and Oxford: Berghahn Books), p. 88.
2. Anon. (1939) The Press: war weeklies, *Time Magazine* (25 September). Accessed 9 April 2013. Available at <http://www.time.com/time/magazine/article/0,9171,761998,00.html>.
3. For discussion of women's varied war roles, responses and experiences explored through the reports and recollections of individuals, see Janet S. K. Watson (2004) *Fighting Different Wars: experience, memory and the First World War in Britain* (Cambridge: Cambridge University Press); Paul Ward (2001) Women of Britain say Go!: women's patriotism in the First World War, *Twentieth Century British History*, 12(1), pp. 23–45. For examples of contemporary evaluations of women's activities in wartime writing, see Susan R. Grayzel (1999) *Women's Identities at War: gender, motherhood, and politics in Britain and France during the First World War* (London: University of North Carolina Press).
4. Christine E. Hallett and Alison S. Fell (2013) New Perspectives on First World War Nursing, in Alison S. Fell & Christine E. Hallett (Eds) *First World War Nursing: new perspectives* (London: Routledge), p. 3.
5. Gail Braybon (1989) *Women Workers in the First World War* (London: Routledge), p. 49.
6. Bernard A. Cook (2006) *Women and War: a historical encyclopedia from antiquity to the present* vol. I (Santa Barbara, CA: ABD-CLIO), p. 238.
7. Anon. (1914) Grenadiers and Scots Guards off to the Front, *The War Illustrated* (26 September), p. 127.
8. Anon. (1915) The Teutonic Wave and the Wreck it Leaves, *The War Illustrated* (22 May), p. 323.
9. Anon. (1915) The Annihilation of a Family, *The War Illustrated* (19 February), p. 16.
10. Nicoletta Gullace (1997) Sexual Violence and Family Honor: British propaganda and international law during the First World War, *The American Historical Review*, 102, pp. 714–747 (pp. 716–717).
11. James Bryce (1915) Report of the Committee on Alleged German Outrages (London). For a reappraisal of the pervasiveness and inevitability of destruction, brutality and gender-specific violence in the conflict, see Alan Kramer, *Dynamic of Destruction: culture and mass killing in the First World War* (Oxford: Oxford University Press, 2007).
12. Anon. (1916) Fortune of War at the 'Estaminet Fortune', *The War Illustrated* (11 March), p. 85.
13. Anon. (1915) Phases of Women's Interest in Men at Arms, *The War Illustrated* (17 July), p. 519.
14. Anon. (1915) War's Diverse Effects on Feminine Temperament, *The War Illustrated* (10 April), p. 184.

15. Krisztina Robert (1997) Gender, Class, and Patriotism: women's paramilitary units in First World War Britain, *The International History Review*, 19(1), pp. 52–65 (p. 54).
16. Anon. (1914) Cossack to the Rescue of a Red Cross Nurse, *The War Illustrated* (28 November), p. 343.
17. Anon. (1915) A Modern Joan of Arc, *The War Illustrated* (23 October), p. 217.
18. Anon. (1914) Brave Nurse who Protected British Wounded, *The War Illustrated* (14 November), p. 314.
19. Anon. (1915) The Murder of Nurse Cavell, *The War Illustrated* (30 October), p. 241.
20. Anon. (1915) Woman Spy guards secret German Telephone, *The War Illustrated* (2 January), p. 476.
21. Tighe Hopkins (1917) The Training of the Spy: how the tools were chosen for doing dirty work, *The War Illustrated* (24 November), p. 289.
22. Anon. (1917) Agents of Prussia's World-Wide Espionage, *The War Illustrated* (17 January), p. 277.
23. Janet S. K. Watson (1997) Khaki Girls, VADs, and Tommy's Sisters: gender and class in First World War Britain, *The International History Review*, 19(1), pp. 32–51 (pp. 36–40).
24. Anon. (1918) Sister Services, *The War Illustrated* (29 June).
25. Anon. (1915) Snap-shots by the Way in War-Time, *The War Illustrated* (10 July), p. 493.
26. Melissa K. Stockdale (2004) My Death for the Motherland is Happiness: women, patriotism, and soldering in Russia's Great War, 1914–1917, *American Historical Review*, 109(1), pp. 78–116.
27. Anon. (1915) War and the Real Triumph of Feminism, *The War Illustrated* (26 June), p. 447.
28. Anon. (1916) Some of the Women Behind the Guns, *The War Illustrated* (4 March), p. 72.
29. Cicely Hamilton (1915) The Manless Homes of England: British womanhood fills the gaps while its manhood lines the trenches, *The War Illustrated* (13 November), p. 292 (my emphasis).
30. Sidney Low (1917) The British Empire After the War, *The War Illustrated* (13 January), p. 506, p. 508; Clement K. Shorter (1917) Literature After the War, *The War Illustrated* (10 February), p. 611, p. 614; George Barnes (1917) Labour After the War, *The War Illustrated* (24 February), pp. 26–28; R. F. Horton (1917) Religion After the War, *The War Illustrated* (17 April), p. 107, p. 110.
31. Millicent Garrett Fawcett (1917) The War's Effect on Women's Work, *The War Illustrated* (6 January), p. 482, p. 484.
32. Jo Vellacott (1987) Feminist Consciousness and the First World War, *History Workshop* 23, pp. 81–101 (p. 87).
33. Claudine Cleve (1916) Women and the War, *Illustrated War News* (15 November), p. 34.
34. Anon. (1915) War's Diverse Effects on Feminine Temperament, *The War Illustrated* (10 April), p. 184.
35. David Monger (2014) Nothing Special? Propaganda and Women's Roles in Late First World War Britain, *Women's History Review*, 23(4), pp. 518–542 (p. 535).
36. Susan Grayzel (2002) *Women and the First World War* (Longman: Harlow), p. 103.
37. Anon. (1916) For Manly Heroism and Womanly Devotion, *The War Illustrated* (23 September), p. 143.
38. Anon. (2012) Gallant Nurses, *Great War London: London and Londoners in the First World War* (26 September). Accessed 26 March 2016. Available at <https://greatwarlondon.wordpress.com/2012/09/26/gallant-nurses/>
39. Grayzel, *Women and the First World War*, p. 118.

3 Suffragettes and the Scottish Press during the First World War

Sarah Pedersen (iD)

ABSTRACT

This article analyses the coverage of the suffrage movement in Scottish newspapers during the First World War. Suspension of militant action and a re-focus on women's war work did not mean the complete disappearance of the suffrage campaign from newspapers. However, while militant and non-militant organisations received press coverage for their war work, there were also stories associating suffragettes with the peace effort—or even conspiracies against the state. Volunteers at the Scottish Women's Hospitals were approvingly described as 'suffragettes' but the appellation retained negative connotations when used about peace campaigners. Brave 'suffragette battalions' were reported to be arriving in France, but at the same time a politician painted the Germans as 'the suffragettes of Europe'. Whilst editors wrote enthusiastically of women's contribution to the war effort, jokes about suffragettes continued to provide light relief. Editorials made the connection between women's war work and achievement of the vote. However, not all readers were happy with this point of view, with some correspondents attacking what they saw as the suffrage organisations' opportunistic use of war work and abandonment of working women.

The start of the First World War led to the suspension of militant action in the campaign for votes for women, and both Emmeline Pankhurst of the Women's Social and Political Union (WSPU) and Millicent Garrett Fawcett of the National Union of Women's Suffrage Societies (NUWSS) urged women to focus their efforts on the war effort. However, this did not mean the complete disappearance of the suffrage campaign from the newspapers. This article demonstrates that there was a continuance of the suffrage campaign in Scotland throughout the war and that the suffrage issue continued to be raised in the Scottish press in a variety of ways. Press coverage of the campaign for votes for women *did* decline sharply in the first half of the war, only reappearing in any major way in 1916 with discussion of the Representation of the People Bill, but the issue did not fully disappear, even in the early years of the war. However, the press portrayal of the suffrage campaign and the figure of the suffragette became more fragmented during the war. This article discusses the ways in which the campaign for the vote became associated in wartime Scottish newspapers with a number of very different groups—war-workers, pacifists, patriots, socialists. The image of the suffragette also continued to be used by newspapers as a means of raising a quick laugh: old jokes from the pre-war years were repeated, with scant regard to the fact that they might share column inches with praise for the work of groups such as the Scottish Women's Hospitals, associated with the NUWSS. In addition, as the WSPU refocused its efforts on war service in order to demonstrate the entitlement of women to citizenship, the voices of other suffrage groups became louder in the Scottish press. Newspaper coverage of women's war work in general also contributed to a change of public opinion on women's right to the vote. Many of the pre-war suffrage organisations were involved in the organisation of women's volunteer war work, meaning an association of such work with the suffrage campaign, although by later in the war and the centralisation of war work under Lloyd George, the origins of such groups became less important. Nonetheless, newspaper editorials discussed women's war work in approving tones and made the connection between war service and citizenship. Since the granting of the vote to women in 1918 there has been debate over the differing contributions of women's war work and militant action to the final decision in favour of women's enfranchisement.[1] However, there was no doubt in the minds of newspaper editors that women had earned the vote through their war work.

In the months prior to the start of the First World War in August 1914, readers of Scottish newspapers would have been presented with a fairly coherent picture of 'the suffragette'. She was a fire-starting vandal whose tactics led to arrest and imprisonment, hunger-striking, force-feeding and release under the 'Cat and Mouse Act'.[2] Coverage of arson attacks on Scottish buildings such as the church at Whitekirk in East Lothian, the grandstand at Ayr Racecourse and Farrington Hall in Dundee, plus the force-feeding of Scottish suffragettes in Perth Prison, ensured that the majority of Scottish press coverage focused on acts of militancy rather than the constitutional suffrage campaign. Whether you supported or argued against women's suffrage, the image of the suffragette in the Scottish press was generally consistent—if not representative of the whole movement—and the term 'suffragette' was used interchangeably to cover members of the two main militant societies, the Women's Social and Political Union (WSPU) and the Women's Freedom League (WFL), and sometimes even the constitutional National Union of Women's Suffrage Societies (NUWSS).[3] This consistent image in the press was completely fractured by the War.

This article draws on reports, editorials and jokes published in Scottish newspapers during the First World War. Newspapers offer a key source for the history of the woman's suffrage movement in Britain, which is not surprising when the importance of the press to the militant movement in particular is considered. The first act of militancy occurred in October 1905 when Christabel Pankhurst and Annie Kenney disrupted a Liberal meeting in Manchester by heckling the speakers. Both were arrested after Christabel spat at a policeman. Faced with the choice of paying a fine or a short prison sentence, both opted to be imprisoned. The press coverage that followed was an educational experience for the leadership of the WSPU and it adopted these new 'tactics' of interrupting meetings and refusing to pay fines in order to gain maximum publicity for the cause. Arguing that the suffrage question had been ignored by the press until that moment, Christabel stated later: 'Where peaceful means had failed, one act of militancy succeeded and never again was the cause ignored by ... any ... newspaper.'[4] The move of WSPU headquarters from Manchester to London also facilitated national press coverage of the 'suffragettes'—and indeed it was the *Daily Mail* that coined this term for the WSPU militants during the 1906 general election to distinguish them from the constitutional suffragists. Whilst it was initially the WSPU that was at the forefront of engagement with the press, other suffrage societies soon followed suit when they realised how beneficial press coverage of the demand for the vote could be—and also that there was a need to get constitutional voices in the press as well as militant ones. The minute books of the Glasgow and West of Scotland Association for Women's Suffrage, for example, offer a fascinating glimpse of one suffrage association's growing acceptance of the need for engagement with the press. By 1912 this constitutional association had appointed its own press secretary to co-ordinate all press communications and authorised her to employ Durrants Press Cuttings to collect relevant press coverage.[5]

The digitisation of newspapers in recent years has made the task of the media historian easier by making access and search facilities much more comprehensive, allowing the historian to read and compare a much greater number of texts in a comparatively shorter time. This article is based on an analysis of local newspapers from Aberdeen to the Scottish Borders which have been accessed via digital resources such as the British Newspapers Archive (BNA). However, as Adrian Bingham warns in his useful review article on the use of digitised newspaper archives, such easy access brings its own issues.[6] For example, scanning and character-recognition problems can hamper digital searches and, more problematically, results can be separated from their original page, meaning that contextualisation is lost. As much as possible I have guarded against these issues by examining articles in their original page-setting. This has made it possible to identify, for example, occasions where jokes about the suffrage movement were placed on the same page as articles in praise of some aspect of suffrage war work. Some newspapers have not been digitised at all, and others have only been partially digitised: these were accessed via the more traditional route of visiting archives.

Studies of press coverage of the suffrage movement offer valuable insights into the way in which the movement was framed by the mainstream media, and a number of studies have analysed the significance of newspaper coverage for our understanding of the suffrage movement and how it was received. Newspaper coverage of events such as suffrage processions and meetings not only reported these events in detail but also provided photographs, thus increasing the visibility of suffrage campaigners and providing a pictorial record of the changes in the tactics of both suffragettes and suffragists during the decades.[7] In her analysis of newspaper coverage of suffrage processions in London, Katherine E. Kelly argues that the press and the suffrage movement were symbiotic: through collaboration, the suffragettes gained visibility and the press provided its readership with spectacle and modernity. However, while press coverage could be enthusiastic, sometimes it was more curious than positive, focusing more on the response of the crowds to the marchers than the cause itself, or even using the suffragettes as a source of humour. Krista Cowman notes the attitude of amused interest demonstrated in some press reports of the suffrage movement, even after it became militant and attitudes hardened.[8] However, the approach of a particular newspaper to the question of votes for women very much depended on individual editors or proprietors and might change with a change of ownership.[9] In Aberdeen, for example, the *Free Press* was of more liberal sympathies than its rival the *Daily Journal* and took a more positive view of the question of women's enfranchisement.[10] Differences might even be found between newspapers owned by the same proprietor. In Dundee, D C Thomson owned both the conservative *Courier* and the more liberal *Advertiser* at the start of the twentieth century, one supportive of the suffrage campaign and one not.[11]

Studies of the press treatment of the suffrage question have so far tended to focus on national, London-based newspapers with very little reference, if any, to newspapers outside London apart from *The Manchester Guardian*, and have also tended to focus on the years before the outbreak of the war. In contrast, this study investigates the ways in which the Scottish press covered the suffrage movement during the less-studied (in suffrage terms) period of the First World War. Jacqueline DeVries' 2013 review of new scholarship on women's suffrage in Britain suggests that the 'politics of location' and the study of regional dynamics is one of the clearest trends in suffrage scholarship in recent years.[12] Thus a renewed focus on press coverage of the campaign for women's suffrage outside London, indeed outside England, is of value in contributing to a wider and more nuanced picture of the women's suffrage movement and also as a contribution to the wider history of women and the media in Scotland.

In June 1914, a few months before the start of the war, Scottish newspapers were full of the events of a suffrage meeting in Glasgow's St Andrew's Halls. Mrs Pankhurst had been re-arrested on the stage under the Cat and Mouse Act by baton-wielding policemen, despite defensive actions by the suffragettes, who threw flowerpots from the stage and used Indian clubs on the policemen. The newspapers were filled with editorials and letters both sympathising with the suffrage cause and criticising the suffragettes and the police, and the controversy rolled on for months as campaigners attempted to take legal action against the police. However, on the outbreak of the war Mrs Pankhurst announced a negotiated peace with the British government. The WSPU promised to cease all militant acts and suffrage prisoners were released from jail with the remainder of their sentences remitted. Soon after, Christabel Pankhurst returned from Paris to join her mother in a campaign to support the war effort and demonstrate to the British public the value of women at this time of crisis for the Empire. The *Aberdeen Journal* reported Christabel's words: 'I feel that my duty lies in England now, and I have come back. The British citizenship, for which suffragists have been fighting, is now in jeopardy.'[13] Press coverage of the militant acts of the suffragettes ceased, but this did not mean that the movement disappeared entirely from the pages of the newspapers.

The *Edinburgh Evening News* greeted the news of the WSPU's commitment to the war effort with approval and had no doubt that the suffragettes would respond well to the amnesty. Its editorial explained that, with the freeing of the militants, the need for able-bodied men to guard public buildings would end and that there was plenty of war work 'for women who wish to do real service'.[14] *The Courier* celebrated the re-opening of Dundee churches on weekdays and that suffragettes were turning their attention to war work. Its article, 'Militants no longer', carried an interview with a local minister stating that 'the Suffragettes, who were associated with the Red Cross Society, had given him their word of honour that no damage would be done. There was a desire in these days to go into churches.'[15]

Thus the image we find in Scottish newspapers in the early months of the war is of the ex-militant suffragette, campaigning for the right to engage in war work and involved in recruiting men for the forces. Scottish newspapers covered events in London such as the 'March of the Women' in July 1915, with the *Aberdeen Journal* commenting approvingly on 'how well Mrs Pankhurst is playing her cards in the supreme crisis',[16] but also reported on the visits of Christabel Pankhurst and Flora Drummond to Scotland to run military recruiting drives. During these visits Pankhurst and Drummond stressed the need for suffragettes to rally to the cause of King and Country. Indeed, in a speech reported in the *Dundee Courier* Christabel made direct connection between suffragettes' previous militancy and their new recruiting role—'[she] said as a militant woman she hoped to do something to rouse the spirit of militancy in men'.[17] While praising such sentiments, the newspapers found time to appreciate the irony of the situation, with the *Aberdeen Journal* suggesting: 'Anyone who watched the activities of the Suffragettes at the meeting must have been amused. They were busy as bees distributing pamphlets, not condemning Mr Lloyd George, but exhorting the young men to go and enlist.'[18] The *Edinburgh Evening News* meanwhile mourned the low attendance of men at one meeting —'It was a pity that eligible young men were not present in their hundreds to be thrilled and inspired by ladies who had "faced death" over and over again'—but hinted that perhaps the days of suffragette speeches and demonstrations were now over:

> Although demonstrations are calculated to keep individuals and organisations in the lime-light, they do not compare, for usefulness, with some of the other activities by which the suffragettes are seeking to play their part in the quiet, splendid and devoted service which is being rendered by the womanhood of the nation.[19]

Overall the press wrote approvingly of this change of tactic from the WSPU and made the connection between war work and the eventual achievement of the vote. Several newspapers commented that the suffragettes' steadfastness of purpose could now be channelled into patriotic war work. As the *Dundee Evening Telegraph* put it:

> That they will perform their functions efficiently no one need have any doubt. In their political campaign they showed a capacity for sticking to their point which compelled a measure of admiration even from those most resolutely opposed to their claims.[20]

The leader of the NUWSS, Millicent Garrett Fawcett, also announced that her organisation would be suspending its ordinary political work. She appealed to members of the Union to 'bind themselves together for the purpose of rendering the greatest possible aid to the country at this momentous epoch'.[21] Local suffrage societies were quick to point out that they could offer established organisation, contacts and offices to the war effort. At a civic meeting in Dundee, the provost read out a letter from the Dundee Woman Suffrage Society offering the use of its organisation and offices to a round of applause and suffrage workers were immediately co-opted onto newly formed committees.[22]

Newspapers reported that not only were suffragettes eager to replace men to free them for service at the front, they might also be dispatched to the front themselves. In spring 1915 a number of Scottish newspapers reported on the arrival of 'Suffragette battalions' in France 'to take up the duties of telephone operators, signallers, telegraphists, and chauffeurs'.[23] The *Dumfries and Galloway Standard* praised the initiative as being a 'really useful and noble channel for their energies' and remarked that they were 'as good as an extra battalion for Sir John French'.[24] Emmeline Pankhurst had often applied military terminology to the suffragettes:[25] in *My Own Story* (1914) she described the WSPU as 'a suffrage army in the field'.[26] Thus the construction by the WSPU of its members as an army was now used to frame women's war work in the press. The newspapers also informed readers that the French press had called for 'three cheers for the suffragettes' and that correspondence from home found on the bodies of German troops contained warnings against them: 'I want to warn you to be very careful when you meet them, and don't let them scratch at your eyes, and, above all, don't let them capture you. That would shame you before the world.'[27] In such descriptions we find hints that the shiny new image of the suffragette war heroine still contained elements of the older version of the shrieking sisterhood aiming to scratch out men's eyes. The *Dundee Evening Telegraph* claimed that the Parisian crowd had rejected the name of 'Suffragettes' for the women, re-Christening them 'Lady Kitcheners' and commenting favourably on their looks—attractive women evidently not corresponding with the popular concept of the suffragette.[28]

Closely associated with the idea of suffragettes at the front is one of the key images of the woman war-worker to be found in the pages of the Scottish press—the volunteers of the Scottish Women's Hospitals. Founded by Dr Elsie Inglis, a member of the Edinburgh branch of the Scottish Federation of Women's Suffrage Societies, this organisation sent several hospitals, fully staffed by women, to work with the French and Serbian armies. While the NUWSS provided a London sub-committee, the headquarters of the hospitals were in Edinburgh. Jane McDermid explains that the name of the hospitals was chosen in order to appeal to both suffragists and anti-suffragists, but that all notepaper, appeals and press notices were headed by the NUWSS logo and all fourteen hospital units flew the NUWSS red, white and green flag below the Union Jack.[29] Fundraising for the hospitals was carried out under the auspices of the NUWSS throughout the war, and scarcely a week went by without a mention in local Scottish newspapers of a flag-day, sale of work, fete or other means of raising money. The sums raised could be very large indeed. In April 1918 an article in *The Edinburgh Evening News* reported that over £300,000 had been raised for the Scottish Women's Hospitals since the start of the war. All such activities name-checked the local branch of the NUWSS (usually with the careful addition of the word 'non-militant'). In addition, returning nurses, doctors or even Dr Inglis herself toured Scotland as speakers. Local newspapers carried articles and photographs of the women who volunteered to work with the hospitals, both when they departed and in the event of their death. Such articles usually made it clear that the volunteers were also suffrage campaigners. For example, when the Misses Gray of Leven departed for the Scottish Women's Hospital at Royaumont in November 1914, several local newspapers covered the story. Even more covered the death of Mary Gray in January 1916, described as a 'heroine's death' by the *Fife Free Press*.[30] The Misses Gray were described as giving their services to 'the Unionist cause, women suffrage (non-militant) and the affairs of Scoonie Kirk', and the newspaper went on to state that 'The Scottish Women's Hospitals (launched by the Suffragette Society) was scarcely proposed ere the sisters were selected'. Note the use of the term 'Suffragette Society' to describe the NUWSS. Even before the war the term had become useful shorthand for the press to describe anyone involved in the campaign for women's suffrage, and it no longer necessarily indicated a member of the WSPU or even a member of a militant society. For example, the *Fife Free* Press described the NUWSS as the 'Suffragette Society' in its discussion of hospital fundraising in Leven[31] while the *Arbroath Herald* similarly praised the work of the hospitals 'under the auspices of the Suffragette association'.[32] However, it should be noted that the press also used the term 'suffragist' to describe members of the militant societies. For example an article in the *Aberdeen Daily Journal* described a visit of Mrs Pankhurst and others to the Welsh coal mines with the headline 'Suffragists as Miners'[33] and Ethel Smyth, composer of *The March of the Women*, 'the battle song of the Women's Social and Political Union' was described by the *Daily Record* as a 'suffragist musician'.[34] Thus the careful distinction made by historians between constitutional suffragists and militant suffragettes was certainly not one being used by this time in the Scottish press and care should be taken before assuming the implications of the use of either term by a newspaper report.

An examination of Scottish newspapers therefore suggests that a dominant press image of the suffrage movement during the war was associated with the Scottish Women's Hospitals and the constitutional NUWSS rather than the militant WSPU. The Scottish Women's Hospitals' fundraising campaign was an extremely prominent 'good cause' in the press, and each advert, report or article re-asserted its connection with the NUWSS. The constitutional societies were also involved with the organisation of other war work, such as war relief for the families of soldiers and sailors, utilising networks built up over the decades in their campaign for the vote. The Edinburgh society, for example, at the start of the war argued that 'their organisation of over 5000 adherents in the district should be utilised in connection with the various schemes for relief, so that there should be coherence in the work and an avoidance of overlapping'.[35]

A similar approach was taken by the more militant Women's Freedom League, which had a strong presence in Scotland, particularly in Glasgow and Edinburgh, and which established the Women's Suffrage National Aid Corps in August 1914. In Glasgow, the constitutional Society for Women's Suffrage also organised an Exchange for Voluntary Workers, while the Liberal Women's Suffrage Union concentrated on fundraising for Belgian refugees. Thus a clear connection was constantly being made between suffrage and women's war work—a connection that was also being made in editorial columns in the press with approving articles explicitly making the connection between suffrage campaigners' war work and their chance of winning the vote post-war.

However, not all newspaper readers were happy about this state of affairs. A letter to the *Perthshire Advertiser* in October 1914 objected strongly to 'the efforts being made in some quarters, not only to continue political controversy during the war, but actually to exploit the war and the sufferings of our gallant troops, to further the ends of a particular section. War-relief efforts put forward by suffragist women are labelled "Suffrage" for the purpose of advertisement.'[36] The writer appealed to the patriotism of readers to see through this ploy. A similar point was made by a correspondent using the pen name 'A Simple Woman' in a letter to the *Dundee Evening Telegraph* the following year:

> Even now you hear suffrage women saying, 'We will get the vote because we are working.' They are little Jack Horners. They are eating their Christmas pie. They are working for an end. We anti-suffragists thank God that we are allowed to help, and only ask that we may do it well to His glory.[37]

Such letters demonstrate that, despite the more positive views of many editors, not all newspaper readers were happy to see the redemption of the suffrage movement through war work and were suspicious of the motives of these workers. This theme came strongly to the fore in the later years of the war in the campaign against women's enfranchisement through the Representation of the People Bill, with letters to the newspapers arguing that such war work should not be rewarded because it had been undertaken only because of self-interest and with political intent. The Anti-Suffrage League protested that it had taken the patriotic course of 'refraining from all propaganda and consecrating the entire organisation and effort in relief to the wounded' while its opponents 'had taken advantage of the war and the excellent service rendered by women to revive the demand for the suffrage in a very controversial form'.[38] In response, the Glasgow trade unionist and suffrage campaigner Margaret H. Irwin wrote to the *Daily Record* arguing that 'all fair-minded persons' appreciated that women now deserved the vote in view of 'the magnificent work which women of every class have rendered and are rendering the nation at this supreme crisis'.[39]

Interestingly, a letter sent to the *Dundee Courier* in 1917 suggests that the close association between the Scottish Women's Hospitals and the NUWSS was not always promoted by the organisers of the hospitals themselves. A correspondent reported turning down a request to fundraise for the Hospitals on the grounds that she was anti-suffrage. She claimed to have received a letter in response stating:

> Out of loyalty to the group of suffrage women who first started the running of hospitals staffed by women at the outbreak of war, we still have to put NUWSS on our notepaper ... but my Hospitals Committee do no suffrage work, and, truth to tell, the hospitals take up so much of our time ... that we really hardly have time to think of suffrage at all.[40]

Such a letter suggests that, while the suffrage associations had been useful starting-points for the organisation of women's war work at the beginning of the war, this work had outgrown its foundations by 1917. It is not surprising that the suffrage societies, particularly the constitutional societies, were useful in establishing women's war-work organisations quickly given the number of civic-minded women involved in such organisations before the war. However, after 1915 and under the growing power of Lloyd George, first as Minister for Munitions and then Prime Minister, the government and local authorities began to impose a more centralised and less personalised approach to voluntary organisations in order to provide a more uniform approach to women's war work.[41] This centralisation process, plus the passing of years and changes in personnel, may have meant that war-work organisations' ties to their founders became weaker.

Despite the more positive views of newspaper editors on the suffrage question, certain stereotypes associated with the figure of the suffrage campaigner did not disappear completely from newspapers. Jokes and stories about suffragettes, originally coined in peacetime, were repeated again and again in the Scottish newspapers. Reports of entertainments put on for the troops or to raise funds frequently featured skits such as 'The Heid o'the Hoose, a Scottish comedy sketch founded on an episode of militant suffragism ... a most delightful performance'.[42] A selection of letters to the *Falkirk Herald* in reference to the 'suffragette battalions' mentioned above humorously offered to sacrifice wives and mothers-in-law for the good of the country, whilst another writer suggested that it was a good thing that the suffragettes were to go since 'they have had practice in destroying ancient places enough.'[43] Meanwhile the *Southern Reporter* sarcastically suggested that the ladies who rushed to Oxford Street to buy wool to make garments for soldiers had merely changed from Suffragettes to Selfragettes[44] and the *Dundee Evening Telegraph* quipped that, with the renaming of *The Suffragette* newspaper as *Britannia* in 1915, 'on the front page should be a symbolical figure of Britannia armed with a strident.'[45] The term 'suffragette' might also still be used to imply mindless violence or aggression. At the start of the war several newspapers picked up the description of the Germans by the

Conservative MP Sir Arthur Stanley as 'the suffragettes of Europe'.[46] As Krista Cowman notes, humour at the expense of the suffragette 'crowded the popular Edwardian daily press'[47] and could also be found in film, the theatre and on picture postcards, so it is not surprising that such an easy target continued to attract jokes during the war. Such jokes might even sit uneasily on the same page as reports of women's war work. For example, the *Dundee Evening Telegraph* carried the joke: '"Women Workers into the Breach" cries a Suffrage paper. "Into the breeches," echo answers' on the same page as an editorial praising the employment of women to replace men leaving for the trenches.[48]

Thus the Scottish press continued to offer some coverage of the women's suffrage movement during the war years, but this was now primarily associated with the war work undertaken by groups established by different suffrage organisations at the start of the war. In addition, the figure of the suffragette was still occasionally used for humorous relief. However, this does not mean that coverage of the campaign for the vote disappeared altogether. Because the Women's Freedom League continued to campaign for the vote throughout the war, the Scottish newspapers still had the possibility of reporting on suffrage meetings and the campaign for the enfranchisement of women. In fact, the need for the female vote was argued to be more urgent than ever during wartime. As a letter to the *Dundee Courier* made clear, the Women's Freedom League 'reaffirms the urgency of keeping the Suffrage flag flying, and especially now, making the country understand the supreme necessity of women having a voice in the counsels of the nation'.[49] Local newspapers continued to report on the meetings of WFL branches in Scotland on the subject of the vote throughout the war, which continually made the point that women needed a voice in the government of the nation in both war and peace. Nina Boyle spoke at a WFL 'At Home' meeting in Dundee in February 1915. Her speech was reported at some length in the local press, including her emphasis that:

> The Freedom League, in taking up relief work at this time, is never for one moment to haul down its suffrage colours, and it is woman's duty to think what her position is to be after the war, and to see that her sex does not come out on the wrong side.[50]

NUWSS branches also continued to offer speakers on political and constitutional matters, mixing topical war concerns with the suffrage. For example, in November 1914 the Edinburgh branch advertised a meeting in the local press to hear about proportional representation in Belgium.[51]

One of the leaders of the Women's Freedom League, Charlotte Despard, was a frequent visitor to Scotland and an indefatigable speaker on a number of different issues. In fact, Mrs Despard spoke on so many different issues, some more popular than others, that her role as President of the WFL might become blurred in newspaper reports. While she spoke on platforms organised by the WFL, her main attraction for the audience in the early years of the war was as the sister of Sir John French, Commander-in-Chief of the British Expeditionary Force. As the *Sunday Post* quipped, 'Lord French's sister was at one time a prominent suffragette, which goes to prove that fighting runs in the family.'[52] However, as a committed vegetarian, she could also be found in newspapers advocating a change in the national diet, and she was also a popular speaker at meetings of Theosophical Societies. In one week in 1917 Scottish newspaper reports show that she spoke at the Perth Theosophical Society on 'The Making of Destiny' on Saturday 6th October; at Aberdeen on 'The Hidden Worlds' on Monday 8th; in Dundee on Tuesday

9th on the work of the Women's Freedom League; was quoted on the doctrine of reincarnation in the *Dundee Evening Telegraph* on Wednesday 10th and returned to speak in Aberdeen on the same day on 'The Hidden Worlds' again. Descriptions of her speeches on these subjects usually included the information that Despard was a well-known suffragette, thus associating the suffrage question with other, possibly more 'cranky', subjects. Vegetarianism was part of the WFL ethos, with the League opening vegetarian restaurants during the war, and Despard saw vegetarianism as 'pre-eminently a woman's question'.[53] As Gifford Lewis points out, she exemplified 'a familiar clustering in the suffragist world of feminism, pacifism, vegetarianism and a working-class base'.[54] However, this mixture might still be alarming for some Scottish newspaper readers, whose views might perhaps better be summed up by the words of the psychiatrist Sir James Crichton-Browne as he opened the Dumfries and District Flower Show in 1915: 'The war is giving an opportunity to the faddists and cranks who are diligently exploiting it on behalf of their favourite whims. The prohibitionists, the vegetarians, the fruitarians, the nutarians, and all the rest of them.'[55] Note that the campaign for women's suffrage was also closely associated with the campaign for prohibition in Scotland.[56]

Charlotte Despard felt that it was still possible for women to be given the vote during wartime, arguing that 'this would be an advisable time for passing a non-party measure, such as Women's Suffrage, to take effect after the war.'[57] In what might be seen as a criticism of the WSPU she argued that this might have been possible 'had all the suffrage societies held together as suffragist'. However, it was her association with the Anti-Conscription League of 1916, and her advocacy of a peace by negotiation that opened her up to more critical remarks in the newspapers. Descriptions of the meetings at which she spoke on these subjects, often in the company of Sylvia Pankhurst, were dismissive if not downright hostile. The *Daily Record* account of a meeting in December 1916 in Trafalgar Square, where both Despard and Sylvia Pankhurst attempted to speak, was headlined 'More Peace Cranks'[58] while the *Aberdeen Journal* referred to the 'insidious campaign' of Mrs Despard and the anti-conscriptionists, who were 'fighting by passiveness ... for a lost cause'.[59] Again, many of these comments linked Despard negatively to the suffrage campaign, such as a letter in the *Dundee Evening Telegraph* of October 1915, which criticised a speech by Mrs Despard and warned 'Woman's Suffrage is against God's law.'[60]

Charlotte Despard's speeches on the subject of peace were, however, reported in some detail in the Scottish newspapers, giving her a good chance of getting her points across to their readership, just as before the war suffragettes' speeches were reported in detail, even by hostile newspapers.[61] When she addressed the Perth Theosophical Society in October 1915, the *Dundee Evening Telegraph* reported:

> Speaking on woman's attitude towards the war, she said that many people said that the present moment was not the time to speak about peace; that they should crush the enemy, and then think of peace. She disagreed with that. At the present moment they ought to be working for and thinking about peace. The attitude of woman towards war should be one of the very sternest disapproval. She should like to see a crusade of women against war, and it would be bound to cease.[62]

In 1915 the WFL established the Women's Peace Council for a negotiated peace with members including Charlotte Despard, Teresa Billington-Grieg and Helen Crawfurd, and throughout the war Scottish press reports of WFL meetings returned to this idea of women's 'natural' abilities as peacemakers. In February 1918 a meeting of the Dundee WFL heard a 'Miss Munro' (possibly the Glaswegian Anna Munro) stating that 'in the past woman's natural outlook was towards peace and the building up of the homes of the people, and it was because of that outlook that they wanted women in the councils of the nations'.[63] Helen Crawfurd and Charlotte Despard were among the founders of the Women's Peace Crusade, which started in Glasgow in July 1916 and spread across the country in 1917. A grassroots socialist movement, the WPC aimed to demonstrate publicly women's demand for a negotiated peace and the end to war.

Of course, the WFL were not the only suffrage campaigners to be associated with the peace movement in the Scottish press. In April 1915 many Scottish newspapers spoke out against the International Women's Congress in The Hague, also known as the Women's Peace Congress, organised by Dutch women's suffrage organisations and attended by over a thousand delegates from twelve countries. The *Stirling Observer* stated, '[t]here is a decided feeling in this country against our women-folk taking part in international conferences and propaganda for terminating the war' and that there was danger of 'more harm than good being done by such conferences'.[64] It noted that Mrs Despard was suggested as one of the participants. Several other newspapers reported the reply of the French author Juliette Adam to an invitation to attend the congress: 'Are you truly an Englishwoman? Although I am but little of a Suffragette I must confess to you that I better understand those Englishwomen who would like to fight.'[65] Note the connection made between the suffrage movement and the war rather than peace despite the fact that many of the women attending the peace congress were also connected to the suffrage movement. In fact, the British delegation, which included Sylvia Pankhurst, was unable to cross the Channel to attend the Congress and only three British women, all of whom were already outside the UK, were able to attend—Emmeline Pethick-Lawrence, Kathleen Courtney and Crystal Macmillan.[66] Courtney and Macmillan were members of a group who had resigned from the Executive Committee of the NUWSS on Mrs Fawcett's announcement of its support of the war effort while Pethick-Lawrence was an ex-member of the WSPU. Mrs Pankhurst issued a press statement declaring that the WSPU would take no part in the Congress: 'She says this is not time to talk of peace.'[67] Later the same year there was also criticism in the press of what was called 'The Ship of Fools', the 'peace ship' organised by the American industrialist Henry Ford. A description of the ship in the *Edinburgh Evening News* pointed out that the 'dining-room was draped with Suffragette colours'.[68] Thus there were confusing and conflicting associations of the suffrage movement with both the war and the campaign for a negotiated peace in the Scottish press.

Mrs Pankhurst attempted to disassociate herself in the press with the suffragettes who campaigned for peace during the war. In the spring of 1917 she was also forced to issue press statements disassociating herself with attempted murder in what was known as the 'Poison Plot Trial'. On 1 February 1917 the newspapers reported that three women and a man—Alice Wheeldon, her daughters Harriet and Winnie and son-in-law Alfred Mason—had been arrested for a conspiracy to murder the Prime Minister and Arthur Henderson, both members of the War Cabinet. 'The three women ... are said to be Suffragettes, and the man is believed to be a conscientious objector.'[69] The WSPU at once issued a statement: 'The officials of the WSPU have no knowledge of the persons as described.'[70]

The trial opened in front of the magistrates in Derby the following week and it was reported that 'Mrs Pankhurst has arrived in Derby, and it is understood she will ask permission to make a statement in Court.'[71] The story presented by the prosecution was that the conspirators planned to make use of a plan previously concocted by the suffragettes before the war to poison the Prime Minister by driving a poisoned nail through his boot. (Note that it is suggested by Sheila Rowbotham that some of the evidence was fabricated in a government attempt to disgrace the anti-war movement.[72]) Witnesses also reported Mrs Wheeldon discussing how she and other suffragettes had used petrol to burn down churches. This reminder of pre-war tactics, plus the suggestion that some suffragettes were now associating with anti-conscriptionists, conscientious objectors and socialists, came at the same time as the House of Commons was debating the recommendations of the Speaker's Conference on franchise reform. Thus readers of the Scottish press could turn from the reports of speeches praising women's contributions to the war effort to reports of other women—and self-confessed suffragettes—plotting to kill the Prime Minister. The *Dundee Courier* reported on the trial on page 4 of its 10th March edition directly after a report on the preceding page of the death of Mrs Harley, a member of the NUWSS executive committee and administrator of a Scottish Women's Hospital in the Balkans. Mrs Harley was another sister of Lord French and was described as 'a worthy sister of a great soldier'.[73] On 12th March the *Aberdeen Journal* juxtaposed a report of the sentences handed out to the plotters on pages 3 and 4, which repeated the statement that the original plot had been conceived by 'the suffragists' (again note the use of a term usually associated with the constitutional NUWSS), with a letter from the Executive Committee of the Edinburgh Branch of the Scottish League for Opposing Women Suffrage arguing that the issue of the enfranchisement of women should not be discussed until all men had returned home from the front.[74] When the trial concluded with the conviction and imprisonment of Mrs Wheeldon and Winnie and Alfred Mason, Mrs Pankhurst was allowed to make a statement to the court, with the recommendation from the Judge that 'the press take note':

> 'There never was,' said Mrs Pankhurst, 'such a plot, nor was any money expended for such a purpose. The whole idea of a plot and the language employed by the prisoners about the war are abhorrent to the officers and members of the Union .... The W.S.P.U. regards the Prime Minister's life as of the greatest value in the present grave crisis, and its members would, if necessary to do so, take great risks themselves to protect it from danger.'[75]

Throughout the war some of the most prominent voices in the Scottish press on the subject of women's suffrage were actually those of men. Like the Women's Freedom League, the Northern Men's Federation for Women's Suffrage continued to campaign and hold meetings in Scotland. Originally established in 1913 through the work of the activist and actress Maud Arncliffe Sennett, the Northern Men's Federation was a formidable group made up of Scottish councillors, bailies, magistrates, trade-council members and others in public life in Edinburgh and Glasgow. The Federation was originally formed to travel to London to deliver a petition to the Prime Minister in July 1913. Asquith refused to see the deputation, a slight that captured press interest and was portrayed as a great insult to Scottish manhood.[76] Having held meetings in Hyde Park, the group returned to Scotland and the core continued its campaign for women's suffrage throughout the war. In August 1916 they returned to London to deliver another petition to the

Prime Minister. Again they were rebuffed, but this time the Prime Minister had changed his opinion on the subject of women's suffrage, and the deputation was informed of this in a meeting with the Chief Whip: 'It was only a matter of time when the women would be given the vote. They might consider women's suffrage as practically safe.'[77] Thus one of the first indications in the Scottish press of the coming franchise reform was through reports on the activities of male suffragists.

Since the enfranchisement of a limited number of women in 1918 there has been debate over the differing contributions of women's war work and militant action to their achievement of the vote. However, there was no doubt in the minds of newspaper editors that women had earned the vote through their war work. As the editor of the *Perthshire Advertiser* put it: 'Women's patriotism has never once been called in question ... .The hand that rocks the cradle is, after all, fit enough to help to rule the world.'[78] The *Evening Express* quoted the *Daily Mail*'s opinion that '[t]he immense services that they [women] have rendered during the war have pretty well revolutionised the average man's ideas of their usefulness'[79] while the women's correspondent of the *Aberdeen Journal* opined that 'women's work in the war has handicapped the opponents of her political emancipation.'[80] She also noted that:

> For the essentially womanly woman it has long been a trial, this dilemma in which women have been placed, that if they were quiet and orderly they were stamped as not wanting the vote; while if they were not quiet and orderly they did not deserve it.

However, not all newspapers were fully in support of the extension of the franchise to women—the editor of the *Dundee, Perth, Forfar and Fife's People's Journal* suggested that newly enfranchised woman 'casts a most portentous shadow' and summed up with the words 'Well, whatever it may be, we are in for it now.'[81]

It is a popular misconception that the suffrage campaign lay dormant or disappeared during the war years as women turned their energies to war work. This short introduction to the coverage of the topic in the Scottish press has shown that the campaign for women's enfranchisement continued throughout the war years. Meetings were held, speeches made and letters written to the newspapers, even if not in the same numbers as before the war. In particular, the activities of groups such as the Women's Freedom League and the Northern Men's Federation for Women's Suffrage continued to prioritise the campaign for the vote, while the association of the NUWSS with the Scottish Women's Hospitals kept that organisation's profile high throughout the war. While coverage of the suffrage campaign did not preoccupy journalists as it had in the few years before the outbreak of war, in particular because of the cessation of acts of militancy, the cause did not disappear from Scottish newspapers. Thus newspaper coverage demonstrates that the suffrage campaign continued, albeit in a reduced form, throughout the war years in Scotland.

The Scottish press also continued to shape public opinion on the suffrage question. In their praise of women for performing their patriotic duty from very early in the war, newspaper editorial columns established a connection in the minds of their readers between women's war work and their achievement of the vote as editors and proprietors became convinced of the need for enfranchisement reform. Whilst historians debate how much women's war work contributed to their achievement of suffrage after the war, there was little question in the minds of contemporary newspaper editors that the two should be connected. The majority of Scottish newspapers were in support of some form of women's suffrage by the end of the war, and made explicit to their readers the connection between women's contribution to the war effort and their achievement of citizenship. However, not all readers were happy with this association of patriotic work and female suffrage, and some correspondents attacked what they saw as the suffrage organisations' opportunistic use of war work to further their political cause.

However, while there continued to be some coverage of the suffrage movement in the Scottish press during the First World War, the image of suffrage campaigners therein was contradictory and fragmented. Suffragettes were presented in the newspapers as both wartime heroines and figures of fun; murderous conspirators and committed reformers. The stereotype of the suffragette was too useful a shorthand for a particular type of enthusiastic woman reformer to be entirely discarded by the press, particularly in terms of her potential as a butt of jokes, which could easily be recycled from before the War. Whilst editors wrote enthusiastically of women's contribution to the war effort, jokes about suffragettes continued to provide light relief. The immediate pre-war press coverage of the suffrage issue had been dominated by the actions of the WSPU, but in wartime—at least in Scotland—other organisations, in particular the Women's Freedom League, came to the fore, perhaps because they continued to hold meetings on the suffrage question but also because of connections to campaigns such as the Women's Peace Crusade. At the same time, the fundraising campaigns for the Scottish Women's Hospitals served as a constant reminder to the general reader of the aims and arguments of the constitutional societies. While groups such as the Women's Freedom League and the Northern Men's Federation for Women's Suffrage benefited from the decision of the WSPU to focus on war work, gaining more newspaper coverage for their continuing campaigns for the vote, a less coherent position on the suffrage question was now presented in the press. While both militant and non-militant organisations received praise for their war work, there were also newspaper stories associating the suffrage movement with the peace effort—or even conspiracies against the state. Volunteers at the Scottish Women's Hospitals were approvingly described as 'suffragettes', but the appellation retained negative connotations when used about peace campaigners. It might also be suggested that, while suffrage associations were efficient and quick ways of establishing women's war work at the start of the war, as the organisation of this work became centralised, the origin of such groups became less important.

It can thus be seen that, although the suffrage campaign did not disappear from the pages of the Scottish press during the First World War, its image became much less consistent than it had been before the war, and the newspapers presented a number of very different, and opposing, discourses on the subject, reflecting the differences of opinion on issues such as a negotiated peace that now appeared within both the constitutional and the militant organisations. Nonetheless, the overall tone of the Scottish newspapers towards the suffragettes' contribution to the war effort was a positive one, and this helped to shape wider public opinion on the subject of women's enfranchisement as the war drew to a close.

Notes

1. See, for example, L. E. M. Mayhall (1995) Creating the 'Suffragette Spirit': British feminism and the historical imagination, *Women's History Review*, 4(3), pp. 319–344.

2. This was the Prisoners (Temporary Discharge for Health) Act of 1913 that dealt with the problem of hunger-striking suffragettes by releasing them on licence and then re-arresting and returning them to prison once their health had improved.

3. Members of the NUWSS were known as constitutional suffragists because they believed that they could achieve the vote for women through peaceful tactics such as non-violent demonstrations, petitions and lobbying MPs.

4. C. Pankhurst (1987) *Unshackled* (London: Century Hutchinson), quoted in K. E. Kelly (2004) Seeing Through Spectacles: the woman suffrage movement and London newspapers, 1906–13, *European Journal of Women's Studies*, 11(3), p. 327.

5. *Papers of the Glasgow and West of Scotland Association for Women's Suffrage: suffrage executive committee minute books*, 30 October 1912. Mitchell Library, Glasgow, 891036/1.

6. A. Bingham (2015) The Digitization of Newspaper Archives: opportunities and challenges for historians, *Twentieth Century British History*, 21(2), pp. 225–231.

7. K. E. Kelly (2004) Seeing Through Spectacles: the woman suffrage movement and London newspapers, 1906–13, *European Journal of Women's Studies*, 11(3), pp. 327–353.

8. K. Cowman (2007) 'Doing Something Silly': the uses of humour by the women's social and political union, 1903–14, *International Review of Social History*, 52, pp. 259–274.

9. J. Chapman (2013) *Gender, Citizenship and Newspapers: historical and transnational perspectives* (Basingstoke: Palgrave Macmillan); R. Nessheim (1992) *British Political Newspapers and Women's Suffrage 1910–1918* (Doctoral dissertation, University of Oslo).

10. S. Pedersen (2002) The Appearance of Women's Politics in the Correspondence Pages of Aberdeen Newspapers 1900–14, *Women's History Review*, 11(4), pp. 657–674.

11. N. Watson (2010) *Suffragettes and the Post* (Dundee: Linda McGill), p. 52.

12. J. DeVries (2013) Popular and Smart: why scholarship on the women's suffrage movement in Britain still matters, *History Compass*, 11(3), pp. 177–188.

13. *Aberdeen Journal* (4 September 1914), p. 6.

14. *Edinburgh Evening News* (11 August 1914), p. 2.

15. *Dundee Courier* (2 September 1914), p. 4.

16. *Aberdeen Journal* (19 July 1915), p. 4.

17. *Dundee Courier* (9 September 1914), p. 2.

18. *Aberdeen Journal* (21 September 2014), p. 4.

19. *Edinburgh Evening News* (1 March 1915), p. 4.

20. *Dundee Evening Telegraph* (26 February 1915), p. 2.

21. *Dundee Courier* (8 August 1914), p. 3.

22. *Dundee Evening Telegraph* (14 August 1914), p. 3.

23. *Dundee Evening Telegraph* (25 February 1915), p. 1.

24. *Dumfries and Galloway Standard* (27 February 1915), p. 4.

25. J. Purvis & M. Wright (2005) Writing Suffragette History: the contending autobiographical narratives of the Pankhursts, *Women's History Review*, 14(3–4), p. 414.

26. E. Pankhurst (1914) *My Own Story* (London: Eveleigh Nash), p. 59.

27. *Dundee Evening Telegraph* (23 March 1915), p. 3.

28. *Dundee Evening Telegraph* (10 March 1915), p. 5.

29. J. McDermid (2008) A Very Polite and Considerate Revolution: the Scottish women's hospitals and the Russian Revolution 1916–1917, *Revolutionary Russia*, 21(2), pp. 135–151.

30. *Fife Free Press and Kirkcaldy Guardian* (29 January 1916), p. 5.

31. *Fife Free Press and Kirkcaldy Guardian* (18 March 1916), p. 5.

32. *Arbroath Herald* (26 May 1916), p. 2.

33. *Aberdeen Daily Journal* (28 September 1915), p. 5.

34. *Daily Record* (24 January 1916), p. 4.

35. *Edinburgh Evening News* (25 August 1914), p. 3.

36. *Perthshire Advertiser* (28 October 1914), p. 2.

37. *Dundee Evening Telegraph* (13 October 1915), p. 2.

38. *Dundee Evening Telegraph* (21 July 1916).

39. *Daily Record* (20 November 1916).

40. *Dundee Courier* (16 October 1917), p. 2.
41. S. Pedersen (2002) A Surfeit of Socks? The Impact of the First World War on Women Correspondents to Daily Newspapers, *Journal of Scottish Historical Studies*, 22(1), pp. 50–72.
42. *Dundee Evening Telegraph* (17 November 1914), p. 2.
43. *Falkirk Herald* (13 January 1915), p. 1.
44. *Southern Reporter* (11 February 1915), p. 7.
45. *Dundee Evening Telegraph* (30 September 1915), p. 2.
46. For example, *Aberdeen Evening Express* (17 September 1914), p. 2.
47. K. Cowman, 'Doing Something Silly', p. 261.
48. *Dundee Evening Telegraph* (25 March 1915), p. 2.
49. *Dundee Courier* (18 August 1914), p. 5.
50. *Dundee Courier* (4 February 1915), p. 3.
51. *Edinburgh Evening News* (14 November 1914), p. 4.
52. *Sunday Post* (24 December 1916), p. 12.
53. *The Vegetarian Messenger and Health Review*, 10(1913), p. 308. Quoted in L. Leneman (1997) The Awakened Instinct: vegetarianism and the women's suffrage movement in Britain, *Women's History Review*, 6(2), p. 278.
54. G. Lewis (1988) *Eva Gore Booth and Esther Roper*, p. 169. Quoted in Leneman, 'The Awakened Instinct', p. 281.
55. *Dumfries and Galloway Standard* (28 August 1915), pp. 4–5.
56. See M. Smitley (2009) The Feminine Public Sphere: middle-class women and civic life in Scotland, c. 1870–1914 (Oxford: Oxford University Press).
57. *Daily Record* (18 October 1915), p. 3.
58. *Daily Record* (26 December 1916), p. 4.
59. *Aberdeen Daily Journal* (15 May 1916), p. 5.
60. *Dundee Evening Telegraph* (13 October 1915), p. 2.
61. Pedersen, 'The Appearance of Women's Politics', p. 659.
62. *Dundee Evening Telegraph* (11 October 1915), p. 4.
63. *Dundee Courier* (18 February 1916), p. 7.
64. *Stirling Observer* (20 April 1915), p. 7.
65. *Dundee Courier* (24 April 1915), p. 3.
66. L. B. Costin (1982) Feminism, Pacifism, Internationalism and the 1915 International Congress of Women, *Women's Studies International Forum*, 5(3), pp. 301–315.
67. *Dundee Evening Telegraph* (9 April 1915), p. 2.
68. *Edinburgh Evening News* (6 December 1915), p. 3.
69. *Aberdeen Daily Journal* (1 February 1917), p. 6.
70. *Aberdeen Daily Journal* (2 February 1917), p. 6.
71. *Dundee Courier* (6 February 1917), p. 4.
72. S. Rowbotham (2015) *Friends of Alice Wheeldon: the anti-war activist accused of plotting to kill Lloyd George* (New York: NYU Press).
73. *Dundee Courier* (10 March 1917), p. 3.
74. *Aberdeen Daily Journal* (12 March 1917), pp. 3–4.
75. *Dundee Courier* (12 March 1917), p. 4.
76. See C. Eustance (1997) Citizens, Scotsmen, Bairns: manly politics and women's suffrage in the Northern Men's Federation, 1913–20, in C. Eustance & A. V. John, *The Men's Share? Masculinities: male support and women's suffrage in Britain, 1890 to 1920* (London: Routledge).
77. *Dundee Evening Telegraph* (18 August 1916), p. 3.
78. *Perthshire Advertiser* (16 January 1918), p. 4.
79. *Aberdeen Evening Express* (11 January 1918), p. 2.
80. *Aberdeen Journal* (16 January 1918), p. 2.
81. *Dundee, Perth, Forfar and Fife's People's Journal* (12 January 1918).

Disclosure statement

No potential conflict of interest was reported by the author.

Funding

The author is grateful to the Carnegie Trust for the Universities of Scotland for a travel grant which has enabled this research [grant number 31880].

ORCID

Sarah Pedersen ⓘ http://orcid.org/0000-0001-8017-4227

4 Antimilitarism, Citizenship and Motherhood

The formation and early years of the Women's International League (WIL), 1915–1919

Sarah Hellawell

ABSTRACT

This article examines the concept of motherhood and peace in the British women's movement during the Great War. It does so by focusing on the Women's International League (WIL)—the British section of the Women's International League for Peace and Freedom (WILPF). Drawing on the WIL papers, the article shows how a section of the movement continued to lobby for female representation during the war alongside its calls for peace. WIL referred to the social and cultural experiences of motherhood, which allowed it to challenge the discourse on gender and to build bridges between women of former enemy nations. This case study examines how maternalist rhetoric influenced feminism and sheds light on how British women attempted to enter the political sphere by linking women's maternal experience to their demands for citizenship.

In April 1915, approximately 1200 women from twelve nations gathered at The Hague, united in the belief that 'the women of the world must come to that world's aid.'[1] Emmeline Pethick Lawrence, a former suffragette who turned her attention to the cause of peace upon the outbreak of war, argued that the Hague Congress 'opened a new chapter in the history of the world-wide women's movement'.[2] A 'significant minority' of British suffragists supported the aims of the anti-war Congress and formed the British Committee of the International Women's Congress in February 1915 to coordinate their efforts to travel to The Hague.[3] Approximately 180 British women from suffrage, social reform and labour backgrounds responded to the invitation from Dutch feminists, but only three—Emmeline Pethick Lawrence, Kathleen Courtney and Chrystal Macmillan—avoided the wartime travel restrictions and reached the event, held from 28 April to 1 May 1915. On their return to London, they co-founded the Women's International League (WIL), the British national section of—what would become known as—the Women's International League for Peace and Freedom (WILPF).[4] By May 1919 British WIL had 4000 members in fifty local branches. The organisation was largely made up of suffragists and combined radical feminist claims to citizenship with calls for peace and international law.

This study of British WIL will shed fresh light on the historical debate surrounding British feminism during the First World War. It examines demands for women's citizenship and peace during the Great War and in its immediate aftermath. The view that the war was a 'watershed' has been quite common, reflected in the argument that the conflict heralded dramatic improvements in the lives of women.[5] More recently, however, this perspective has been increasingly questioned.[6] Susan Kingsley Kent claims that the women's movement lost its radical edge during the Great War as it seemingly accepted traditional notions of difference between the sexes and reaffirmed the notion of separate spheres, yet she overlooks the prevailing influence of maternalism on feminism before 1914.[7] The relationship between maternalism and feminism has a complex history, which this article will highlight. Women's activism was both aided and constrained by gendered assumptions about women's roles. For example, 'caring' work and philanthropic efforts permitted some middle-class women access to the public sphere, yet romanticised versions of motherhood placed burdens on working women.[8] Furthermore, women's international humanitarian relief work could contribute to ideas about empire-building whilst upholding maternal ideals. The latter aspect has recently been illustrated by Emily Baughan's research on the Save the Children Fund, which was co-founded in 1919 by WIL member Dorothy Jebb Buxton and her sister Eglantyne Jebb.[9] Although WIL was not a relief association, such work influenced the feminism and pacifism of those members who undertook humanitarian efforts before, during and after the Great War.[10]

WIL's roots were entangled with the suffrage campaign, which had argued for equality on the dual grounds that men and women shared a common humanity and that recognition of women's roles would balance society.[11] A leading group of suffragists resigned from the Executive Committee of the National Union of Women's Suffrage Societies (NUWSS) during the war, considering their support for peace to continue 'the principle for which our long fight has been waged', based on the 'essential duty of women to uphold the ideal of moral force in human affairs'.[12] These suffragists were involved in the foundation of WIL in 1915. The example of WIL thus illustrates how a prominent section of the British women's movement remained active during and beyond the Great War. As the article will show, feminists asserted women's 'moral force'—often linked to maternal roles—as an integral part of their ideology and methodology in the campaign for women's rights and peace, which represents continuity with the maternalist rhetoric of the pre-war women's movement. WIL stressed the impact of war on women, whilst underlining that feminism was unequivocally opposed to militarism. Furthermore, this article will reveal how feminists of WIL used their understanding of war to demand female citizenship. The discourse of motherhood allowed WIL to operate in the realm of international politics—a traditionally male domain—to demonstrate that women had a valuable contribution to make to the public sphere. Finally, the article will consider the association's humanitarian and political campaign against the Allied blockade in 1919, demonstrating that maternal rhetoric could unite women from former enemy nations and that women had much to offer to international relations.[13]

Feminist Attitudes to Militarism

Martha von Tilling, the protagonist in Bertha von Suttner's pacifist novel *Die Waffen Nieder!* based her revulsion to war on her experience as a mother.[14] Suttner, the first female recipient of the Nobel Prize for Peace, expressed a gendered response to the issues of war and peace that inspired many of the delegates to the 1915 congress.[15] War had long been a concern of the women's movement: the International Council of Women's (ICW) standing committee on peace and arbitration was formed in 1899, coinciding with both the first peace conference at The Hague and outbreak of war in South Africa. Motherhood and its relationship to war, nation-building and the British Empire became a highly politicised issue during the conflict of 1899–1902: Emily Hobhouse, a leading critic of the Boer War, and Millicent Garrett Fawcett, president of the NUWSS, produced contrasting reports on the impact of the war. Both women employed gendered arguments about military conflict and penetrated the male sphere of international politics, thus preceding WIL's similar campaigns.[16]

A discourse of nationalism, imperialism and patriotism in the context of the Boer War permeated feminist rhetoric.[17] Anna Davin's influential work demonstrates that a 'powerful ideology of motherhood emerged' from the late nineteenth century and that concerns over the birth rate at the turn of the century had imperialist implications for maternal responsibility.[18] The Great War reinvigorated concerns for non-combatants and the question of child welfare, as the crude demand for 'cannon fodder' increased, with obvious implications for women's patriotic duty.[19] The use of maternal rhetoric during the 1914–1918 war was complex; it was employed by both patriots and feminist-pacifists alike.[20] Patriotic propaganda evoked images of mothers' national service and imperial visions of women as 'mothers of the race'.[21] Yet, WIL also used maternal rhetoric alongside its radical opposition to militarism, adopting a language of motherhood in relation to the loss of human life.

For example, Catherine Marshall, the first Honorary Secretary of WIL, condemned militarism as an 'outrage on motherhood' as she considered war to be a waste of women's work in raising sons.[22] Marshall resigned her post as an Honorary Secretary of the NUWSS in March 1915, a month after attending meetings in Amsterdam with German, Belgian and Dutch feminists to plan the women's peace congress.[23] Marshall was amongst the wave of leading suffragists who resigned from the NUWSS Executive Committee when the organisation refused to support the pacifist aims of the congress. Jo Vellacott has documented the divergence between the patriotic Fawcett and the anti-war suffragists, who went on to found WIL.[24] Fawcett promoted support of the war effort to legitimise the Union's claim to the franchise, whereas Marshall believed the best way to 'serve our country, and the best way in which we could continue to serve the cause of Women's Suffrage' was to promote peace. Marshall saw the campaign for a just settlement of the war as 'the natural and almost inevitable development' of the work of the suffrage movement.[25] Her commitment to democracy and peace, which motivated her work for suffrage and involvement with WIL, is also reflected in her leadership of the No-Conscription Fellowship during the war as she campaigned to protect the rights of Conscientious Objectors. Likewise, WIL Chair Helena Swanwick was highly critical of war, which she described as a 'silly, bloody game of massacring sons of women'. Although many of WIL's members never had children— Swanwick 'was indeed glad I had none' during the war—the organisation condemned war as a devastating loss of human life: not just sons, but husbands, brothers and friends.[26]

Many women, whether they opposed or supported the war, used maternalist arguments alongside their claims for equal rights. WIL asserted that motherhood was more than simply a biological function and the association linked the social status of mothers to its radical feminist pacifism. Yet, WIL did acknowledge that not all women were opposed to the Great War: Maude Royden, a member of WIL's Executive Committee, wrote that her belief that women were innately more pacifist than men had 'been severely shaken, if not altogether destroyed' during the war.[27] Female patriotic support and pro-war propaganda frequently emphasised women's roles as mothers of the nation. WIL too used maternal rhetoric during its formative years, illustrating that both patriotic and pacifist feminists were deeply influenced by prevailing discourse on maternal duty and the nation. However, some scholars have concluded that the movement's use of maternalism signalled a decline in its claim to equality.[28]

Maternal rhetoric informed WIL's feminist-pacifist strategy alongside more radical feminist campaigns and its wider concern with the subjugation of women. Laura Beers has demonstrated that women's historical experience of oppression influenced WIL's interpretation of war and international relations.[29] Militarism, as the pinnacle of patriarchal oppression, reduced women to mere 'breeders and slaves'.[30] Swanwick's 1915 pamphlet on *Women and War* argued that 'men make wars, not women', driven by a masculine thirst for honour and domination; while Hobhouse described women as 'chief sufferers from war's curse'.[31] War was portrayed as a direct threat to the progress of feminism, meaning that 'militarism and the woman's movement cannot exist together.'[32] Thus Carol Miller, Leila Rupp and Jo Vellacott have portrayed WILPF as the most ambitious international women's organisation of the interwar years due to its radical feminist critique of international relations alongside its campaign to raise the status of women.[33]

WIL's feminist pacifism was by no means confined to the rhetoric of maternal duty. Its members controversially referred to the use of sexual violence as a weapon of war, as 'the horrible violation of women which attends all war'.[34] The organisation also objected to the wartime repression of civil liberties that influenced women's lives. Feminists challenged the unequal moral standard enshrined in regulation 40D of the Defence of the Realm Act (DORA), which reintroduced police powers to conduct compulsory medical examinations on prostitutes over fears of the spread of venereal disease. Helen Ward, a member of WIL's Executive Committee, described the procedure as 'insidious menaces to the freedom of women'.[35] The regulation did not subject men to the same examination, thus feminist protest against 40D mirrored the movement's earlier opposition to the controversial Contagious Diseases Act.[36] Similarly, activists highlighted the direct impact that aerial technology and disruption to food supplies had upon women as non-combatants on the home front.[37] Dismissing the popular argument that men were 'fighting for hearth and home', Swanwick claimed that 'security as a result of militarism is an illusion'.[38] Feminist pacifists also utilised women's non-combatant status to give voice to their antimilitarism. Free from patriotism bound up in expectations of military service, WIL argued that women could freely oppose war and enter a political space beyond masculine defined boundaries.[39] Challenging the militarist threat to the home, WIL used women's experiences, including motherhood, to contest the political status quo. The organisation argued that female maternal roles and prolonged subjugation provided women with a unique understanding of war and peace.

Historians of the British peace movement, however, have too often dismissed WIL's pacifism as incoherent and historians of feminism have rarely analysed the unique nature of WIL's feminist pacifism and its radicalism.[40] In a pamphlet published by the antimilitarist Union of Democratic Control (UDC), Swanwick wrote that pacifists would only be successful when they recognise a 'woman's claim to freedom'.[41] Her writing demonstrates the intricacies of feminist pacifism, which considered the movements for peace and women's rights as intimately connected, yet at times seemed to suggest that women possessed an innate natural pacifism. Whilst veering close to essentialist claims about female nature, she also asserted that 'we women are pacifists at heart, but we have been too much passivists.'[42] To Swanwick—whose ideas deeply influenced WIL—peace was an active quality, tied to a progressive vision of internationalism and women's rights.[43] As committed pacifists, a number of WIL's Executive Committee also joined other anti-war associations in protest against the Great War: for example, Catherine Marshall effectively led the NCF and Swanwick was the only woman on the UDC's Executive Committee. WIL also supported NCF and UDC campaigns, sharing their opposition to conscription, militarism and secret diplomacy. WIL, however, deemed their own status as a feminist pacifist association to be unique, as there was 'none which makes just the connection that we do between feminism and the abolition of war'.[44] Rather than subsume its feminism to join forces with other anti-war groups or sacrifice its calls for peace to concentrate on the campaign for women's suffrage with the NUWSS, WIL saw the campaign for women's rights and peace as one.[45]

Citizenship to Balance Militarism

During the war, the concept of British citizenship was tied up with notions of national duty and service in the armed forces.[46] Vilified for their unpatriotic stance, pacifists and conscientious objectors eschewed expectations of service; the press scorned the 'peacettes' in 1915 for their participation in the 'German' congress.[47] For the majority of suffragists and suffragettes, national loyalty expressed through their support for the war effort could legitimise their claim to citizenship rights.[48] Ideas about gender, patriotism and pacifism were complex. Many women conformed to their roles as 'mothers of the race', whereas some female patriots, including those who distributed white feathers to 'shirkers' or wore military uniforms, disrupted traditional notions of feminine passivity.[49] In contrast, male anti-militarists, pacifists, Quakers and conscientious objectors subverted conventional concepts of masculinity and patriotic service.[50] Much of the literature on female service during the war, however, seems to confirm contemporary assumptions that pacifism and patriotism were mutually exclusive.[51] Nonetheless, WIL did not consider itself to be unpatriotic. Feminist pacifists advocated that it was their duty, as women, to protect society from the destruction of war by securing peace. Swanwick questioned jingoistic, anti-German patriotism, asserting that 'it is not necessary for a man to hate other countries because he loves his own'; rather, she considered herself a patriotic anti-militarist and internationalist.[52] Drawing on popular discourse of service to the family and nation, Marshall stressed that it was women's duty to ensure that 'the sacrifices our men are making shall not have been made in vain.'[53] WIL also questioned whether a 'defensive' war could protect the home as claimed by anti-German propaganda.[54] In so doing, WIL both adhered to, and challenged, prescribed gender roles, thus creating a space for women's contribution to the political sphere.

Wartime upheaval reopened the parliamentary debate on the terms of the British franchise, creating an opportunity for suffragists, including WIL members, to renew their calls for voting rights.[55] WIL claimed that 'there would be great injustice in confining an extension of the franchise to sailors and soldiers'; the devastation of war illustrated that 'never before was the need so great for the enfranchisement of the whole people, and especially of women.'[56] It thus highlighted both the innate value of women's votes and their wartime national loyalty. Like the more 'patriotic' suffragists, WIL used the language of national service to demand female citizenship.[57]

Moreover, leading WIL members challenged anti-suffragist 'physical force' claims. Opponents of female suffrage had long used women's (lack of) physical strength and their omission from the armed forces to deny the extension of the franchise.[58] The 'physical force' debate had further implications for imperial and international relations, as the claim implied that political power was maintained through physical means, ensuring the dominance of stronger nations over smaller states, creating a survival of the fittest competition.[59] Swanwick and Royden argued that this preference for physical strength created unnecessary rivalry and an uneasy system of shifting alliances with 'the eternal necessity of war'.[60] WIL linked 'physical force' to both the oppression of women and small states, campaigning for 'an assertion of moral force as the supreme governing force in the world'—moral force was linked to progress, democracy and equality, which would create peace.[61] Swanwick went further: she dismissed the exclusion of women on the grounds of 'physical force', arguing that, as child bearers, women possessed a positive form of physical force.[62] Feminist pacifists, therefore, contributed to an ongoing discussion among suffragists and anti-suffragists on the 'Woman Question', in particular reference to female maternal roles and their contribution to society.[63] They also linked militarism and female oppression, whilst promoting the value of 'moral force'.

WIL's position within the suffrage movement subverted traditional notions of citizenship based on militarism, using women's position as mothers and non-combatants to justify both their opposition to war and demands for greater equality, which has often been overlooked in the history of the British suffrage campaign.[64] Despite her work on the organisation, Jo Vellacott represents the formation of WIL as an irrevocable split within the suffrage movement, rather than an ongoing development of existing feminist theories on militarism and female subjugation.[65] She also overlooks the ongoing cooperation between WIL and the suffrage movement, particularly at the local level. For example, the Manchester branch of WIL worked closely with suffrage organisations throughout the war years.[66] WIL was represented in the suffrage deputation to Lloyd George in March 1917 and continued to work for equal suffrage in the 1920s alongside the NUWSS's successor, the National Union of Societies for Equal Citizenship.[67] That said, WIL did represent a different strand of thought within the women's movement, which—although present in the movement before 1914—found its own voice during the Great War.[68] Feminist pacifists employed the language of service to underscore the valuable contribution that women could make to both national and international politics.

One of the most defining features of WIL was its commitment to internationalism. Unlike other international women's organisations—including the ICW and the International Women's Suffrage Alliance (IWSA), which created loose coalitions of existing national women's associations—WILPF was a truly international organisation from the beginning, encouraging its members to form branches in their home countries. Members of WILPF's International Executive Committee were elected as individuals, rather than as national representatives, and the Executive had powers to act without the consultation of national branches.[69] For WILPF, the principles of peace and feminism would best be achieved internationally, and both its feminism and pacifism reflected pronounced transnational commitments. Many delegates at the 1915 Congress saw themselves as citizens of the world, claiming to 'advance a step further and think for the whole world'.[70]

At the international level, feminist pacifists worked beyond the traditional confines of their gender, demonstrating that women were capable of international political work. After the 1915 Congress, two envoy groups travelled across Europe to present their plan for continuous mediation to government ministers. The envoys reported positively that officials in both neutral and belligerent nations 'apparently, recognized without argument that an expression of the public opinion of a large body of women had every claim to consideration in questions of war and peace'.[71] The mission demonstrated that women were able to traverse the lines of war to facilitate diplomacy, arguing that it was their duty to articulate the popular will for mediation.[72] Although the aims of the envoys were not realised, and war continued until the declaration of the Armistice in 1918, the delegates demonstrated that women could operate within the international political sphere.[73] At the second international congress of women, held between 12 and 17 May 1919 in Zurich, WILPF's Feminist Committee produced a Women's Charter outlining a wide-reaching programme for women's rights. Although post-war restrictions prevented the congress from being held in Paris as planned, a WILPF delegation presented the peacemakers with their strategy for a permanent peace. This lobby group included two British representatives, Charlotte Despard and Chrystal Macmillan. WILPF subsequently was one of the first international associations to condemn the Treaty of Versailles. The peace settlement, it argued, would breed tension within Europe and overlooked the need to emancipate women to secure progress and peace.[74] The Women's Charter also linked peace with feminist concerns, such as the endowment of motherhood, trafficking, prostitution and the moral standard—campaigns with pre-war origins. Notably, the Charter urged the 'recognition of women's service to the world, not only as wage-earners, but as mothers and home-makers', underlining that the empowerment of women in traditional gender roles would be 'an essential factor in the building up of the world's peace'.[75]

WIL's Response to the Aftermath of the Great War

Founded on the resolutions of the 1915 congress, WILPF was committed to securing women's rights and peace through international law. Maintaining a transnational network, however, was difficult; it relied on global travel, regular correspondence and meetings but, most importantly, a strong sense of a shared identity in order to transcend nationalism. Leila Rupp has demonstrated that international women's organisations, including WILPF, asserted a 'collective identity' through an assumption that women shared certain characteristics.[76] One of the ways WILPF created a sense of 'we' was its use of female identity, including women's experience of motherhood, described by Hobhouse in 1915 as the 'perfect unanimity of motherhood that seeks but to save the life it has given the world'.[77] The demonstration of transnational unity based on motherhood, or as 'protectors of true civilisation and humanity' may have simply been a rhetorical device.[78] For most, it was the organisation's unique and radical combination of feminism and pacifism that drew women to its ranks. Yet, the use of maternalist discourse demonstrates the prevailing influence of maternalism on feminism at the international level, which is demonstrated through one of WIL's post-war campaigns.

In the immediate aftermath of the Great War, WIL responded to a call from its feminist colleagues in famine-stricken Germany and Austria. The association coordinated a gendered campaign that aimed to reconstruct relations between women of former enemy nations. In 1919, reports reached Britain of famine in Central Europe caused by the Allied blockade. WIL responded by raising funds to send rubber teats to German women who were struggling to feed their babies. The rubber-teat campaign was a highly gendered operation that aimed to provide practical and moral support for 'enemy' women in relation to their experience of motherhood. WIL worked with the Red Cross in Britain and Frankfurt to distribute over one million teats in Germany, which they sent with 'a message of goodwill from the senders to their German sisters'.[79] The blockade became a central concern for WIL in the immediate aftermath of the war, particularly because of its impact on children. In response to pleas for assistance from the Austrian section of WILPF, Ethel Williams, a British WIL member, visited Vienna in 1919 and reported on the famine for WIL's publication *Towards a Permanent Peace*. She condemned the Allied blockade as it caused malnutrition and rickets amongst children in the city, urging the British Government to 'remember that such warfare is directed against children'.[80]

WIL, however, had conflicted attitudes to the provision of aid. Although many of its members participated in relief work during the Great War—including Kathleen Courtney, who worked in Salonika and Corsica—WIL did not organise wartime relief work, opting to focus on political campaigns for peace. Swanwick argued that 'if we abandoned that, we should indeed be surrendering to the age-old notion that women had no concern in public life except to wipe up the mess made by men.'[81] Swanwick believed that relief work could prolong the war and confine women to traditional gender roles, whereas other WIL members found relief work compatible with their feminist pacifism. Nonetheless, WIL's foray into the provision of humanitarian relief in 1919 highlights the organisation's focus on the transformation of public attitudes to 'break(ing) down the barriers of hate, in the name of a common humanity'.[82] WIL's opposition to the blockade also aimed to create a platform for women in the reconstruction of Europe that 'went beyond the humanitarian', as its members focused on the politics of international relations.[83] On 6 April 1919, WIL held a demonstration in Trafalgar Square to campaign against the blockade. WIL's Emmeline Pethick Lawrence, Barbara Ayrton Gould of the Fight the Famine Council and representatives of the Women's Co-operative Guild addressed the 10,000-strong crowd. WIL evocatively portrayed the blockade as 'extermination which begins with the children' and appealed to women, as mothers, to assist mothers in former enemy nations.[84] WIL thus continued to adopt a highly gendered discourse, making particular reference to women's roles as mothers—a role shared by women from all nations. Significantly, WIL's concerns were focused on the plight of children. The child became a symbol of the loss of innocence and hope for a new internationalism for humanitarian associations like the Save Children Fund in the aftermath of the Great War.[85] WIL used maternal rhetoric combined with its radical feminism to demand that women be heard in discussions about the blockade and post-war reconstruction in the interest of permanent peace.[86]

In 1919 WILPF assembled in Zurich 'in the consciousness of our common responsibility in order to seek a common solution and a common deliverance through our united efforts'.[87] WIL's commitment to internationalism, women's rights and a peaceful reconstruction of society provided the organisation with a clear collective identity, which was often expressed through women's experiences of motherhood. However, WIL's feminism was rooted in the ideas of Western suffrage movements. Its leaders were well educated, white and middle-class, which obviously influenced their particular vision of motherhood. WILPF struggled to expand beyond the 'West' and the organisation's relationship with empire remained complex.[88] Although the group's use of maternalist rhetoric decreased after 1920, WIL's campaigns for women's rights during the interwar period included dynamic debates over protective legislation for women in the workplace, the endowment of motherhood and the provision of birth control, which also related to the female experience of motherhood. Notwithstanding its obvious limitations, WILPF attempted to create a transnational feminist pacifist association through its shared aims and rhetoric. Transnational maternal unity was a particularly effective rhetorical device used by the organisation to bridge the divides between women of belligerent nations in the aftermath of war. WIL's response to the blockade also aimed to demonstrate the role that women could play in international politics.

Writing in 1915, Helena Swanwick described 'two pieces of work for the human family (that) are peculiarly the work of women: they are the life-givers and the home-makers'.[89] This article has examined how feminist pacifists were both influenced by maternalism and used maternal rhetoric to further their goals during the Great War. This case study of the Women's International League is instructive for a broader understanding of the women's movement during wartime, as it highlights the continuities between pre-war and interwar feminist ideas about citizenship and motherhood, in relation to the nation and international political sphere. Ultimately, this article has demonstrated how a significant section of the women's movement saw feminism and antimilitarism as inextricably linked. Feminism continued to be influenced by prevailing gender discourse on women's roles as mothers, whilst the movement attempted to challenge women's exclusion from the public sphere. WIL confronted anti-suffragist arguments that blocked women's route to citizenship by highlighting the positive physical and moral force inherent within women's roles and experiences. They argued that women's understanding of war and their duty to 'foster life and to protect the helpless' would allow them to make a unique contribution to the making of peace and the reconstruction of international society after the Armistice.[90] Moreover, WIL also used maternalist pacifism to convey loyalty to both the nation and international law. Between 1915 and 1919 WIL members were united through their wartime experiences as women: as unenfranchised non-combatants and as mothers.

Notes

1. Emily Hobhouse (1915) *Bericht-Rapport-Report* (Amsterdam: International Women's Committee of Permanent Peace). Swarthmore College Peace Collection (SCPC), Women's International League for Peace and Freedom Collection (DG043), Part II: WILPF international office, *Reports of the International Congresses, 1915–1998*, Reel 141(1).
2. Emmeline Pethick Lawrence (1915) *Towards Permanent Peace*, p. 17. The Women's International League for Peace and Freedom Papers, 1915–1978, Reel 16.

3. Alison Fell & Ingrid Sharp (Eds) (2007) *The Women's Movement in Wartime: international perspectives, 1914–19* (Basingstoke: Palgrave Macmillan), p. 12.

4. The International Committee of Women for Permanent Peace (ICWPP) changed its name to WILPF at its Congress held in Zurich from 12 to 17 May 1919. In keeping with the association's own use of acronyms, in this article I use WILPF to refer to the international organisation and WIL to distinguish the British national section.

5. For example, women's wartime work led to an assumption that the Great War had an emancipatory effect on women: Arthur Marwick (1965) *The Deluge: British society and the First World War* (London: Bodley Head); see also Gail Braybon & Penny Summerfield (1987) *Out of the Cage: women's experiences in two world wars* (London: Pandora Press).

6. Gail Braybon (2003) *Evidence, History and the Great War: historians and the impact of 1914–18* (Oxford: Berghahn Books); see also David Monger (2014) Nothing Special? Propaganda and Women's Roles in Late First World War Britain, *Women's History Review*, 23(4), pp. 518–542.

7. Susan Kingsley Kent (1988) The Politics of Sexual Difference: World War I and the demise of British feminism, *The Journal of British Studies*, 27(3), p. 232; Harold Smith (1990) *British Feminism in the Twentieth Century* (Aldershot: Edward Elgar); Ann Taylor Allen (2005) *Feminism and Motherhood in Western Europe 1890–1970: the maternal dilemma* (Basingstoke: Palgrave Macmillan); Eileen Yeo (1999) The Creation of Motherhood and Women's Responses in Britain and France, 1750–1914, *Women's History Review*, 8(2), pp. 201–218. For a more positive account of the British women's movement after the Great War see Adrian Bingham (2004) 'An Era of Domesticity'? Histories of Women and Gender in Interwar Britain, *Cultural and Social History*, 1(2), pp. 225–233.

8. Jane Lewis (1984) *Women in England, 1870–1950: sexual divisions and social change* (Brighton: Wheatsheaf); Joy Damousi & Marilyn Lake (1995) *Gender and War: Australians at war in the twentieth century* (New York: Cambridge University Press).

9. Laura Beers (2016) Advocating for a Feminist Internationalism between the Wars in Glenda Sluga & Carolyn James (Eds) *Women, Diplomacy and International Politics Since 1500* (New York: Routledge); Emily Baughan (2013) 'Every Citizen of Empire Implored to Save the Children!' Empire, Internationalism and the Save the Children Fund in Inter-war Britain, *Historical Research*, 86(231), pp. 116–137; Heather Jones (2009) International or Transnational? Humanitarian action during the First World War, *European Review of History*, 16(5), pp. 697–713; Bruno Cabanes (2014) *The Great War and the Origins of Humanitarianism, 1918–1924* (Cambridge: Cambridge University Press).

10. Dorothy Jebb Buxton's experience of the Balkan Wars influenced her support for WIL and SCF. Similarly, Kathleen Courtney worked in Salonika and Corsica during the war. Hilda Clark and Edith Pye set up a maternity hospital in France in 1914 before becoming active in WIL.

11. Les Garner (1984) *Stepping Stones to Women's Liberty: feminist ideas in the women's suffrage movement 1900–1918* (New Jersey: Associated University Presses); Melanie Phillips (2004) *The Ascent of Woman: a history of the suffragette movement and the ideas behind it* (London: Abacus).

12. Margaret Ashton, Letter to the Secretaries of Societies and Federations of the NUWSS, 14 April 1915. Women's Library, WILPF/4/1.

13. For more on the international women's movement see Carol Miller (1994) 'Geneva—the Key to Equality': interwar feminists and the League of Nations, *Women's History Review*, 3(2), pp. 219–245; Leila Rupp (1997) *Worlds of Women: the making of an international women's movement* (New Jersey: Princeton University Press); Ellen DuBois & Katie Oliviero (2009) Circling the Globe: international feminism reconsidered, 1920 to 1975, *Women's Studies International Forum*, 32(1); Francisca De Haan, Margaret Allen, June Purvis & Krassimira Daskalova (Eds) (2012) *Women's Activism: global perspectives from the 1890s to the present* (London: Routledge); Marie Sandell (2015) *The Rise of Women's Transnational Activism: identity and sisterhood between the world wars* (London: I.B. Tauris).

14. Bertha von Suttner (1908) *Lay Down Your Arms: the autobiography of Martha von Tilling* (London: Longmans Green & Co; first published 1889), p. 48.
15. Regina Braker (1995) Bertha Von Suttner's Spiritual Daughters: the feminist pacifism of Anita Augspurg, Lida Gustava Heymann and Helene Stocker at the International Congress of Women at The Hague, 1915, *Women's Studies International Forum*, 18(2), pp. 103–111.
16. Rebecca Gill (2013) *Calculating Compassion: humanity and relief in war, Britain 1870–1914* (Manchester: Manchester University Press).
17. Heloise Brown (2003) 'The Truest Form of Patriotism': pacifist feminism in Britain, 1870–1902 (Manchester: Manchester University Press).
18. Maternal duty was stressed by authorities as a key factor in maintaining racial superiority within the British Empire and wider world: Anna Davin (1978) Imperialism and Motherhood, *History Workshop*, 5, pp. 9–65; Ellen Ross (1993) *Love and Toil: motherhood in outcast London, 1870–1918* (Oxford: Oxford University Press).
19. Davin, 'Imperialism and Motherhood'.
20. Susan R. Grayzel (1999) *Women's Identities at War: gender, motherhood and politics in Britain and France during the First World War* (Chapel Hill: University of North Carolina Press).
21. Yeo, 'The Creation of Motherhood'.
22. Catherine Marshall (1915) Women and War in Margaret Kamester & Jo Vellacott (Eds) (1987) *Militarism versus Feminism: writings on women and war* (London: Virago Press), p. 40.
23. The four other British representatives at the preliminary meetings in February were: Chrystal Macmillan, Theodora Wilson, Kathleen D. Courtney and Emily Leaf. ICWPP (1915) *Towards Permanent Peace, A Record of the Women's International Congress*. WILPF Papers, Reel 16.
24. Letter from Millicent Garrett Fawcett to Secretaries of Federations and Societies, 23 April 1915. Women's Library, WILPF/4/1; Jo Vellacott (2007) *Pacifists, Patriots and the Vote: the erosion of democratic suffragism in Britain during the First World War* (Basingstoke: Palgrave Macmillan); see also Angela K. Smith (2005) *Suffrage Discourse in Britain during the First World War* (London: Aldgate).
25. Catherine Marshall, Letter to the Executive Committee, 9 March 1915. Women's Library, WILPF/4/1. Kathleen Courtney, Alice Clark, Isabella Ford, Katherine Harley, Margaret Ashton, Emily Leaf, Helena Swanwick, Maude Royden and Cary Schuster also tendered their resignation to the NUWSS Executive Committee, March/April 1915.
26. Helena Swanwick (1935) *I Have Been Young* (London: Victor Gollancz), p. 246. Notably, the loss of her brother and fiancé led Vera Brittain to condemn war. She became a WIL vice-president in the late 1930s.
27. Royden, *War and the Woman's Movement*, p. 6.
28. Richard J. Evans (1987) *Comrades and Sisters: feminism, socialism and pacifism in Europe 1870–1945* (Brighton: Wheatsheaf Books); Susan Kingsley Kent (1993) *Making Peace: the reconstruction of gender in interwar Britain* (New Jersey: Princeton University Press).
29. Beers, 'Advocating for a Feminist Internationalism'.
30. Helena M. Swanwick (1915) *Women and War* (London: Union of Democratic Control), p. 7. SCPC, CDGB GB, Swanwick, Box 1.
31. Ibid; Hobhouse, *Bericht-Rapport-Report*.
32. A. Maude Royden (1915) *War and the Woman's Movement* (London: George Allen & Unwin). Women's Library, 7AMR.
33. Miller, 'Geneva—the Key to Equality'; Rupp, *Worlds of Women*; Vellacott, *Patriots, Pacifists and the Vote*.
34. Women's Peace Party (1915) *Report of the International Congress of Women* (USA: Roy G. Harper), p. 11. WILPF Papers, Reel 16.
35. Helen Ward (1929) *A Venture in Goodwill, Being the Story of the Women's International League, 1915–1929* (London: WIL), p. 23.
36. Vellacott, *Pacifists, Patriots and the Vote*.

37. Susan R. Grayzel (2012) *At Home and Under Fire: air raids and culture in Britain from the Great War to the Blitz* (Cambridge: Cambridge University Press).

38. Swanwick, *Women and War*, p. 7.

39. Jane Addams (2003; first published 1915) Factors in Continuing the War, in Jane Addams, Emily Greene Balch, & Alice Hamilton (Eds) *Women at The Hague: the International Congress of Women and its results* (Chicago: University of Illinois Press).

40. Martin Ceadel asserts that 'the W.I.L. was doctrinally too confused ever to become important': Martin Ceadel (1980) *Pacifism in Britain, 1914–1945* (Oxford: Oxford University Press), p. 61. Anne Wiltsher, Jo Vellacott and Jill Liddington have researched WILPF, but have not analysed in depth the organisation's decision to maintain a separate feminist-pacifist organisation, see Anne Wiltsher (1985) *Most Dangerous Women: feminist peace campaigners of the Great War* (London: Pandora Press); Vellacott, *Pacifists, Patriots and the Vote*; Jill Liddington (1989) *The Long Road to Greenham: feminism, pacifism and anti-militarism in Britain since 1820* (London: Virago).

41. Swanwick, *Women and War*, p. 5.

42. Helena Swanwick (1919) Evening Speech, *Report of the International Congress of Women, Zurich*.

43. Vellacott, *Pacifists, Patriots and the Vote*.

44. Helena Swanwick (1920) A Regiment of Women, *Monthly News Sheet* (January), p. 2.

45. Ibid.

46. Lucy Noakes (2006) *Women in the British Army: war and the gentle sex, 1907–1948* (London: Routledge); Marilyn Lake (1994) Between Old Worlds and New: feminist citizenship, nation and race, in Caroline Daley & Melanie Nolan (Eds) *Suffrage and Beyond: international feminist perspectives* (New York: New York University Press).

47. *Daily Mail*, 3 May 1915, p. 3.

48. Nicoletta Gullace (2002) *'Blood of Our Sons': men, women, and the renegotiation of British citizenship during the Great War* (Basingstoke: Palgrave Macmillan).

49. Lucy Noakes (2008) Playing at Being Soldiers? British Women and Military Uniforms in the First World War, in Jessica Meyer (Ed.) *British Popular Culture and the First World War* (Leiden: Brill Academic Publishers).

50. Gullace, *The Blood of Our Sons*.

51. Vellacott, *Patriots, Pacifists and the Vote*; Paul Ward (2001) Women of Britain Say Go: women's patriotism in the First World War, *Twentieth Century British History*, 12(1), pp. 23–45.

52. Swanwick, *Women and War*, p. 9.

53. Marshall, 'Women and War'.

54. Swanwick, *Women and War*, p. 2.

55. Millicent Garrett Fawcett, Order of Deputation (March 1917). Women's Library, 6B/106/7/MGF/90A/WWI.

56. WIL (1916) *Monthly News Sheet* (August), p. 4.

57. Martin Pugh (2000), *Women and the Women's Movement in Britain* (Basingstoke: Palgrave Macmillan); Sandi E. Cooper (1991) *Patriotic Pacifism: waging war on war in Europe, 1815–1914* (New York: Oxford University Press).

58. Brian Harrison (1978) *Separate Spheres: the opposition to women's suffrage in Britain* (London: Croom Helm); Melanie Faraunt (2003) Women Resisting the Vote: a case of anti-feminism? *Women's History Review*, 12(4), pp. 605–621.

59. Swanwick rejected Darwinist theories of competition, which confined women to the role of 'breeder'. Swanwick, *Women and War*; see also Anna Davin, 'Imperialism and Motherhood'.

60. Swanwick, *Women and War*, p. 5.

61. Royden, *War and the Woman's Movement*.

62. Swanwick, *Women and War*, p. 4.

63. Julia Bush (2007) *Women Against the Vote: female anti-suffragism in Britain* (Oxford: Oxford University Press); the suffrage movement contributed to a shift in perceptions of women, see

Maroula Joannou & June Purvis (Eds) (1998) *The Women's Suffrage Movement: new feminist perspectives* (Manchester: Manchester University Press).

64. Despite Jill Liddington's seminal text, much remains to be understood about feminism and anti-militarism: Jill Liddington, *The Road to Greenham Common*. Martin Pugh is dismissive of WIL, claiming its significance was limited: Pugh, *Women and the Women's Movement in Britain*, p. 10.
65. Vellacott, *Pacifists, Patriots and the Vote*; Brown, 'The Truest Form of Patriotism'.
66. Women's International League, Special Conference of Representatives of Woman Suffrage Associations in Manchester, 24 November 1915, Manchester Branch Minute Book, 1915–1919. LSE Archives, WILPF/BRAN/1/1; Alison Ronan (2011) Fractured, fragile, creative: a brief analysis of wartime friendships between provincial women anti-war activists, 1914–1918, *North West Labour History*, pp. 21–30.
67. The deputation included Charlotte Despard and Mary Macarthur, members of WIL's Executive Committee. Millicent Garrett Fawcett, *Order of Deputation* (March 1917); WIL was a member of the Equal Political Rights Campaign Committee (1927) *Equal Political Rights for Men and Women*. Women's Library, 5ERI.
68. Swanwick, *Women and War*, p. 13; Royden, *War and the Women's Movement*.
69. WIL (1919) *Towards Peace and Freedom*. WILPF Papers, Reel 17.
70. Hobhouse, *Bericht-Rapport-Report*, p. x. This also mirrors the infamous 1929 remarks by the Hungarian feminist Rosika Schwimmer: 'I have no sense of nationalism, only a cosmic consciousness of belonging to the human family', WILPF (1929) *Pax International* (July), p. 2. WILPF Papers, Reel 111.
71. Emily Greene Balch (1915) At the Northern Capitals, in Jane Addams, Emily Greene Balch, & Alice Hamilton (Eds) *Women at The Hague*, p. 52. See also Lela B. Costin (1982) Feminism, Pacifism, Internationalism and the 1915 International Congress of Women, *Women's Studies International Forum*, 5(3), pp. 301–315; David S. Patterson (2008) *The Search for Negotiated Peace: women's activism and citizen diplomacy in World War I* (London: Routledge).
72. Aletta Jacobs, Chrystal Macmillan, Rosika Schwimmer, Emily G. Balch, & Jane Addams (1915) *Full Text of the Manifesto, Issued by Envoys of the International Congress of Women at The Hague to the Governments of Europe, and the President of the United States* (New York, 15 October). WILPF Papers, Reel 16.
73. They met with the Prime Ministers and Foreign Ministers of the Great Powers; the King of Norway; the Presidents of Switzerland and the United States; and the Pope. Ibid.
74. WILPF (1919) *Report of the Second International Congress, Zurich, 12–17 May*. WILPF Papers, Reel 17.
75. Ibid.
76. Leila Rupp & Verta Taylor (1999) Forging Feminist Identity in an International Movement: a collective identity approach to twentieth-century feminism, *Signs*, 24(2), pp. 363–386.
77. Hobhouse, *Bericht-Rapport-Report*, p. x.
78. Lida Gustava Heymann (1915) Women of Europe, When Will Your Call Ring Out?, *Jus Suffragii* (February), p. 232.
79. WIL (1919) British Section Report, *Report of the International Congress of Women*.
80. Ethel Williams (1919) A Visit to Vienna, *Towards Peace and Freedom*, p. 10. WILPF Papers, Reel 17.
81. Swanwick, *I Have Been Young*, p. 315.
82. WIL (1919) In Aid of Germany's Starving Babies, *Monthly News Sheet* (February), p. 3.
83. Vellacott, *Pacifists, Patriots and the Vote*, p. 184.
84. WIL (1919) Demonstration at Trafalgar Square, *Monthly News Sheet* (May); A number of WIL's leading members were involved with the creation of the Fight the Famine Council and Save the Children Fund, including Dorothy Jebb Buxton, Maude Royden, Marian Cripps (Lady Parmoor), Kathleen Courtney and Mosa Anderson, see Clare Mulley (2009) *The Woman Who Saved the Children: a biography of Eglantyne Jebb founder of Save the Children* (Oxford: Oneworld Publishers).

85. Michael Barnett (2011) *Empire of Humanity: a history of humanitarianism* (London: Cornell University Press), p. 86.
86. WIL delegates corresponded with President Wilson during his time at the peace talks in Paris. Telegram from President Woodrow Wilson (May 1919). WILPF Papers, Reel 17.
87. Clara Ragaz (1919) Address of Welcome, *Report of the International Congress of Women, Zurich.*
88. Antoinette Burton (1994) *Burdens of History, British Feminists, Indian Women and Imperial Culture, 1865–1915* (Chapel Hill: University of North Carolina Press); Angela Woollacott (2006) *Gender and Empire* (Basingstoke: Palgrave Macmillan); Sandell, *The Rise of Women's Transnational Activism.*
89. Swanwick, *Women and War*, p. 2.
90. Jane Addams (1915) Presidential Address, *Bericht-Rapport-Report.*

Disclosure statement

No potential conflict of interest was reported by the author.

5 'Giddy Girls', 'Scandalous Statements' and a 'Burst Bubble'

The war babies panic of 1914–1915

Catherine Lee

ABSTRACT

During a few short months following the outbreak of war in 1914, Britain's press was rife with reports of what was heralded as a new 'social problem'. The alleged impending birth of thousands of 'war babies' to unmarried young women and girls, said to have been fathered by men recently departed for the Western Front, was widely discussed but ultimately proved to be largely fallacious. This article examines the extraordinary 'war babies' episode through the lens of the moral panic, focusing on the impact of exceptional wartime circumstances upon the shifting and conflicting sets of gendered, moral values and attitudes of the period.

A New 'Social Problem'

… all over the country in districts where large masses of troops have been quartered a great number of unmarried girls will become mothers within a few weeks of the present time. I have information of one county borough, which is said not to be exceptional, where there are more than two thousand women and girls in this condition. The total number of illegitimate children shortly to be born is very many thousands … [1]

With these words, in April 1915 Ronald McNeill, MP, fanned the flames of a rumour that had been smouldering since the previous autumn. Writing in the *Morning Post,* the Conservative Unionist member for the Canterbury area drew attention to the alleged imminent birth of thousands of so-called 'war babies'. This impending 'new social problem' had attracted escalating comment during the preceding months, filling the columns of the local, provincial, national and even international press.[2] McNeill's letter was immediately taken up by numerous other titles across the country, many of which reprinted it verbatim. Thus the claim that, in many British towns, several hundred women and girls (and, in one often-repeated but unsubstantiated anecdote, 400 residents of a single street) had been impregnated by soldiers recently departed for the Western Front gained widespread currency.[3]

The rumour grew sufficiently potent over the following weeks as to trigger speeches in the Houses of Commons and Lords, mention at the Convocation of Canterbury, extensive social inquiry and the issue of a notice from Scotland Yard. By the time it was put to rest two months later, having been denounced as 'fiction', 'romance', 'delusion' and 'myth' by the very medium that had been instrumental in promoting it in the first place, a range of prominent figures had been drawn into the affair.[4] These included the Archbishops of Canterbury and York, the Duchess of Bedford, Lord Kitchener, novelist and playwright Emma Orczy, feminist activists Louise Creighton and Margaret Llewelyn Davies, together with some of the foremost women physicians of the day.

Moral Panics

In examining this extraordinary episode through the lens of the 'moral panic', this article focuses on the impact of the exceptional circumstances of wartime on the shifting and con-flicting sets of moral values and social attitudes of the period, as reflected in the press and in public discourse. First defined in the 1970s by Stanley Cohen, the moral panic model has been argued to play a significant role in moral regulation.[5] It has thus proved to be a particularly valuable theoretical tool for historians studying the construction of deviancy.[6] Its focus on the complex relationship between discourses and attitudes, broader fears of the loss of social control at moments of instability or crisis, and the identi-fication of a 'folk devil' group or phenomenon, allows the social and cultural construction of deviancy and the identification of scapegoat groups to be analysed. A common theme has been the demonisation of youth, from the juvenile street criminal of the 1840s to the sexually active teenager of the 1960s. It is thus a particularly useful model for an explora-tion of the discourses surrounding the unmarried mothers of so-called 'war babies' in 1915.

The role played by the media in the construction of deviancy makes press reportage a particularly appropriate source material for the study of the 'war baby' panic. The mass digitisation of newspapers allows the trajectory of the rumour to be traced through the local, provincial, national tabloid and broadsheet, as well as professional press, to a level of detail barely possible previously. Notwithstanding the well-documented methodological challenges that digital newspaper searching poses for historians, the ability to trace the life-cycle of the moral panic (as Adrian Bingham argues) is one of its compensatory advan-tages.[7] The continual addition of new titles, particularly regional ones, over the past few years provides an illuminating insight into the reach of the 'war baby' rumour at commu-nity level and has gone some way to address the problems of selectivity that Bingham raises. It also allows close examination of the ways in which social and official attitudes were reflected in reported public discourse, given that the 'war baby' rumour was posi-tioned at the intersection of a range of political, moral and legal debates brought into con-flict on the declaration of war. These touched on themes of sin and corruption, charity and Christian forgiveness, patriotism and the war effort, public health, as well as the sexual double standard.

Unmarried Wives

The search for the origins of the rumour begins amongst the multiple strands of debate concerning the separation allowances payable to the dependants of men serving in the armed services and, specifically, the definition and identification of who was, and who was not, eligible to receive them. This debate placed the question of extra-marital birth

under the spotlight since it quickly became apparent that strict adherence to official definitions of eligible recipients left vast numbers of dependent families unsupported following the swift mobilisation of the armed forces. The first group of such families were those
of servicemen who had married 'off the strength', that is to say, without the required permission from military authorities. These legally recognised but militarily unacknowledged
families found themselves in a particularly vulnerable position in August 1914 amidst the
rapid deployment of forces overseas, despite the Prime Minister's assurances in the House
of Commons that, for the duration of the war, wives 'off the strength' and their families
were to be officially recognised for the purposes of financial support.[8] For territorials
and recruits to Kitchener's Army, a separation allowance was payable to the 'dependents
of married men' and 'children of widowers'.[9] In the exceptional conditions of the first
weeks of war, the hastily assembled mechanisms for the payment of these allowances,
and for identifying qualifying recipients in the men's absence, ground slowly and left
dependent families financially vulnerable.

The suggestion that the definition of soldiers' 'dependents' might be broadened placed
private lives under the public spotlight. *The Times* claimed on 3rd September, in reporting
the acute financial distress suffered by the wives of some men at the front, that '[n]ot every
woman who at the moment is claiming to be a soldier's wife has a right to the title.'[10] The
question of common-law wives' entitlement to financial support was raised in November
by the War Emergency Workers National Committee.[11] Chaired by Labour MP Arthur
Henderson, this pressure group, an alliance between the Labour Party and organisations
such as the Trades Union Congress, the Co-operative movement and the Fabian Society,
demanded that the War Office grant 'unmarried wives' and their children the 'full status of
dependents'.[12] The Select Committee on Naval and Military Services (Pensions and
Grants) responded favourably.[13] At this stage it is clear that both the War Office and
the Soldiers and Sailors Families Association (SSFA, which had been appointed by the
government to distribute financial assistance on its behalf), understood and defined
non-married dependents in terms of the households of established relationships that
were marriages in all but name. The oxymoronic term 'unmarried wife' was introduced
into official parlance and policy in the Select Committee's interim report issued on 2nd
February. This move, however, provoked a swift rejoinder from the Southwark Diocesan
Conference, regretting the State's decision not to privilege lawful (and, by implication,
Christian) marriage. The conference passed a resolution pledging to safeguard 'morals
and manners'.[14]

The ensuing debate brought into relief the inherent tension between conflicting strands of
Christian values: on the one hand calls for charity, compassion and care; on the other
demands for strict adherence to the Church's moral teachings. These currents were additionally overlaid with themes of patriotism, articulated in terms of the nation's duty to provide
and care for the dependents of men who were at the front and making the ultimate sacrifice.
A correspondent to the *Evening Telegraph*, for example, deplored the state of affairs in which
'women and children are living in starvation while their supporters are fighting for King and
Country' purely because they were unable to produce a marriage certificate.[15]

This theme, of the shared moral responsibility to care for non-married soldiers' babies,
also reflects contemporary public-health concerns over critically high infant mortality
levels. Links between these rates, the physical degeneration of the poor, inadequate nutri-
tion, poor housing and mothers' working conditions had been prominently highlighted a

decade previously.[16] Yet, as the work of Anna Davin and others has shown, these inter-connected political and public-health factors were reduced to a simplistic narrative focussing on individual mothers' role in 'the bearing and rearing of children—the next generation of soldiers and workers, the Imperial race'.[17] Official reaction to the report of the Committee on Physical Deterioration pointed, amongst other things, to its findings in relation to mothering skills and its implications for empire. In the ensuing House of Lords debate the Bishop of Ripon had referred to child-bearing-aged women as the 'birth force of the country' and questioned whether the 'English-speaking people' would, in the future, be able to 'populate', 'direct' 'govern' or even 'hold' its 'great inher-itances' given the physical degeneration of the population.[18]

Thus the suggestion, ten years later and following the declaration of war, that thousands of 'war babies' were about to be brought into the world tapped into a range of pre-existing social concerns. The Registrar General's statistics for 1912 had once again revealed a sig-nificant disparity in mortality rates between infants of non-married parents compared with those whose parents were legally married.[19] The infants of unmarried men serving abroad and unable to provide for them were understood to be doubly vulnerable. Philan-thropic agencies such as the SSFA, according to Susan Grayzel, exploited the supposed connection between babies classed as 'illegitimate' and discourses of children of the patrio-tic fallen 'whether it was accurate or not'.[20]

These tensions were brought to a head at an SSFA Special General Meeting held at Caxton Hall at the end of January 1915. Opposing a resolution that financial aid should only be granted on the production of marriage and birth certificates, William Hayes Fisher, MP, moved an amendment upholding the principle (previously established during the Boer War) that help be given to unmarried mothers and their children pro-vided that 'there is a real home' and the 'connection is not merely a casual one'.[21] Lord St Audries commented that this principle was 'in accordance with the dictates of Chris-tianity and humanity' and the amendment was carried by 329 votes to 120. The Times reported the meeting's outcome under the heading 'Soldiers' Morals', a choice that reflects the blurred boundaries in discussions about financial arrangements and moral rhetoric.

This debate also highlighted the private versus public responsibility dichotomy that was characteristic of the discourses surrounding the early twentieth-century infant-welfare movement. Between 1910 and 1916, the Local Government Board issued five reports which conceptualised infant mortality as an individual problem and as a 'failure of motherhood'.[22] Angela Smith has argued that the 'punitive tone and substance' of this movement, underpinned by the idealisation of marriage, placed upon women the respon-sibility of improving the nation's 'stock'.[23] Thus the prospect of large numbers of births outside of wedlock was seen as a rejection both of the 'moral obligation' of motherhood and the construction of the 'ideal mother'.[24] Aristocrat Lady Gwendoline Cecil was among those who publicly mixed moral and pecuniary discourses in posing the question: 'Is the unhappy tax-payer to be further burdened in order to place such girls in a position of peculiar honour and privilege?'[25] This reference to the 'unhappy tax-payer' alluded to maternity benefits for working mothers, irrespective of marital status, recently introduced under the National Insurance Act 1911.[26] The Suffragette, reflecting its broad feminist agenda, argued in contrast for collective responsibility and reminded readers that the war babies 'are everybody's children and have a claim on the community as a whole'.[27]

Khaki Fever

As debates over maintenance rumbled on, an additional strand of discourse emerged to fully ignite the spark of the war-baby rumour. An alleged outbreak of 'khaki fever', a sickness to which the nation's girls and young women were reported to have been succumbing, had been attracting increasing press attention from August 1914 onwards. The alleged epidemic was said to be the direct consequence of the mass mobilisation of troops and hasty establishment of temporary training camps throughout the country.[28] Many of these camps consisted of tented cities on open ground, commons and municipal parks in, or on the outskirts of, urban areas. As a result of these significant disruptions of population, large numbers of girls and young women were soon reported to have been affected by the presence of so many young men in the locality, a phenomenon described in many quarters as the 'excitement aroused by war'.[29] In one south London example, girls were reported to have been attracted to visiting Crystal Palace, where the Naval Brigade was encamped, from all surrounding districts and to be losing their heads in expressing 'open admiration' for the men.[30] The girls' 'flighty conduct', according to *The Times*, made them 'liable to quite unwarranted aspersions'.[31] Other commentators were considerably more damning, referring to the women and girls attracted to military camps as the 'vilest of women' and 'bad lots'.[32] This discourse echoes Penny Summerfield's observations in relation to the class dimensions of constructions of women's sexual deviance in wartime.[33] Whilst not explicitly couched in class terms, the language used ('vilest', 'bad lots') contributed to the construction of working-class girls and women as most susceptible to 'khaki fever'. Thus, the focus of moral opprobrium was transferred from stable, if common-law, marriages (which belonged to the private sphere) to casual relationships between young girls and soldiers (which were visible and largely conducted in public space).

The tone and extent of the press coverage dedicated to the so-called 'soldier and girl problem' exemplifies Cohen's definition of the mass media's role in the moral panic.[34] This, he argued, made use of tropes and stereotypes to represent either an episode or individuals as a threat to social values. In the press reportage of the 'war baby' rumour, women and girls were portrayed with reference to a spectrum of stereotypes from 'careless' to 'immoral'.[35] This characterisation was in direct contrast to that of the idealised woman on the Home Front who was imagined as hard-working and committed to rectitude and self-sacrifice. Given the widespread preoccupation with war's supposed negative impact on young women's morals, it was perhaps only a matter of time before there were reports of expectations of 'thousands of war babies all over the country'.[36] Indeed, one newspaper made the direct connection by entitling a piece on the story 'khaki babies'.[37]

War Babies' and Mothers' League

In this climate, the formation of a philanthropic organisation dedicated to the amelioration of the new social problem of war babies was soon announced in the press. As early as 26th August 1914, the *Coventry Herald* carried a small notice about the formation of an organisation to 'help the babies and little children of men serving with the colours'.[38] The Honorary Secretaries were named as Mrs Helen Best of 411, Oxford Street and

Mrs Gertrude Hope of 7, South Molton Street. This was followed by a more detailed item in *The Times* three weeks later, naming the organisation as 'The War Babies' and Mothers' League' and its patron as Lady Shaftsbury. A message from Lord Kitchener wished the League every success and Mrs Churchill (about to give birth herself) was reported to have made a donation of baby clothes. It is notable that this article referred to 'soldiers' babies' and the 'mothers of babies' rather than to 'wives' and their children. This language suggests that the families of non-married men were being discreetly included.[39] The League promised not to limit its support to 'recognised' wives but to help all those women whose 'immediate future' was threatened by enlistment.

Over the following weeks the League brought its cause repeatedly to the attention of the public in a series of emotive letters written by its well-connected patrons to the press. The *Daily Express* published letters from novelists Gertrude Baillie Reynolds on the 31st October appealing on behalf of 'the children to be born in Britain during this time of trouble and stress' and from Baroness Emma Orczy (author of the *Scarlet Pimpernel*) on 4th November.[40] The latter wrote, in an item entitled '"Unwanted" War Babies', of 'wee mites that now, as at all times, alas! come into the world unwanted', thus defining 'war babies' definitively as those of non-married parents.[41]

Elsewhere, as has been seen, the media had been drawing escalating attention to 'the moral questions raised by war-time conditions' and 'the behaviour of the women and girls who congregate in the neighbourhood of the camps now scattered over the country'.[42] These reports gathered momentum, culminating in a report in the *Manchester Guardian* to the effect that the War Babies' and Mothers' League had received an 'ambiguously worded' statement to the effect that no fewer than 39,000 unmarried mothers in London were dependent on soldiers' pay.[43] The *Daily Herald* reported with conviction that 400 'illegitimate' births were expected at one un-named south-coast town 'this month alone'.[44] This statement is all the more remarkable for the fact that the month being referred to was April, the last day of which was only 39 weeks from the declaration of war.

At this juncture the publication of McNeill's letter to the *Morning Post*, with which this article opened, fully ignited the war baby rumour and, as a result, the press intensified its coverage of the subject. The *Daily Express* published an item on war babies almost every day until 3rd May, together with numerous letters to the editor on the subject.[45] The story was carried in national, provincial and local titles across the country, in 'nearly every newspaper' according to the *Daily Herald*.[46] In Kent, the location of McNeill's constituency and home to large numbers of stationed troops, the letter was published in full in the *Folkestone, Hythe, Sandgate and Cheriton Herald*.[47] His emotive rhetorical question: 'Are they, the offspring of the heroes of the Marne, of Ypres, of Neuve Chapelle, to carry through life the stigma of shame for "irregular birth"?' was to be much repeated in the following weeks.

The *Observer* reported McNeill's intention to arrange a meeting with the Archbishop of Canterbury in order to persuade religious leaders to make a statement to the effect that 'the mothers of our soldiers' children should be treated with no scorn or dishonour, and that the babies themselves should receive a loyal welcome.' He also sought reform, even if temporary, of the bastardy laws.[48] *The Times* reacted swiftly in providing a moral backlash against such proposals to treat the families of all soldiers equally. Under the headline 'The New Social Problem', it identified khaki fever as the source of the dilemma, deploring the 'great wave of emotional nonsense' that had been spoken in support of young women and their babies, and claimed that such proposals were 'subversive both of the principles of morality and of the foundations of the state'.[49] *The Times* called for voluntary philanthropic action in preference to state intervention. The *Sunday Mirror* appealed to women suffragists who 'before the war [had] fought hard for a vote' to mobilise the same energies and determination in seeking legislative change to facilitate marriage in the exceptional conditions of wartime in order to legitimise children whose parents subsequently married.[50]

On 23rd April the Bishop of Oxford used a sermon at St George's Chapel Windsor to deplore the 'lamentable decay in domestic discipline' that was said to have caused the present situation. Observing that there had been 'much excitement' among young girls he called on his congregation to deal with the problem with kindness but urged it not to turn 'this shame' into a 'kind of glory'.[51] The War Babies and Mothers' League fuelled the debate further by reminding the public that it had helped 'hundreds' of cases of unmarried mothers who had been cared for and helped 'regain and retain their self-respect'.[52]

Investigation

In this heated climate, on the afternoon of 22 April 1915 a remarkable, and, according to the *Daily Mirror*, 'comic' scene played itself out on the pavements of Hanover Square in London.[53] A large group of women, supposedly 'disappointed' and 'indignant' at having been refused entrance to a meeting being conducted in one of the offices there, had gathered on the pavement outside, so noisily as to prompt a complaint from a neighbour. The crowd was reported to include well-known novelists, suffragette leaders and a number of women who had 'obviously come in hopes of amusement', according to the disdainful *Mirror* correspondent. A room in the Women's Imperial Health Association's suite of offices at Number 7, where a meeting on the subject of war babies was in progress, was said to be crowded 'almost to suffocation' with upwards of seventy people, with the result that many would-be attendees, including representatives of the press, had to be refused admittance. Delegates included representatives of the Local Government Board and of some of the country's most established and well-respected organisations. These included the Salvation Army, the Young Women's Christian Association and the Women's Co-operative Guild. The allegation of up to 400 pregnant girls in a single street was refuted.[54] Many speakers, readers were told, noted that war baby rumour-mongering represented a slur on the characters of the men 'who had come forward patriotically to fight for their country'.[55] The meeting, presided over by Dr Christine Murrell, resolved to set up a committee to investigate the problem, not only of alleged war babies, but of illegitimacy more widely.

From this point onwards, a clear note of scepticism is discernible in the press coverage of McNeill's claims, suggesting that the 'war baby' tide had begun to turn. The *Yorkshire Evening Post* quoted doctors in Leeds who had encountered no cases of imminent 'war baby' births. According to one, the story had been a gross exaggeration and he professed that he did not 'believe a quarter' of what had been reported in the press on the subject.[56] Similarly, the Archbishop of York told the Rescue and Preventative Association on 26th April that those he had consulted believed the claims to be 'wildly exaggerated'.[57] Dr Barbara Tchaikovsky, who worked with Sylvia Pankhurst in the East End, had also been unable to ascertain any precise figures from her enquiries. As a consequence of the rumour-mongering, Dundas White, MP, tabled an Early Day Motion in the House of Commons proposing the legitimation of babies by their parents' subsequent marriage, whilst the Archdeacon of Surrey raised the question at the Lower House of Convocation of Canterbury on 27th April.

Numerous independent investigations were immediately set in motion in an attempt to ascertain the truth of the war baby reports. The *Manchester Guardian* of 24th April reported its own inquiries carried out in Manchester, Southport, Blackpool, Morecambe and Lancaster, which had failed to discover any evidence of raised pregnancy rates amongst unmarried women. The *Birmingham Gazette* likewise commissioned its own investigation, which reported similar findings. Community workers at an unnamed provincial town of some 4,000 inhabitants, where in the region of 2,000 troops had been regularly billeted since August, expected no change in the rate of illegitimate births compared with the previous year, based on the evidence of their recent experience in the area.[58] On 26th April Lambeth Palace announced that the Archbishops of Canterbury and York, together with a number of other prominent figures such as physician Dr Mary Scharlieb, had requested the establishment of a committee under the auspices of the National Union of Women Workers. Headed by its president Louise Creighton, this was to investigate properly the extent and nature of the war babies problem.

Bubble Burst

When, a little over two months later, the NUWW investigation completed its investigation the rumours were pronounced 'beyond doubt to have no foundation in fact'.[59] Reporting to the Committee on Illegitimate Births during the War, chaired by the Archbishop of York, the findings were based upon the results of fifty-five enquiries across the country. These included one un-named 'northern city' where 'the wildest statements had been made' but where only one pregnancy had been discovered in a factory employing 3,000 women. This was followed swiftly by the similar findings of a separate and exhaustive enquiry made by the National Society for the Prevention of Cruelty to Children (NSPCC), using its extensive network of inspectors.[60] In most cases, these reported that there was not likely to be any increase in the illegitimate birth rate in their districts and that, in many cases, 'not a single case' could be traced.[61] The NSPCC concluded that 'Generally inspectors express the opinion that the conduct of the troops has been very good.' The Local Government Board, on behalf of the government, had instigated enquiries carried out by local Medical Officers of Health, the Salvation Army, and the Charity Organisation Society. All had similarly negative results.[62]

Meanwhile the War Babies and Mothers League had continued to publicise its work and its founder, Helen Best, wrote to the *Observer* about her organisation's aid to 'these unfortunate little ones and their mothers' and to announce her intention of holding a public meeting.[63] In contrast to the sympathetic hearing that communications from Mrs Best's organisation had previously met from the press, on this occasion, although the letter was printed, it was appended with a note from the editor. This was to the effect that, since 'it is now evident that the whole matter has been grossly exaggerated', no further correspondence on the subject would be published. This shift was reflected elsewhere in the press. The story was carried by titles as far afield as the USA and Australia. Readers of the *Victoria Advocate* were informed that Mrs Best 'still maintains it is happening, but there is no evidence to support her fears'.[64] In New York State, the *Massena Press and Norfolk Times* implied scepticism of Mrs Best's credentials in noting that she was 'by profession an electrolysis operator'.[65]

By the 11th June, the date on which the War Babies and Mothers' League was due to have held a meeting in London, aspersions were being publicly cast upon its financial affairs. The *Manchester Guardian* reported the short-notice cancellation of the meeting to enable the League to have its full report and financial accounts properly audited. Only a few days previously the Metropolitan Police had issued a notice advising the public not to subscribe to the organisation.[66] William Anderson, MP for Sheffield Attercliffe, took the opportunity to bring the matter to the attention of the Home Secretary, asking him to take steps 'to protect 780 philanthropic ladies from the temptation to benefit war babies which, as far as this League is concerned, appear to be mainly apocryphal'.[67] The Home Secretary responded that he hoped 'that the police warning will make philanthropic persons more careful in selecting the societies or leagues which they support'.

The 'apocryphal' nature of the war babies appeared to be publicly affirmed the following year as Medical Officers of Health up and down the country reported the 1915 birth and death statistics to their local authorities and, as was customary, these were published in local newspapers. These reflected some variation from place to place but, overall, no significant increase in the number of births recorded as 'illegitimate'. The Rhonda Urban District reported an increase from 139 to 146.[68] Birmingham's figures were up by four births from 698 to 702 though this represented a drop from the 1913 figure.[69] In Portsmouth the number was lower than it had been for 1914.[70] Grantham, the site of a large military camp since 1914, likewise witnessed a reduction.[71] Most press titles, in reporting these statistics, made reference to the war baby rumour. In Devon, Dr Steele-Perkins, Medical Officer of Health for the Honiton Rural District Council commented:

> After all the rubbish we have read in the papers as to war babies, it is refreshing to come up against actual facts. In our district we have had soldiers billeted with us since war commenced, and I have only one illegitimate birth to report and, as far as I can gather, this child is not a so-called war baby. It surely goes to show that these scandalous statements, made by a certain section of the press, are purposely and solely for the sake of advertising themselves.[72]

As these first reports of the 1915 figures, which were often framed as a denunciation of the war baby scare, were circulated, commentators and the press immediately launched into in a discourse of shock at the slur on soldiers' morals represented by the rumour. The Bishop of London expressed 'righteous indignation' that men in training could be believed to have been 'behaving badly'. 'The cry of "war babies"', which he laid firmly at the door of the press, had proved to be 'a large bubble that had now exploded'.[73] The rumour had, he said, been given credence purely on the basis of the behaviour of a few 'young, giddy girls excited by the presence of so many young men in khaki'.[74]

The press and others now embarked upon a campaign of ridicule waged against what the *Manchester Guardian* called 'ordinarily sober-minded people' who had fuelled the war baby rumour by 'accepting and passing on wild statements'.[75] The *British Medical Journal*, more sympathetically, attributed public credulity to 'excitement' and a 'disturbance of the public nerves'.[76] The Archbishop of Canterbury, however, speaking in the House of Lords, claimed to be 'justified in the scepticism we had entertained as to the nature of the allegations made'.[77] In the House of Commons, war babies were said by Irish Nationalist MP Michael Reddy to be one of the 'extraordinary delusions' created by wartime.[78]

Evaluation

The benefits of hindsight and long-term perspective, denied to the 1916 Medical Officers of Health and other contemporary commentators, allow for a more measured consideration of whether expectations of a sharp rise in 1915 extra-marital births were realised and whether the panic surrounding those expectations was, in any way, justified. Such an appraisal is not, however, unproblematic. The first difficulty is one of definitions and meanings. Historians face challenges in dealing with a constructed category such as 'illegitimate', which, arguably, reveals more about gendered contemporary attitudes and belief in the ability of statistics to reflect reality than it does about that reality itself. Moreover, as Andrew Hobbs has argued, the category 'illegitimate' was applied to a variety of different circumstances.[79] It has been seen that 1914 debates over dependents' allowances revealed the extent of common-law marriage. Never-married women, by contrast, accounted for only one-third of the 'illegitimacy' statistics but yet they attracted most attention and comment.[80] Thus the statistics have to be approached with caution and with the above caveats in mind.

Even when taken at face value as demographic data, however, the statistics are not without problem. Amidst a falling general birth rate (a common demographic wartime phenomenon and set against a longer-term background decline), 36,245 births were officially recorded as 'illegitimate' for 1915.[81] The comparable figure for 1914 was 37,329.[82] This decline in raw numbers, when expressed as a percentage of all births, reflects a small increase of 0.2% from 4.25% to 4.45%. This compares with ratios of 3.97% for 1900, 4.01% for 1905, 4.08% for 1910, and 4.3% for each of 1912 and 1913.[83]

However, as the Registrar General observed at the time and as demographers emphasise, the expression of extra-marital births as a ratio of the total is problematic statistically because it is affected by two independent factors. These are the number of births inside marriage and the number of unmarried women of fertile age available to produce births outside marriage.[84] Illegitimacy rates could be 'better studied', a subsequent Annual Report advised, relative to numbers of possible mothers. Using this ratio, the rates for 1915, 1916 and 1917 expressed per 1,000 women between the ages of 15 and 45 were 7.4, 7.6 and 7.4 compared with an average of 8.1 for the period 1906–1910.[85] Reflecting on this trend, the Registrar General had this to say:

> Throughout the greater part of the war, from the second quarter of 1915, the first seriously affected by war conditions, to the first quarter of 1918 inclusive, the rates [of extra-marital births] ruled low, notwithstanding the apprehensions expressed of an alarming number of 'war babies'.[86]

There was, however, an upward trend, from the second quarter of 1918, of those births classified as 'illegitimate' as a proportion of the whole and the 1919 rate rose to 8.3. This common phenomenon, of increased numbers of 'illegitimate' births recorded in the years following warfare, is attributed by demographers to changes in men's and women's relative 'bargaining power' and women's reduced 'marriage market prospects' by the short-fall of men.[87] This explanation cannot, however, be satisfactorily applied to the period of the most intense 'war baby' headlines (early 1915, several quarters in advance of the recorded upturn) nor to the 'giddy girls' to whom the majority of the scare headlines referred.

Sexual Governance

This article turns finally to consider why what has been described as the 'excited atmosphere' created by total war should provide such fertile ground for the moral panic.[88] This atmosphere was played out against a backdrop of what D'Cruze and Jackson have described as the 'recasting of youthful femininity in terms of sexual agency' in early twentieth-century Britain, leading to what Pamela Cox describes as the 'sexual governance' of girls and young women.[89] The perceived need to protect this group from 'sexual danger', Cox has argued, was the main focus of regulatory, as well as informal, control frameworks. The exceptional circumstances of wartime (including whole-scale dislocations of population, profound uncertainty and the disruption of the patterns of everyday life) served to exacerbate this propensity to sexualise youthful femininity whilst at the same time framing women's sexual agency in terms of deviance. A number of historians have noted the connection between wartime and patterns of heightened anxiety over women's sexual agency. Expressions of women's sexuality that took place in public space, as the discourse surrounding 'khaki fever' demonstrates, were seen as especially problematic. Woollacott points to the months following the declaration of war as 'climactic' with regards to the articulation of fears about women's social and sexual behaviour while Sonya Rose has argued that such 'out-pouring of moral discourse' is to be expected specifically at moments when national identity is put under the spotlight, wartime being a notable example.[90] Furthermore, as Dean Rapp has argued, exceptional wartime conditions served to heighten social purists' anxieties because perceived threats to social and moral standards were conceptualised more broadly as threats to the state, and thus to the patriotic cause. In other words, the 'war baby' scare represented a perceived threat not only to moral values but also to social stability and order precisely because it happened at a moment of intense social crisis—a state of total war. The successful moral panic, as Cohen observes, finds 'points of resonance with wider anxieties'.[91]

The final word on the subject of the 'war babies' must go to Col. Arthur Lee, MP, personal commissioner to Kitchener, who was tasked in 1916 with reporting on medical services in the field. In a House of Commons debate Ronald McNeill (who, it will be remembered, had played such a prominent part in the war babies story), criticised the standard of field medical services in France. In response, Lee accused McNeill of being too 'easily misled by over-zealous informers'.[92] Using the recent 'war-babies' debacle to reinforce McNeil's gullibility, Lee reminded the House, with a rhetorical flourish, of the '2,000,000 impending war babies, which [...] after most careful investigation dwindled down to two false alarms and one case of twins'.

Notes

1. *Morning Post* (11 April 1915).
2. *The Times* (19 April 1915), p. 5.

3. *Daily Express* (23 April 1915), p. 1.
4. *Derby Daily Telegraph* (18 December 1915), p. 2; *Washington Times* (12 June 1915), p. 2.
5. Stanley Cohen (2004, 3rd edn.) *Folk Devils and Moral Panics* (London: Routledge); Sean P. Hier, Dan Lett, Kevin Walby & André Smith (2011) Beyond Folk Devil Resistance: linking moral panic and moral regulation, *Criminology and Criminal Justice*, 11, pp. 259–276.
6. See for example: Judith Rowbotham & Kim Stevenson (Eds) (2003) *Behaving Badly: social panic and moral outrage – Victorian and modern parallels* (Aldershot: Ashgate); Peter King (1998) The Rise of Juvenile Delinquency in England 1780–1840: changing patterns of perception and prosecution, *Past and Present*, 160, pp. 116–166; Clive Emsley (2008) Violent Crime in England in 1919: post-war anxieties and press narratives, *Continuity and Change*, 23, pp. 173–195; Steven Angelides (2012) The 'Second Sexual Revolution', Moral Panic, and the Evasion of Teenage Sexual Subjectivity, *Women's History Review*, 21(5), pp. 831–847.
7. Seth Cayley (2012) Digitization in Teaching and Learning: the publisher's view, *Victorian Periodicals Review*, 45(2), pp. 210–214; Bob Nicholson (2013) The Digital Turn: exploring the methodological possibilities of digital newspaper archives, *Media History*, 19(1) pp. 59–73; Adrian Bingham (2011) The Digitization of Newspaper Archives: opportunities and challenges for historians, *Twentieth Century British History*, 21(2), pp. 225–231.
8. *Hansard*, House of Commons Debate (10 August 1914) 65, c2261.
9. *The Times* (28 August 1914), p. 6.
10. *The Times* (3 September 1914), p. 4.
11. War Emergency Workers' National Committee (1914) *The Workers and the War: a programme for labour* (London: Co-operative Printing Society, Warwick Digital Collections). http://contentdm.warwick.ac.uk/cdm/ref/collection/tav/id/3507 [last accessed 25/04/2016].
12. *The Times* (9 November 1914), p. 5.
13. HMSO (1914–16) *Select Committee. Naval and Military (Pensions and Grants)*; IV.189, p. 46.
14. *Evening Telegraph* (3 February 1915), p. 3; *Sunday Times* (22 November 1914), p. 4.
15. *Evening Telegraph* (23 September 1914), p. 2.
16. HMSO (1904) Inter-Departmental Committee on Physical Deterioration, *Report of the Inter-Departmental Committee on Physical Deterioration*.
17. Anna Davin (1978) Imperialism and Motherhood, *History Workshop*, 5, pp. 9–65, p. 12.
18. Hansard, House of Lords Debate (20 July 1905) 149 cc1304–52.
19. HMSO (1913) *Seventy-fifth Annual Report of the Registrar-General of Births, Deaths, and Marriages in England and Wales*, 7028: XVII(7), pp. xii–xxiii.
20. Susan. R. Grayzel (1999) *Women's Identities at War: gender, motherhood, and politics in Britain and France during the First World War* (Chapel Hill: University of North Carolina Press), p. 96.
21. *The Times* (29 January 1915), p. 6.
22. Jane Lewis (1980) The Social History of Social Policy: infant welfare in Edwardian England, *Journal of Social Policy*, 9(4), p. 465.
23. Angela Smith (2010) Discourses of Morality and Truth in Social Welfare: the surveillance of British widows of the First World War, *Social Semiotics*, 20(5), p. 521.
24. Ibid. p. 522.
25. Cited in *Yorkshire Evening Post* (1 April 1915), p. 5.
26. Paula Bartley (2000) *Prostitution: prevention and reform in England, 1860–1914* (London: Routledge), p. 110.
27. Cited in *Yorkshire Evening Post* (1 April 1915), p. 5.
28. See Angela Woollacott (1994) "Khaki Fever" and Its Control: gender, class, age and sexual morality on the British homefront in the First World War, *Journal of Contemporary History*, 29(2), pp. 325–347.
29. *The Times* (31 December 1914), p. 3.
30. *The Times* (28 January 1915), p. 5.
31. *The Times* (31 December 1914), p. 3.
32. Lady Gwendoline Cecil, cited in *Yorkshire Evening Post* (21 April 1915), p. 5.

33. Penny Summerfield (1997) Gender and War in the Twentieth Century, *International History Review*, 19(1), pp. 2–15.
34. *Yorkshire Evening Post* (2 March 1915), p. 4.
35. *Grantham Journal* (12 December 1914), p. 4.
36. *Daily Express* (23 April 1915), p. 1.
37. *Aberdeen Daily Journal* (27 April 1915), p. 3.
38. *Coventry Herald* (26 August 1914), p. 4.
39. *The Times* (19 September 1914), p. 11.
40. *Daily Express* (31 October 1914).
41. *Daily Express* (4 November 1914).
42. *Daily Mail* (14 October 1914), p. 6; *The Times* (13 October 1914), p. 9.
43. *Manchester Guardian* (23 February 1915), p. 16.
44. *Daily Herald* (10 April 1915), p. 9.
45. 14th, 16th, 22nd, 23rd, 24th, 26th, 27th, 28th, 29th, 30th April and 1st and 3rd May.
46. *Daily Herald* (17 April 1915), p. 3.
47. *Folkestone, Hythe, Sandgate and Cheriton Herald* (17 April 2015), p. 7.
48. *Observer* (18 April 1915), p. 15.
49. *The Times* (19 April 1915), p. 5.
50. *Sunday Mirror* (18 April 1915), p. 6.
51. *Daily Express* (24 April 1915), pp. 4–5.
52. *Sunday Times* (18th April 1915), p. 7.
53. *Daily Mirror* (23 April 1915), p. 2.
54. *Daily Express* (23rd April 1915), p. 1.
55. Ibid.
56. *Yorkshire Evening Post* (14 April 1915), p. 5.
57. *Daily Express* (27 April 1915), p. 5.
58. *Birmingham Gazette* (26 April 1915), p. 5.
59. *The Times* (18 June 1915), p. 11.
60. *Manchester Guardian* (14 June 1915), p. 6.
61. *Birmingham Daily Post* (14 June 1915), p. 6.
62. *The Times* (25 June 1915), p. 10.
63. *Observer* (2 May 1915), p. 12.
64. *Victoria Advocate* (14 June 1915), p. 3.
65. The reference given by the digital provider of the *Massena Press and Norfolk Times*, (nyshistoricnewspapers.org) is 9 February 1915, p. 1. It seems clear from the digital image, however, that the page is torn in two and that the bottom half is from a different edition. From the content of the 'War Babies' article (e.g. reference to the Metropolitan Police notice) it seems more likely that it appeared in mid-June.
66. *Manchester Guardian* (12 June 1915), p. 5.
67. *Hansard*, House of Commons Debate (17 June 1915) 72 cc779-80 779.
68. *Western Mail* (7 September 1916), p. 3.
69. *Birmingham Daily Post* (15 September 1916), p. 8.
70. Reported in the *Essex Newsman* (12 August 1916), p. 1.
71. *Grantham Journal* (27 May 1916), p. 2.
72. *Exeter and Plymouth Gazette* (10 April 1916), p. 3.
73. *The Times* (11 June 1915), p. 11.
74. *Washington Times* (12 June 1915), p. 2.
75. *Manchester Guardian* (14 June 1915), p. 6.
76. *British Medical Journal* (26 June 1915), p. 1090.
77. *Hansard*, House of Lords Debate (24 June 1915), 19 cc143-8 143.
78. *Hansard*, House of Commons Debate (26 July 1916) 84 cc1679-82.
79. Andrew Hobbs (2008) It Doesn't Add Up: myths and measurement problems of births to single women in Blackpool, 1931–1971, *Women's History Review*, 17(3), pp. 435–454, p. 438.
80. Ibid.

81. HMSO (1915) *Annual Report of the Medical Officer of Health to the Local Government Board Report on National Mortality in Connection with Child-Bearing and Its Relation to Infant Mortality*, [Cd. 8085] XXV(157), p. 13; John C. Caldwell (2004) Social Upheaval and Fertility Decline, *Journal of Family History*, 29(4), pp. 382–406.

82. HMSO (1915) *Seventy-Eighth Annual Report of the Registrar-General of Births, Deaths, and Marriages in England and Wales*, [Cd. 8484] 53, p. 124.

83. Based on ibid. p. 4 Table 2.

84. Hobbs, 'It Doesn't Add Up', p. 443.

85. HMSO (1919) *Eighty-Second Annual Report of the Registrar-General of Births, Deaths, and Marriages in England and Wales*, [Cd. 1017] Xl(1), Table X.X, p. xxxv.

86. Ibid.

87. Dirk Bethmann & Michael Kvasnicka (2012) World War ll, Missing Men and Out of Wedlock Childbearing, *Economic Journal*, 123, pp. 162–194.

88. Wollacott, '"Khaki Fever"', p. 325.

89. Pamela Cox (2007) Compulsion, Voluntarism, and Venereal Disease: governing sexual health in England after the contagious diseases acts, *Journal of British Studies*, 46(1), 91–115, p. 113; Shani D'Cruze & Louise Jackson (2009) *Women, Crime and Justice in England Since 1660* (Basingstoke: Palgrave Macmillan), p. 150

90. Wollacott, '"Khaki Fever"', p. 325; Sonya O. Rose (1998) Sex, Citizenship, and the Nation in World War II Britain, *American Historical Review*, 103(4), pp. 1147–1176.

91. Cohen, *Folk Devils and Moral Panics*, xxxvii.

92. *Hansard* House of Commons Debate (16 March 1916), 80 cc2307-445.

Acknowledgements

The author wishes to thank the anonymous reviewers for their very constructive and helpful comments.

Disclosure statement

No potential conflict of interest was reported by the author.

6 'A Matter of Individual Opinion and Feeling'

The changing culture of mourning dress in the First World War

Lucie Whitmore

ABSTRACT

Mourning dress, the typically black costume worn to mark a bereavement was once a well-established part of funeral and mourning culture in Britain. The First World War is generally understood to have caused a major breakdown in mourning practices; the explanations offered for this breakdown include patriotism, practicality, concern for morale, and respect for the war dead. This paper will address the changes that took place within the culture of mourning dress between 1914 and 1918, while simultaneously considering how attitudes towards death and the rituals associated with bereavement were altered by the conflict. This will include an analysis of the developments in fashionable mourning dress during the war, assessing changes both in aesthetics and etiquette, in an attempt to determine the reasons for the breakdown. This paper will also discuss what comfort the ritual of mourning dress offered the war widow, and what constituted 'war appropriate' mourning in wartime.

Introduction

Writing in July 1915, a journalist for society magazine *The Queen* commented that: 'extraordinarily modified as her dress is, there is no mistaking the young widow. She is, alas! a far too prominent personage just now.'[1] It is this 'extraordinary modification' of female mourning attire during the First World War in Britain that comes under question in this paper. The dramatic change in the appearance and role of mourning dress at this time has been commented upon by dress historians such as Lou Taylor, who claimed that 'it was the terrible slaughter of the First World War that undoubtedly caused the major breakdown in funeral and mourning etiquette'.[2] This paper seeks to establish how mourning dress—the typically black costume worn after the death of a relative—was changed by the war between 1914 and 1918, and why these changes took place. The details of these changes have not been analysed in any great detail elsewhere, so this paper offers a unique insight into the world of fashionable mourning dress during the war. It also attempts to establish the significance of mourning dress as a ritual for women who could not afford the latest fashionable styles.

In the limited literature available on this subject a few suggestions have been made as to *why* mourning dress changed at this time, but with little insight into *how* it changed.

Within his analysis of mourning culture in twentieth-century Britain, Geoffrey Gorer has proposed that traditional black mourning was not widely worn during the war as it could appear depressing and weaken morale, both for those at home and soldiers returning on leave.[3] Dress historians Valerie Mendes and Amy de la Haye have intimated that the reasons for change were more rooted in practicality: 'the rules of funeral and mourning etiquette were relaxed because many women working for the war effort were unable to adhere to them.'[4] Finally, in the most comprehensive discussion of this subject, Lou Taylor has suggested that during the war it was felt that a different expression of grief was required to adequately mark the death of a soldier. Traditional mourning dress was not considered to be an appropriate expression of respect for those who had died fighting for their country.[5]

Within these three sources, and the few other works that tackle this subject,[6] the same conclusion is drawn: that the cultural practice of mourning dress was forever altered by the First World War, and never recovered. This paper does not refute this, but seeks to add some depth to the discussion. The quotes cited above suggest that mourning dress was no longer considered to be a valued ritual, that it lost favour because it was thought to be irrelevant, impractical or disrespectful within the context of war. This paper argues that while there may be some truth in each of these statements, the function of mourning dress was more diverse and dynamic, and the ritual remained significant for many women. Furthermore, it hopes to show that by understanding mourning dress both as a material ritual and as a fashionable practice, it can be used to understand the emotional experiences, social concerns and public role of women who lived through the First World War.

This work is fundamentally a dress history study, and although it engages with broader historical narratives, the methods used are primarily suited to the study of dress objects and dress culture. The study of dress, and the relationship women had with their clothing, offers us an alternative interpretation of wartime life. The colour, form, fabric and ornamentation of a garment might not only signal the wearer's economic status but also her taste, cultural influences, political or religious affiliations and daily routine. Framing women's dress, both surviving garments and their representation in printed media, within this material culture framework helps us to understand the narrative strength of such objects and their power to communicate social and cultural information beyond their intended purpose. In the words of archaeologist Sarah Tarlow, 'If we find an ancient shoe [...] the least interesting thing it tells us is that people in the past had feet.'[7]

When studying fashion and dress there often exists a bias towards the upper classes; those who could afford to shop. Of the available source material for a dress history study, the garments that survive in museum collections are rarely those well-worn and repaired items that belonged to the lower classes, and the styles featured in magazines were aimed at those who could spend for pleasure rather than out of necessity. The wartime women's magazines and 'society' newspapers that were an invaluable source in the writing of this paper are no exception. However, it should be noted that many of the widely unaffordable styles featured in such magazines would have been aspired to by a broader demographic, and would have filtered down through cheap copies or home-made versions. Even for the upper classes, it is not possible to ascertain how closely the advice given in these magazines was followed, yet the content is indicative of the interests and concerns of the war generation, and the magazines offer an insightful commentary on the changes that took place in mourning dress culture at that time.

Mourning culture

To understand how mourning dress culture was changed by the war, it is important first to outline the style and etiquette associated with pre-war mourning, and its role within British culture. Historically, mourning dress was understood to indicate the changed social status of the widow while marking her chastity and piety,[8] but it also had a long association with fashionable dress. Black had been the accepted colour of British mourning since the eighteenth century,[9] and fashionable black mourning experienced a boom in popularity during the second half of the nineteenth century.[10] During this period, mourning clothes 'were made up in every nuance of style',[11] and were featured 'in the most prominent style publications'.[12]

The mourning wardrobe of the mid nineteenth century onwards was marked by strictly defined periods, each with firm guidelines that depended on the closeness of the relationship to the deceased. As with any trend in fashionable dress, the idealised version of mourning dress as dictated by these guidelines, and depicted in magazines, would only have been affordable for a small elite. But a version, however altered, would have been worn or aspired to by women of every class, the practice of mourning dress having reached even 'the very poorest levels of society' by the early twentieth century.[13] That very little has been written on the mourning dress worn by widows of previous wars comes as no great surprise after reading Janis Lomas' work on the status and treatment of war widows. She notes that in the Victorian era, the wives of soldiers and sailors 'were thought to be, at worst, "drunken slatterns" and, at best, on a par with servants and therefore in need of "watching"'.[14]

While the war made a huge impact on mourning dress, and indeed other aspects of mourning culture, the developments that led to the eventual breakdown started long before 1914. A backlash against ostentatious Victorian mourning practices emerged around 1880 after many decades of extravagant mourning rituals, which had come to be regarded as wasteful and disrespectful. The *National Funeral and Mourning Reform Association* formed in 1875 and campaigned for 'moderation' and 'simplicity' instead of 'unnecessary show'.[15] The primary motivation was to save expense, particularly for the poor, for whom a bereavement and the 'terror of inevitable expense' was a serious cause for concern.[16] Another significant change in the roughly thirty-year period prior to the outbreak of war in 1914 was the decline in death rates in Britain. David Cannadine has suggested that the British of 1914 'were less intimately acquainted with death than any generation since the Industrial Revolution'.[17]

The shift in attitudes towards death that coincided with these developments has been written about by Sarah Tarlow, Pat Jalland, and David Cannadine. Tarlow has observed that the 'manner and location of remembering the dead' changed from the nineteenth to the twentieth century. She suggests that the associated practices evolved from 'the flamboyantly individual to the intensely personal', and moved 'from the cemetery to the home'. She adds that this shift 'gathered greater momentum' during the war.[18] These sentiments are echoed in Pat Jalland's work on the subject, who further suggests that the developments were connected to changes in religious belief.[19] The association between mourning dress and religion goes back, as noted by Lou Taylor, to the early years of the Christian Church.[20] The potential link between changes in religious belief and changes in mourning dress as impacted by the war have not been expanded upon within this article due to a lack of evidence, but should relevant source material become available it would be interesting to see how the findings correspond with the conclusions drawn in this paper.

It does not seem surprising, given the death toll of the First World War, that attitudes towards death and bereavement, as well as religious belief, would be shaken at the very least. There were no comparable conflicts in terms of casualties or impact on everyday life in living memory when war broke out in 1914. While many thousands of families received the terrible news that loved ones had been killed, only in some cases were they returned a body to bury. Perhaps even more difficult to cope with was the uncertainty when men were reported as missing, and often never found. The rituals of bereavement and mourning had been established in a period of comparative peace; they relied on the tangible presence of a body, a known date of death, a site of burial to visit. For thousands of First World War soldiers a burial place was never identified.[21] As Jalland and Cannadine have observed, during the war 'Victorian death practices seemed both inadequate and inappropriate, especially in the absence of bodies to bury'.[22]

Jalland has also commented on the gender divide in mourning culture, suggesting that women 'experienced the emotions of loss more acutely and would demonstrate those feelings more openly'.[23] This included the observance of material rituals—mourning dress was worn almost exclusively by women[24]—and so any changes in mourning culture could be presumed to have had a greater impact on women and the way they experienced bereavement. It is important to note that for a large portion of the female population the material rituals of mourning would have been unaffordable, however their loss was manifested. For those who could not afford to adhere to the rules of mourning dress, it could be assumed that the changes to etiquette wrought by war would have made little impact on their bereavement practices. However, this was not always the case. The subject is discussed further in the final part of this paper.

Fashionable mourning in the First World War

Despite growing dissention towards the traditional rituals of mourning, and the many varied challenges of wartime life, the subject of mourning dress remained present both in women's magazines and national newspapers between 1914 and 1918. In March 1915, *The Queen* magazine noted that the subject of mourning dress was 'absorbing far more than the usual share of attention [...] for very obvious reasons'.[25] Most department stores boasted a mourning section, and some businesses specialised solely in producing mourning dress in the latest fashionable styles. For those who wished to keep up with the latest trends in mourning, ample advice was offered in the fashion pages and correspondence columns of society magazines such as *The Queen, The Gentlewoman* and *The Lady's Pictorial.* These weekly 'society' magazines were aimed at a readership of middle and upper class women, and discussed such issues as etiquette, fashion, children, women's work and recent news. While some magazines chose to continue as if nothing unusual was going on, these three titles all altered their content and remained reasonably sensitive to the difficult circumstances of life in wartime. This included their discussion of mourning dress.

The magazines regularly advocated particular garments or suggested the best shops and tailors to frequent, yet the manner in which the subject of mourning was addressed suggests that selling the latest styles was not their sole intention. The mere presence of mourning garments, displayed alongside the season's latest furs and millinery, speaks volumes about women's everyday familiarity with death and grief. The journalists acknowledged the exceptional circumstances of war and tried to help their readers, whether this meant advising on the most charming half-mourning frock for a dinner party, or relaxing the rules of mourning for those who needed distraction more than seclusion. In 1915 *The Queen* advised one reader to wear light mourning, 'under the circumstances' of her 'very sad case'. She was instructed to keep things as 'simple and plain as possible', and to 'drown [her] grief by helping others'.[26] Another woman bereaved three times by the conflict wrote to *The Queen* for advice on which mourning periods to follow, based on her relationship to each of the deceased. Not unfeeling, the magazine attempted assistance and added: 'We sympathise greatly with you in your threefold sorrow.'[27]

The mourning ensembles illustrated in magazines varied in practicality, formality and affordability, but all reflected at least to a small degree the prevailing fashions in everyday dress. This was not a wartime innovation; mourning dress had long born resemblance to the most popular styles of the day in structure and silhouette, with some obvious alterations. This relationship with popular fashion resulted in wartime mourning dress styles that featured layered skirts, tapered sleeves, asymmetric drapes, and apron style bodices. Buttons and braiding were common forms of ornamentation, as were sashes or other waist detailing. Certain details, such as colour, length, trim and accessories, separated mourning from everyday dress; but the silhouettes could be otherwise indistinguishable.

The Gentlewoman featured a mourning outfit in March 1915 that was decorated with military style braiding, a popular wartime trend that reflected the romanticism and hopeful heroism that surrounded all things military in the early stages of war.[28] The outfit was not an anomaly; a Manchester department store advertising their latest mourning collections in 1915 boasted a range that included military style collars, military braiding and smart military double-breasted coats.[29] This inclusion of military braiding appears particularly poignant and insensitive if, as was implied, worn by the widow or bereaved family member of a soldier killed at war. These styles were perhaps designed with the proud and patriotic widow in mind; those that wore mourning as a badge of pride. This was in keeping with the idealised behaviour that the state demanded of its war widows. They were expected to uphold the memory of their heroic husbands, to function as 'living symbols of the glorious dead',[30] regardless of their own needs or desires. Though the uptake of these styles cannot be known, it does seem unlikely that any less enthusiastic widows would wish to engage with such a romanticised notion of conflict in their bereavement practices.

The colours and fabrics of wartime mourning

The colours and fabrics associated with wartime mourning were well documented in magazines, newspapers and advertisements, and are revealing of the traditions and beliefs embedded in the practice. The fabric synonymous with nineteenth century mourning was crape: a crimped, dull silk with a notably matte finish. Its role and purpose would have been universally known; it was worn to signify a bereavement. This association was still well understood in 1915, when a journalist writing for weekly journal *The Sketch* observed that the wearing of crape 'is certainly a protection against intrusive curiosity, as it is always significant of the loss of a near relative'.[31] However, it seems that by the time war broke out it was no longer a prerequisite that widows must wear crape to indicate their status. *The Sketch* noted that it was 'now largely a matter for individual taste'.[32] Courtaulds, who dominated the market through the 1800s, experienced a 55% value loss in profit of crape sales on the home market between 1903 and 1912.[33] Crape was generally considered to be ugly, uncomfortable, impractical,[34] and even detrimental to the health of the wearer.[35] Softer, more practical fabrics such as poplin and alpaca gained popularity over crape. One correspondent of *The Gentlewoman* seeking a fashionable and *patriotic* mourning fabric was advised in September 1914 that English-made crepe-de-chine, a softer and lightweight silk, was 'one of the very nicest mourning materials'.[36]

It does not appear that there was any great change in attitudes towards the colours of mourning during the war. Black for mourning was introduced by the Christian church as early as the sixth century; as declared by *The Sketch* magazine in August 1915, 'in this country, black has always been associated with grief'.[37] Black was worn for full mourning, black armbands were worn by bereaved soldiers at the front, and it was even possible to purchase special black corsets or black crepe de chine underwear specifically for mourning, suggesting that the significance of the colour was taken as seriously as it had ever been. Greys, soft purples and white were worn in the latter stages of mourning. *The Gentlewoman,* advising a correspondent on a half-mourning dinner dress, suggested a 'soft pale grey frock, with silver delicately introduced'.

Black, grey, purple and white were not only worn for mourning. It was stated in *The Gentlewoman* in October 1914 that: 'It seems almost useless to talk about colour, since so much black is worn',[38] and a year later, black was still 'more worn than anything today', according to *The Queen*.[39] Black was a fashionable and practical colour in which garments were widely available. It was worn across age, class and gender, and journalists observed that the colour was in keeping with the general mood of a country at war. It was commented in *The Lady's Pictorial* that 'unrelieved black [...] in these days of war, proclaims a nation's, as well as a woman's, loss of one of her fighting men'.[40] It was also advised that the wearing of black was a 'courteous' choice 'for the sake of the feelings of others'.[41]

A journalist writing for *The Queen* in April 1915 commented on the practice of buying and wearing mourning as a pre-emptive gesture, not to denote a bereavement, but to avoid the fruitless purchase of colourful clothes that would be rendered redundant should a relative be killed in action. 'The luckiest of us goes through spells of short mourning, if nothing deeper, these days, and greys, purples, black, and white combinations are bought by many for prudence' sake for their spring outfits.'[42] Her words of warning would only have been of relevance to those who could afford to purchase seasonal wardrobes, but her intention in part was to save expense. The article illustrates the climate of impending bereavement; it seems that for some British women widowhood was not only dreaded, it was expected. Far from being avoided to keep up morale, as has been suggested elsewhere, these examples indicate that black was widely worn and for a variety of reasons, not just by women in mourning. The colour appears synonymous with the home front, as khaki was for the fighting fronts; worn not only for personal bereavement, but for a nation bereaved.

Wartime mourning etiquette

The complex etiquette of mourning dress was discussed with surprising regularity in society magazines during the war. The wealthier readers of these publications would have been very familiar with the rules; the periods of mourning with their associated restrictions on clothing, jewellery and lifestyle were precisely laid out in the decades preceding 1914. It is easy to see how these rules, meticulous and pernickety, would seem ridiculous and outdated to many in the context of war. For many, they would be irrelevant and impossible to follow due to the associated costs. Perhaps in an attempt to balance tradition with the harsh new realities of war, the advice on etiquette printed in magazines became increasingly confused.

An example of relatively straightforward advice was offered in weekly magazine *The Sketch* in August 1915, where it was noted that changes in mourning dress were 'particularly marked in widows' mourning, the period of which has been reduced from two years to eighteen months with half-mourning for a few months more'.[43] Less helpful was the advice given by *The Queen*, which differed month-by-month. In January 1915, for example, one correspondent was advised that 'the period of mourning is twelve months, and you can either wear half-mourning after ten months or [...] eight months',[44] while a year later they advised another that:

> the longest period of mourning is two years: black should be worn for a year and nine months and half-mourning for three months [...] Diamonds may be worn before gold, pearls before colour stones, the latter after the first year of mourning.[45]

The most insightful comment from *The Queen* came in April 1915, when another correspondent was informed that:

> mourning in its every phase has come to be much more a matter of individual opinion and feeling than was hitherto the case. Rules that were adamantine in bygone days are now waived aside.[46]

For those who could afford to follow the rules of mourning it would seem that, like the dress itself, mourning etiquette was slowly adapting to suit the wartime lifestyle. However, the discrepancies between these examples are illustrative of the complex and ever changing attitudes towards mourning dress conventions at this time, fuelled by increasingly diverse opinions as to the purpose and relevance of the practice within the context of war. The idea that mourning had become a matter of 'individual opinion and feeling' was contradicted by the complicated and severe advice of a year later. Despite the social, cultural and emotional upheaval wrought by involvement in a global conflict, the often-confusing Victorian rules of mourning were still evident in the mid war years.

Wartime developments

The changes in both the appearance and etiquette of mourning dress that occurred between 1914 and 1918 were neither immediate nor drastic, but part of a gradual evolution influenced in part by the natural progression of dress trends, and in part by the very particular circumstances of war. The commentary in wartime magazines would suggest that it was the multitude of *young* war widows that made the most significant impact on mourning dress culture at this time. Angela Smith has suggested that the treatment of widows and their role in society had been set, understandably, on the assumption that widows were older women. Yet it was 'highly likely' that war widows would be 'much younger'.[47] Men as young as 18 could enlist, and consequently the equivalent generation of women faced widowhood. These younger widows, regardless of class, would have had expectations of long and active lives ahead of them. As pointed out by Geoffrey Gorer, it was no longer 'socially realistic' to expect that all widows would renounce their interest in having an emotional or sexual life,[48] or that they would exile themselves from work or social occasions.

The Queen commented in May 1915 that 'young widows are especially adventurous, and have broken a vast deal of ground'.[49] One journalist claimed to be most 'struck' by the growing trend for individuality in mourning dress, and her comments offer an insight into the gradual fragmentation of mourning traditions:

> All the old firm and fast decrees appear to have vanished into thin air [...] The dainty white weeds are still worn but remain correct, according to tradition only, so far as the cuffs are concerned, considerable licence being taken with the collar.[50]

In July of that year it was observed that young widows 'appear to have entirely discarded the conventional weeds'.[51]

However, it was not only the comparative youth of war widows that necessitated change in fashionable mourning dress. Many upper-class women found themselves working for the first time as a part of the increased professional and charitable female contribution to the war effort. As a result, magazines needed to advise their readers on mourning dress that was adapted to suit busier and more physically active lives. It was observed by journalists that 'simplicity, unobtrusiveness, excellence of cut' and 'good materials' were now associated with mourning dress, and in August 1915 *The Sketch* commented that mourning wear in recent years had become lighter, and 'more becoming in character'.[52] A quote from *The Queen* towards end of the war in August 1918 highlights this change in lifestyle that was experienced by some of Britain's widows:

> Seclusion is, at the present day, of the briefest, and many young widows resume their usual occupations and engagements in this time of war at a very early date, often six weeks after their bereavement, if the interests of their work demand it.[53]

An October 1914 cover of French fashion magazine *Le Petit Echo de la Mode* appears to shows nurses working while wearing mourning;[54] however, it should be noted that this author has found no evidence of British women wearing mourning dress, or altering their uniforms to denote a bereavement, in any workplace during the war.

Relaxations of the previously rigid mourning dress regulations included shorter hemlines and lower necklines. It was mentioned in *The Queen* that a 'small V-shaped décolletage is quite permissible',[55] a stylistic detail seen in the illustration of a c.1917 mourning dress available from Miss Bowers, a Glasgow based mourning specialist (see Figure 1). The lower 'V' neckline is also evident on a half-mourning dress dated 1916–1920, now in the National Trust collection at Killerton House (see Figure 2). The lavender half-mourning dress has a sheer black overlay in matte silk, and white bands on the hem, sleeves and neckline. The silhouette is typically fashionable for the era, with a low calf length hem and an emphasised waist. Both physically and aesthetically, the dress fits the description

Figure 1. "Mourning from Miss Bowers" in The Gentlewoman, March 17, 1917. With kind permission of the National Museums of Scotland © National Museums of Scotland.

of the simpler, modern mourning garments that were popular with younger widows. It therefore helps to prove the existence of such garments beyond the pages of magazines. The white bands on the dress were quite possibly added at later stages by the wearer, to indicate the progression away from bereavement and towards normal life. Signs of wear, and the rough tacking stitches holding the now damaged ribbons in place, are indicative of the emotion imbued in this object.

Figure 2. Half mourning dress c.1916–1920, Killerton House 1365782 © National Trust Collections/ Sophia Farley & Renée Harvey.

This dress is the only known preserved item of First World War mourning dress.[56] It is a great pity that such garments have lost their stories; we do not know who wore it, when, or why, and that so few items of wartime mourning have been saved. It is understandable, however, that the widows and bereaved mothers of the war would not wish to preserve the garments so intrinsically connected with grief and loss. Perhaps the lack of such garments says more than their survival ever could.

War-appropriate mourning

While the prescribed colours and codes of mourning appear to have been well established, it is difficult to assess whether and how these material rituals provided comfort to the bereaved women of the First World War. Furthermore, it could be questioned whether the wearing of mourning dress was an appropriate response to a war death. The plight of war widows, and particularly those of the lower or working classes, has been addressed in the work of Janis Lomas,[57] and more recently Angela Smith.[58] While neither author has written specifically about dress, their analysis of the financial hardship and social pressures faced by widows clearly illustrates that for many, what to wear could be presumed to be the least of their worries.

The possibility that mourning dress could hold any comfort or emotional significance for the recently bereaved was rejected by the historian David Cannadine, who addressed the issue in his 1981 article 'War and Death, Grief and Mourning in Modern Britain':

> It remains undemonstrated exactly how—if at all—the elaborate rituals of mourning actually helped to assuage the grief of survivors [...] At the most trivial level, even the wearing of mourning clothes might be more of a sartorial torture than it was psychologically therapeutic.

He further suggested that the 'ostentatious wearing of black' prevented widows from being 'treated as normal human beings'.[59] It could be argued that the emotional benefits of ritual are not something that can be tangibly demonstrated, as demanded by Cannadine, and that mourning rituals played a more intangible role. The idea that mourning dress was not a valuable practice suggests a hierarchy of appropriate mourning rituals, in which dress is deemed frivolous within the context of conflict.

Whether mourning dress, or indeed any other ritual of mourning, was an appropriate response to the many deaths brought about by the First World War is debatable. As Jay Winter has observed, 'how healing occurs, and what quietens embitterment and alleviates despair can never fully be known', but it is the 'responsibility' of historians to ask the questions.[60] Perhaps in this case the more relevant questions to ask would be whether the mourning rituals brought any comfort to the bereaved, whether it was felt to be a fitting tribute to the deceased, and whether it was important that these rituals were specific to a war, as opposed to a civilian, death. That these rituals were changed by the war suggests that the latter was indeed significant, and the question of comfort could only be fully answered by those who experienced a bereavement during the war. Ensuring that a tribute to the dead was 'fitting' may come down to the question of patriotism. For women to have 'given a man' to the fight would most probably have been considered patriotic, and it was felt important that the 'noble endurance' of these women was properly recognised.[61] Mourning dress was one way in which this sacrifice could be visibly manifested. Interestingly, for some German soldiers and their families, mourning dress was considered *un*patriotic. Claudia Siebrecht has written about soldiers sending letters from the front to their wives and mothers asking them not to wear mourning dress should they be killed, to show that their bereavement was a 'proud' one, and that they shared the same ideals of sacrifice.[62] A not entirely dissimilar conclusion was reached by a number of British women at the very start of the war.

The subject of a patriotic and war-appropriate mourning was widely discussed in the contemporary press. One particular suggestion, the wearing of black, white or purple mourning armbands, was debated in a series of letters published in *The Times*. On 17 August 1914, Mrs Edward Lyttleton, wife of the headmaster of Eton School, suggested that 'usual' mourning should be dispensed with and people should instead wear a purple armband on their left arm to represent their mourning for a loved one killed at war.[63] Days later, the Duchess of Devonshire and a group of her peers proposed that a white armband would 'express the pride we feel in knowing that those who are nearest to us and dearest have given their lives in their country's cause'. The women wrote that they all had 'near relations serving with the colours', and should those relations be killed in service, they would 'not show our sorrow as for those who came to a less glorious end'.

There is unfortunately very little evidence as to whether either suggestion was adopted by the British public. Only one mention has been found, in a Scottish newspaper, of an armband actually being worn as an expression of mourning in January 1915, though in this case the armband was white with two black stripes at the edges. In this story it was pointed out that mourning armbands were 'not yet very familiar in Dundee', and that 'quite a number of people prefer the old fashioned mourning in heavy black'.[64] While the suggestion was praised theoretically within some other newspapers, it was commented in February 1915 that 'the white band is never seen',[65] and a writer for *The Sketch* went so far as to claim that 'the suggestion died of inanition. It scarcely aroused interest.'[66]

It is clear from the scope of this debate that, while the women proposing the armbands had patriotic ideals and sensible concerns about saving expenditure, they had not considered the emotional significance or material role of mourning dress in the grieving process. A printed rebuttal to these letters, which included the voice of Miss Henderson, a Red Cross worker from Sutton Coldfield, showed that some British women did not welcome the suggestion. Her words are a powerful reminder that the purpose of ritual could mean very different things to different people:

> Anyone who has worked among the poor knows that to rob them of the right of donning mourning for their dead would be to leave them very poor indeed. The average rich person has not the slightest idea of the enormous importance that working women attach to mourning. They will even starve themselves and their children in order to obtain money for its purchase. To urge them at such a time to dispense with mourning is to add a sting to the terrors of death.[67]

It is unfortunate that the social background of Miss Henderson is not known, but in her letter she gave a voice to working-class women; however correct or misguided her chosen words we will never know. She also divided the genders in her discussion of mourning dress culture, emphasising the emotional significance of mourning dress within women's lives, yet going on to suggest that a simple black band would suffice for men and children. This reinforces the idea that the rituals and expressions of mourning were more significant for women. It is clear that Miss Henderson passionately believed that women would suffer if they could not wear mourning dress, and that its power, however intangible, should not be underestimated by anyone.

It has already been observed in this paper that there would have been many widows who could not afford mourning dress. This does not signify, however, that they would not wish to wear it, or that it would have no meaning for them. More affordable alternatives to the styles in magazines were available, for example to make your own, to dye existing garments black, or to wear black clothes donated by wealthier women through various schemes. The cost did not stop some women, who considered the ritual of mourning more important than financial hardship. The *Yorkshire Evening Post* printed a story in July 1916 in which a Judge reprimanded a parent (presumably a mother) for having spent £14 she did not have on putting herself and a 'large family of girls' into full mourning. The Judge was highly critical of the practice, calling it 'shocking', 'ostentation' and 'mere parade'.[68]

The debate that surrounded war-appropriate mourning dress highlights the challenges that were faced by a culture adapting to the realities of war. The war widow as a 'prominent personage' was a new addition to British society, and the concern expressed by women seeking to wear the correct mourning dress perhaps represents the uncertainty they felt about their new status. It is clear that there was a class divide in the experience of war widows,[69] but all were pressured to varying extents to appear patriotic, loyal, humble and good. As an immediate visual symbol of their status, perhaps mourning dress became a tool to help them navigate the complex life of the war widow.

Conclusion

The aim of this paper was to discover how the First World War changed mourning dress in Britain, and what these changes meant for women bereaved by that conflict.

The available evidence has resulted in a documentation of the 'fashionable' mourning dress worn primarily by the upper classes, but it has also been shown that many of these changes impacted on a wider social group of women. These changes included the relaxation of previously strict rules, which never regained authority in the post-war period. Wearing an armband may not have been the norm, but it seems it was an acceptable substitute for traditional mourning within the context of war. When full mourning dress was worn the style became more relaxed, in keeping with the fashions of the day and with the changing expectations women may have had of their clothing. Most significantly, personal choice played a more dominant role in the wartime culture of mourning dress. Even fashion journalists, accustomed to dictating what should and should not be worn, acknowledged that it was important for women to make their own decisions about what they wore to express their grief. The tight rules that had previously controlled mourning had moved from a hierarchical system to something more idiosyncratic; perhaps to the surprise of those titled ladies who had outlined their own vision of war-appropriate mourning for the country in August 1914. Echoing the more general change in attitudes towards death at this time, mourning was no longer primarily associated with power and social status but became 'a matter of individual opinion and feeling'.

This paper has also sought to contextualise these developments within a wider discussion of the 'appropriate response' to war fatalities, and changing attitudes towards death and bereavement. In his denunciation of mourning dress, Cannadine asked 'What point was there in donning widows' weeds when the husband lay mutilated, unidentified and unburied on the fields of Flanders?'[70] It is understandable that for many the convoluted etiquette of mourning dress seems an entirely inappropriate response to the unspeakable deaths of so many young men. If this were the case, it could be concluded that the culture of mourning dress diminished during the war because it was no longer considered a helpful or functional practice. However, this paper has found that there was comfort in the very ritual and restraint that rendered mourning dress ridiculous in others' eyes. The remnants of Victorian mourning culture, the collected visual symbols of colour, fabric and function, created a code that transcended age and class. Whether fashionable or humble, mourning dress still functioned as a semiotic object: it transmitted a message to the world that the wearer was recently bereaved and in an altered emotional state. For many, the ritual and material traditions of mourning dress were considered an integral part of the grieving process. What right have we to criticise the mourning practices that may have brought comfort to even just a few women.

Mourning dress in this paper has been discussed both as a fashionable activity and as a material ritual. Perhaps it is this duality that renders the relevance and purpose of mourning dress so unclear within the context of war. It is clear that many people wanted to establish war-specific mourning rituals, perhaps to delineate a departure from the fashion system, but cultural practices cannot be altered overnight. For Jay Winter, mourning is defined as 'a set of acts and gestures through which survivors express grief and pass through stages of bereavement'.[71] Mourning dress and other visual symbols of mourning continued to play a part in this process throughout the war. Indeed these material rituals were more, and not less, significant at this time when so many women were never returned a body to mourn. Without the usual activities that followed a bereavement, such as dressing the body or attending a funeral, mourning dress could provide an alternative point of focus, a tangible manifestation, an outward expression of grief.[72] The commemorative war memorials that erupted around the country in the post-war period offered sites of mourning that represented the shared experience of grief. As a more individual response, mourning dress allowed the bereaved to make an immediate and visible reaction to a war death. This small and personal act of commemoration depended on their agency alone.

Notes

1. *The Queen* (July 3 1915), p. 24.
2. Lou Taylor (1983) *Mourning Dress* (London: George Allen & Unwin), p. 266.
3. Geoffrey Gorer (1965) *Death, Grief & Mourning in Contemporary Britain* (London: The Cresset Press, 1965), p. 6.
4. Valerie Mendes & Amy de la Haye (1999) *20th Century Fashion* (London: Thames & Hudson), p. 52.
5. Taylor, *Mourning Dress*, p. 269.
6. The only other works that give noteworthy attention to the subject are an article by Sonia A. Bedikian titled 'The Death of Mourning', in which Bedikian pinpoints the First World War as the period in which mourning culture declined, and the chapter titled 'Widow's Weeds' within Lucy Adlington's 2013 publication *Great War Fashion*, which offers some anecdotal insight into how mourning fashions changed through the war period. Sonia A. Bedikian (2008) The Death of Mourning: from Victorian crepe to the little black dress, *Journal of Death and Dying*, pp. 35–52. Lucy Adlington (2013) *Great War Fashion* (Gloucestershire: The History Press), pp. 167–173.
7. Sarah Tarlow (2010) The Archaeology of Emotion and Affect, *Annual Review of Anthropology*, 41, pp. 169–185.
8. Taylor, *Mourning Dress*, p. 65.
9. Ibid. pp. 251–252.
10. The period is well documented in Lou Taylor's *Mourning Dress*.
11. Taylor, *Mourning Dress*, p. 150.
12. Bedikian, The Death of Mourning, p. 37.
13. Taylor, *Mourning Dress*, p. 120.
14. Janis Lomas (2000) 'Delicate Duties': issues of class and respectability in government policy towards the wives and widows of British soldiers in the era of the great war, *Women's History Review*, 9(1), p. 137.
15. David Cannadine (1981) War and Death, Grief and Mourning in Modern Britain, in Joachim Whaley (Ed) *Mirrors of Mortality: studies in the social history of death* (London: Europa), p. 191.
16. Ibid. p. 191.
17. Ibid. p. 196.
18. Sarah Tarlow (1997) An Archaeology of Remembering: death, bereavement and the First World War, *Cambridge Archaeological Journal*, 7(1), p. 105.
19. Pat Jalland (2010) *Death in War and Peace: loss and grief in England, 1914–1970* (Oxford: Oxford University Press), pp. 1–2.
20. Taylor, *Mourning Dress*, p. 66.
21. Jalland, *Death in War and Peace*, p. 49.

22. Ibid. p. 8.
23. Ibid. p. 3.
24. Mourning dress for men lessened through the nineteenth century, with only a crape armband worn beyond 1900: Taylor, *Mourning Dress*, pp. 134–136.
25. *The Queen* (13 March 1915), p. 446.
26. *The Queen* (13 February 1915), p. 309.
27. *The Queen* (1 April 1916), p. 524.
28. It should be noted that the romantic military trend did not last far beyond 1916.
29. *The Manchester Guardian*, 26 November 1915, p. 4.
30. Angela Smith (2013) *Discourses Surrounding British Widows of the First World War* (London: Bloomsbury), p. 146.
31. *The Sketch* (18 August 1915), p. 136.
32. Ibid.
33. D. C. Coleman (1969) *Courtaulds, An Economic and Social History: volume ii rayon* (Oxford: Clarendon Press), p. 72.
34. Taylor, *Mourning Dress*, p. 204.
35. Cannadine, *War and Death*, p. 190.
36. *The Gentlewoman* (26 September 1914), p. 356.
37. *The Sketch* (18 August 1915), p. 136.
38. *The Gentlewoman* (31 October 1914), p. 504.
39. *The Queen* (28 August 1915), p. 399.
40. *Lady's Pictorial* (7 August 1915), p. 199.
41. *The Manchester Guardian*, 26 October 1914, p. 3.
42. *The Queen* (10 April 1915), p. 610.
43. *The Sketch* (18 August 1915), p. 136.
44. *The Queen* (30 January 1915), p. 187.
45. *The Queen* (1 April 1916), p. 524.
46. *The Queen* (17 April 1915), p. 651.
47. Smith, *Discourses*, p. 5.
48. Gorer, *Death, Grief & Mourning*, p. 6.
49. *The Queen* (29 May 1915), p. 928.
50. Ibid.
51. *The Queen* (3 July 1915), p. 31. The term 'weeds' in these examples refers to the trimmings or finish associated with formal mourning outfits.
52. *The Sketch* (18 August 1915), p. 136.
53. *The Queen* (17 August 1918), p. 137.
54. *Le Petit Echo de la Mode*, 25 October 1914, cover.
55. *The Queen* (29 May 1915), p. 928.
56. There may well be others that are not yet known to this author.
57. Janis Lomas (2000) 'Delicate Duties'; (1994) 'So I Married Again': letters from British widows of the First and Second World Wars, *History Workshop* no. 38, pp. 218–227.
58. Smith, *Discourses*.
59. Cannadine, *War and Death*, p. 190.
60. Jay Winter (1995) *Sites of Memory, Sites of Mourning: The great war in European Cultural History* (Cambridge: Cambridge University Press), p. 116.
61. Susan R. Grayzel (1999) *Women's Identities at War: gender, motherhood, and politics in Britain and France during the First World War* (Chapel Hill & London: University of North Carolina Press), p. 228.
62. Claudia Siebrecht (2014) The Female Mourner: gender and the moral economy of grief during the First World War, in Christa Hämmerle Birgitta Bader-Zaar & Oswald Überegger (Eds) *Gender and the First World War* (London: Palgrave Macmillan), pp. 144–162.
63. *The Times*, 22 August 1914, p. 3.
64. *Dundee, Perth, Forfar, and Fife's People's Journal* (23 January 1915), p. 8.
65. *The Plymouth Evening News*, 20 February 1915, p. 2.

66. *The Sketch* (18 August 1915), p. 136.
67. *The Times*, 2 September 1914, p. 4.
68. *Yorkshire Evening Post*, 29 July 1916, p. 7.
69. Lomas, 'Delicate Duties', p. 128.
70. Cannadine, *War and Death*, p. 218.
71. Winter, *Sites of Memory*, p. 29.
72. *The Times*, 14 December 1914, p. 11.

Disclosure statement

No potential conflict of interest was reported by the author.

Funding

This work was funded by the Arts and Humanities Research Council.

7 Gendered musical responses to First World War experiences

Laura Seddon

ABSTRACT

This article investigates how women composers have responded to and commemorated the First World War. It juxtaposes works written between 1915 and 1916 by Susan Spain-Dunk, Morfydd Owen and Adela Maddison, with contemporary responses as part of the centenary commemorations (2014–2018) by Cecilia MacDowall, Catherine Kontz and Susan Philipz. Pierre Nora's concept of 'sites of memory', Benedict Anderson's 'imagined communities' and Judith Butler's theory of mourning provide a framework in order to analyse the different functions of this music in terms of our collective memory of the War. The article ultimately argues that this music contributes to a re-evaluation of how female composers experience the cultural impact of the War. By anachronistically discussing these stylistically disparate works alongside one another, there is the possibility of disrupting the progressively linear canonical musical tradition.

In August 1914, London's musical society was taken by surprise at the outbreak of war. As it was outside the main concert season, only the Proms concerts, then held at the Queen's Hall, had to immediately consider their programming choices. On 15 August the decision was taken to cancel a performance of Strauss, and two days later an all-Wagner programme was replaced with works by Debussy, Tchaikovsky and a rendition of the Marseillaise.[1] This instigated a debate in the musical press, which continued throughout the War, questioning nationalistic tendencies in music, the role of musicians in wartime, and how the War would influence musical composition. Meanwhile, women's music, which had increasingly gained currency from the early twentieth century, continued with some vibrancy throughout the War, albeit often in non-mainstream venues and private contexts. Here seemed to be a chance for women composers to further the cause of women's music in general, and their individual status as composers. One hundred years later, new musical works have featured prominently as part of the current centenary commemorations (2014–2018).[2] New works by women have re-evaluated and re-worked dominant narratives of the War and contributed to the plurality of voices heard in an extended act of collective mourning.[3] Therefore, three instrumental works by composers Susan Spain-Dunk (1880–1962), Morfydd Owen (1891–1918) and Adela Maddison (1866–1929) written in 1915 and 1916 provide snapshots of very different experiences of the War. These are then juxtaposed to recent works by contemporary composers Cecilia McDowall, Catherine Kontz and Susan Philipsz, in order to open a connective dialogue across time between historical and contemporary women's musical practices. This raises the question of how both sets of works function within collective memory in relation to their individual temporalities and performance histories.

The works are all analysed within the context of collective memory (or indeed collective remembrance), specifically considering whether they function as what Pierre Nora has labelled *lieux de mémoire* (sites of memory).[4] Sites of memory are understood as being created through interaction between history and memory, where in the absence of spontaneous memory 'moments of history are plucked out of the flow of history, then returned to it—no longer quite alive but not entirely dead, like shells left on the shore when the sea of living memory has receded'.[5] A site of memory needs to contain the will to remember, as distinct from other historical artefacts. Particularly pertinent to the musical analysis of women's music is the distinction between 'dominant' sites of memory which are imposed from above by governments or official organisations and include official memorial services, compared to 'dominated' sites which Nora considers 'places of refuge, sanctuaries of instinctive devotion and hushed pilgrimages'.[6] There is also consideration of how the musical works contribute to the construction of the nation at time of war, which Benedict Anderson defines as 'imagined communities'. Here the nation is 'conceived as a solid community moving steadily down (or up) history'.[7] Women's music, however, lacks this continued, canonical linearity that is present in the mainstream heritage of the male musical canon: 'Women were caught in a constant state of rediscovery in which the story of women composers' history had to be re-invented each time ... '[8] Thus, women's music also has the potential to both contribute to and disrupt nations' narratives. Finally, issues surrounding the process of mourning in relation to collective remembrance are examined in terms of how women composers construct personal voice as well as representations of historical voices in their work. Here Judith Butler 'codes mourning as a potential eruption of "unspeakable" losses into public life that would revise the frames by which grief is organized'.[9]

Music and the First World War

Debates on the nature of British and, more specifically, 'English' music preceded the War. Constructs of nationalism were also being discussed in the arts more generally, especially in a European context. In British art, these debates were seen most prominently in *volk* culture such as in the writings of Walter Flex and Edward Thomas 'who felt that Europe's new cities were destroying regional and national cultural identities'.[10] Music, therefore, was perhaps unusual as its canonical repertory was almost exclusively based on German/Austrian composers and their associated forms.[11] British composers had been encouraged by wealthy musical philanthropist Walter Willson Cobbett (1847–1937) to explore 'English' forms such as the Phantasy, which was based on sixteenth-century English fancies. The Phantasy was a free-form style representing a continually evolving musical fragment with no exact repetition. However, in reality many Phantasies remained reliant on German sonata form which, by contrast, was highly structured with an interplay between a main and secondary musical theme culminating in a recurrence of material and a tonal resolution.[12]

Proportionally, there were few contemporary works performed during the War, instead programmes of well-known canonical works contributed to the construction of what Benedict Anderson has defined as 'imagined communities' where 'regardless of the actual inequality and exploitation that may prevail in each, the nation is always conceived as a deep, horizontal comradeship'.[13] Thus, the ability to imagine simultaneity of events beyond direct experience and across time, instils a sense of belonging within a particular group and is an essential part of the concept of the nation.

Large-scale occasional works, such as Edward Elgar's *Carillon* (1914) for orchestra and narrator, attracted mass audiences in the main urban centres and acted as unofficial propaganda for Britain declaring war and significantly contributed to the sense of solidarity between Britain and Belgium.[14] Within the listening experience of a musical work, therefore, the emphasis in terms of 'imagined communities' lies in the ritual of performance rather than pitch or form. As Vanessa Williams has argued, this manifests in the participation of this act of collective memory through listening, singing along, anticipating final chords, reading reviews or remembering past performances.[15] Less canonical chamber works, as will be analysed here, also contributed to the 'imagined community' of the nation. They provided, particularly in the case of the phantasies, an unbroken link to the past and, therefore, the possibility of a post-war future. Jay Winter and Geoffrey Cubitt refer to this as the construction of collective memory—in this case triggering collective emotional memory through sound. Indeed, although Winter argues for a collective remembrance rather than memory, in this case the transient but immediate nature of a group listening to live music performance lends itself to the term 'collective memory'.[16]

Despite fewer opportunities for performance, living composers responded to the War in numerous ways. First, dedications to individuals such as Frank Bridge's *Lament* in 1915 dedicated to a young girl Catherine who drowned on the Lusitania. Second, collective, monumental requiems such as Frederick Delius' *Requiem* (1913–1916), and finally, and most unusually, by invoking sonic resonances of the battlefield such as Gian Francesco Malipiero's *Pause del Silenzio* in 1917.[17] While, as Kate Kennedy describes, there were multiple reasons for immediate compositional responses to the war, including as a means of making sense of the escalating situation, Jeffrey Wood argues that the musical works produced tended to display heroic, denunciative, elegiac or reconciliatory qualities.[18] Yet the creative responses of women composers were not so publically identifiable, classifiable or indeed considered 'valid'. Winter reflects on Joan Scott's interpretation of the authority of direct experience of the moral witness as not something the witness *has* but something out of which the sense of self emerges.[19] This was an authority which the majority of women were denied within their war roles, as they tended to be distanced from the battlefields, despite the fact that many established male composers were equally distanced from active military roles. Women composers were also in an artistic double-bind of the mutually exclusive roles of 'woman' and 'creator', resulting in an identity with diminished authority on two fronts.

Women composers had, however, been making strides in gaining professional status. By the early twentieth century, they were increasingly entering composition classes at London's musical conservatoires including the Royal Academy of Music (RAM) and the Royal College of Music (RCM). This increase had been slow due to the harmony and counterpoint aspects of the entry tests, as these were not commonplace in women's musical education at this time, which tended to emphasise performance. Women who were the 'exception' such as Ethel Smyth (1858–1944), Liza Lehmann (1862–1918) and Maude Valerie White (1855–1937), had previously achieved prestigious orchestral and opera performances in London and in Germany. Lehmann and White also became household names with the publication of their popular songs. This group represented a generation of women who had studied privately in Europe and were held as role models for the younger generation who were more likely to have studied within a musical institution. Yet, as Smyth lamented as late as 1933, 'there is not at this present moment one single middle-aged woman alive who has had the musical education that has fallen to men as a matter of course, without any effort on their part, ever since music was'.[20] On graduation from the conservatoires, women's musical disadvantage was compounded by the fact that, while individuals were supportive of their compositional endeavours, musical society in general was not inclusive. For example, it was difficult to gain regular performances of work at the established concert series in London or to gain financial musical patronage.

In the years immediately preceding the War, women's music benefited from the instigation of the Society of Women Musicians (SWM) in 1911. It was founded by three women, Marion Scott (1877–1953), Katherine Eggar (1874–1961) and Gertrude Eaton (1861–?) who, throughout the war years, were influential in the day-to-day organisation of SWM events as well as disseminating their position on the development of women's music. SWM services were clearly needed; between 1911 and 1920 there were approximately 423 female members and forty-nine associates.[21] The SWM existed as part of a milieu of musical societies before the War, including those organised by women for women such as the Oxford Ladies' Musical Society; however, the political nature of the SWM was through their focus on composition. Activities included Eggar's composers' group, conferences and concerts of members' works and career advice. Although still active until the early 1970s, the SWM had become less influential as an advocate for women in the music industry and more of a social musical group. Thus, the years of the First World War, expanding into the inter-war years, represent the peak of the SWM's political campaigns, which included lobbying the BBC to include women in their orchestra and the Associated Board of the Royal Schools of Music to employ women examiners. Despite arguing, at the inaugural meeting in 1911 that the SWM was not a suffragist society, Eggar did acknowledge that 'In both political and musical life there is a great deal of wire pulling and party policy; one does not need to know much about musical dealings in general to know this.'[22]

Despite Eggar's above comparison, it was rare for SWM members to contribute musical skills to the suffrage movement. Well-known members, such as cellist May Mukle were politically active in the suffragette movement and as has been widely documented composer Ethel Smyth contributed *March of the Women* as a suffrage anthem as well as participating in direct action. However, the feminist movement prior to and during the War did not seek to assist the position of women as composers. As Amanda Harris's study has shown, the radical feminist press tended to disregard music, whereas when woman composers were mentioned in moderate feminist publications such as *The English Woman*, *The Vote* and *The Suffragette* they were referred to as exceptions rather than being exemplary of their sex.[23] The refusal to recognise compositional careers in music as a 'site of radical activism' has been argued to be due to both the association between the feminine and music, and the domestic nature of much of women's music-making in the nineteenth and early twentieth centuries.[24] However, there was a lack of engagement between women musicians and the feminist movement at this time and the musicians were criticised for advancing their own cause rather than acknowledging the wider movement.[25]

Some women composers either chose not to engage, or had a sporadic relationship with the SWM. The most notable of these was Ethel Smyth who, while having work played at SWM concerts and speaking at SWM conferences, did not actively support other women in their music-making through SWM activities or outside of the Society. Other than SWM concerts, women made gains in performances of their works during the War. In spring/ summer 1915, one of the Thomas Dunhill Chamber Music concerts was dedicated to works by SWM members, and Adela Maddison performed a concert of her vocal works on her London return. The London String Quartet also performed Smyth's String Quartet in E minor at the Aeolian Hall, and her opera *The Boatswain's Mate*, whose Frankfurt performance had been cancelled, was produced at the Proms concerts. Both Dora Bright and Maude Valerie White additionally had works performed at the same season of the Proms.[26] However, throughout the war years, women's music did not often overtly reflect wartime themes.

Women's compositional responses during the War

Susan Spain-Dunk is representative of a SWM member during the War, she was educated at the RAM studying harmony with Stewart MacPherson and winning the Charles Lucas medal for composition.[27] She was a friend of Cobbett, playing viola in his private string quartet, and was married to composer Henry Gibson. She was, therefore, at the centre of a young group of women composers who used their connections within musical society, and opportunities afforded them by SWM membership, to further their compositional careers. Although she increasingly composed orchestral music in the 1920s, in the 1910s she was a prolific Phantasy composer. Therefore, Spain-Dunk, alongside composers such as Frank Bridge and Thomas Dunhill, can be considered at the forefront of musical explorations of this revived 'English' form in the context of wider debates on nationalism in music. Indeed, Glenn Watkins highlights the increasing intensity in discussions of identity in British and, specifically, English music.[28] Music was exceptional as an art form at this time, as it was not only so dependent on German forms, but also the ingrained structures and processes that valued tradition in musical performance seemed to set itself at odds with the political/social debates in the War.[29] Contemporary musical commentators were aware of this unique position:

> of all the arts, music is the most cosmopolitan; the regular daily interchange not only of composition but of performers has meant that Europe is virtually a single country so far as the process of music is concerned.[30]

Therefore, Spain-Dunk's Phantasy Quartet in D Minor, published by Goodwin and Tabb in 1915, is a musical response produced in the context of debates on English music. It was also part of the SWM's conviction that women's music would be advanced by moving away from its association with small-scale vocal and piano works, towards instrumental chamber music. The piece can, therefore, be considered to be building on previous phantasies written by women, such as Ethel Barns's (1873–1948) *Fantasie* 1905 and Alice Verne-Bredt's (1868–1958) *Phantasie* 1908. In the twentieth century the Phantasy, as advocated by Cobbett, had become a short piece of instrumental music that progressed through a variety of tempi and styles, with equality among its instrument parts.[31] Despite this, most phantasies at this time were, in practice, heavily reliant on Germanic sonata form featuring the distinctive duality of main theme versus subsidiary theme and, crucially, exact repetition of musical material in the recapitulation at the end of the work. Spain-Dunk's Phantasy is more subtle in its approach, however, combining some sonata principles such as the return of the main theme in the original key but not including any passages of exact repetition. The musical material is equally distributed between the instruments with movement between the instrumental lines and textual variety. The slower middle section acts as a condensed sonata before returning to a florid, evolving phantasy style. Marion Scott commented on the work: 'Each of the four parts has an individuality, and there is significance in the phrases, which marks a great advance in musical thought.'[32] Although not explicitly linked to her wartime experience, Spain-Dunk's Phantasy can be considered a working-through of her musical concerns relating to nationalism and gender.

Audiences would have heard Spain-Dunk's chamber works in private rooms (At Homes), by playing them at chamber music socials and through attending formal concert series. Her Phantasy can be situated within the increasing interest in chamber music, which resulted in the widening of the audience demographic. For example the People's Concert Society founded in 1878 provided low cost tickets in London and other counties, and immediately post-war in 1921 free quartet concerts in Portsmouth attracted an initial audience of 1100.[33] Therefore, the Phantasy can be analysed for its role in the creation of an 'imagined community' by allowing the listener to return to both a pre-war experience and a time before German influence in musical form. The musical cues within the work would have been understood by a musically knowledgeable audience in a communal act of listening that bolstered the possibility of a post-war musical future that was not necessarily based on apocalyptic modernist deconstruction. The preference for the traditional and the canonical, as was prevalent during the War in other art forms, manifested differently in a British music scene that was slow to engage with the European avant-garde, whereby 'the need for hope, nostalgia, comfort and ritual overpowered questions of music's national origin', or we could argue, the composer's sex.[34] Thus for an audience well versed in sonata form, the composer's deviations from this in the Phantasy can be argued to have been an audible disruption to the linearity of historical narrative.

Morfydd Owen's Piano Trio was written in November 1915 and, unlike Spain-Dunk's Phantasy, was written in direct response to the War. Entitled *The Cathedral at Liège* and *The Cathedral at Rheims*, the two movements of the Trio were a musical representation of these sites which had been virtually destroyed in zeppelin attacks a month apart at the beginning of the War. The outcry in the allied press in response to the Rheims offensive forced the German authorities to issue a statement: 'we regret the necessity but the French fire came in that direction. Orders have been issued to save the cathedral.'[35] In the British press reports of atrocities 'rapidly became exaggerated and embellished not least by wounded soldiers'.[36] Therefore, it is highly likely that Owen had read the newspaper coverage of these events while studying in London. While, as Susan Grayzell describes, the fronts were certainly gendered with the home front regarded as 'female', these boundaries were porous. The fronts could be crossed particularly through letters, newspaper accounts and conversations with soldiers on leave.[37] This can be argued to be part of the process of a woman composer gaining increased validity to write on a military theme.

Undoubtedly, Owen was deeply troubled by the outbreak of war, writing to her friend Kitty Lewis on 8 September 1914 (after the cathedrals' destruction): 'Everything is awful and ghastilly [sic] horrible.'[38] Originally from Wales, she had entered the RAM in 1912 principally to study composition under Frederick Corder, obtaining the position of sub-professor before her tragic early death. The Trio, written while Owen was still a student, is likely to have been a competition piece and remains in manuscript form; therefore, it may have only received one performance. Arguably Owen benefited from the increased opportunities for women at the RAM during the War, when Principal Alexander Mackenzie noted the zeal and discipline of the female students who made up by far the majority of the student body.[39]

Owen's Trio was composed in the context of an initially fervent and patriotic atmosphere. Owen does use military-style motifs to invoke sounds of war; however, the work is written for an intimate and reflective instrumental ensemble of violin, cello and piano. This can be compared to other women's works such as Marian Arkwright's (1863–1922) jingoistic *Requiem Mass* for full orchestra, which premiered seven months earlier in Newbury, and was also based on a wartime experience filtered by censored letters and newspaper accounts.[40] By contrast, the smaller Piano Trio includes a military theme, a lyrical theme, a folk tune and a chorale. Within the work it is significant that Owen experiments with silence, which acts to isolate and emphasise particular moments. The use of complete silence—which would have rarely occurred on the front—also contributes to her use of musical narrative. As Byron Almén argues, narratives in music do not necessarily need text or titles, rather narrative can be found in multiple elements within a piece of absolute music: 'For the individual, then, narrative patterns are psychological templates illustrating possible responses to conflict.'[41] The strongly evocative musical features of the themes in the Trio allow a narrative reading. For example, although the military and lyrical themes are not tonally distinctive, they do not flow into one another. Alternatively the lyric theme takes over from the military theme with a sudden shift to a soft dynamic, and the military theme is only reintroduced after a full bar of silence. The two movements, and thus the two cathedrals, of the work are bound together by the military theme; it is this theme that is ultimately musically triumphant with its final return in a jubilant major key. This can certainly initiate multiple readings, rather than being either clearly patriotic or pacifist. These readings include a statement of the inevitability of futile destruction as a product of conflict, a position of solidarity with the increasing numbers of Belgian refugees within the musical community in London, or as the hope for a military triumph. It is a subtle, intellectual response from a young woman which sets itself apart from the kinds of patriotism displayed by the women's movement or the SWM.

The significance of the cathedrals' destruction resonates within collective memory. Therefore, the possibility of multiple interpretations of the musical semiotics within the work, create the possibility for a collective experience of a musical and, indeed, architectural space. It is however, likely that there were no further listening experiences of the work beyond its first performance. Thus it acts as a *potential* site of memory in that it contains a will to remember, yet as argued by Nora, the archive (in this case the score) only becomes a site of memory if the imagination invests it with symbolic aura.[42] The fate of Owen's Trio can be compared to Elgar's previously mentioned orchestral work *Carillon*. His work formed part of a widely disseminated collective response to the invasion of Belgium, is scored for large instrumental forces and received multiple performances across Britain. Owen's Trio was a response by a woman composer who had considerably less influence in musical society. Although both works aurally represent symbols of Belgium (bells and the cathedrals), it is notable that *Carillon* has received recent performances as part of the centenary commemorations of the War.[43] Therefore, at the point of interaction between history and memory essential for sites of memory, Owen's work requires future performances to fulfil its potential in this regard.

While Owen's experience of war remained physically distant, the War had a dramatic effect on the personal and professional circumstances of established composer Adela Maddison. She had a career in both Paris and Berlin as an opera composer, initially leaving her husband and children in London to study with Gabriel Fauré in the late 1890s. By the outbreak of war, she was living in Berlin under the artistic patronage of the Princesse de Polignac and was the lover of the Princesse's German secretary Martha Mundt.[44] After managing to escape Germany in 1914 and return to London, the couple were in straightened circumstances as demonstrated in the tone of Maddison's letter to her friend, the singer Mabel Batten:

> I feel a brute writing all this. *I don't want money* and hate anyone thinking I am begging at this terrible moment but if a roof can be provided somehow—I can for a time manage our food etc.[45]

However, Mundt was ultimately forced to return to Berlin, while Maddison remained in London, and the couple were only reunited in Switzerland in 1921.

Maddison's Piano Quintet (1916) did not receive its first performance until after the War in 1920. The work maintains intellectual connotations of the piano quintet as a genre, while in the fourth movement there is waywardness in the use of continually evolving repetition and corruption of the legacy of sonata form, which was easy for critics to interpret as a shortcoming especially in a work by a woman. 'But surely there is something to be said also for "the little creature" ... this Quintet leaves us very doubtful.'[46] Such criticisms, however, miss the point of a work that places itself in opposition to what Judith Butler and David McIvor consider the 'monumental' and public acts of mourning, which become part of the discourse of the state.[47] Thus, disrupting the narrative formation of imagined communities. Rather, this work represents a personal working-through of mourning a loss which 'becomes unspeakable when certain kinds of mourning are not allowed'.[48] Here, instead of the process of interminable, inconsolable, irreconcilable mourning as described by Derrida, no name is evoked overtly, either in terms of sexuality or nationality. When finally performed after Maddison's post-war reunion with Mundt, the disintegration of the musical form in the final movement of the work was unreadable by an audience who were unable to access a particular collective memory.[49]

The corruption of sonata form in the final movement results in the main theme fracturing into increasingly small fragments accompanied by very subtle changes in rhythm, morphing into a more improvisatory feel. The piece shows Phantasy-like tendencies as Maddison appears to be experimenting with this freestyle form which was entirely under the control of the individual. Thus, the work can be considered both a personal negotiation of uncontrollable circumstances and a mode of political resistance. A temporal distance is perhaps required to enable the listener to move towards a response where, as McIvor suggests, the meanings and significance of traumatic events are contested and revised. Indeed if it can now be identified as a site of memory, through revived performance for the first time in eighty-seven years at the Wigmore Hall in 2007, radio broadcasts and a CD recording by the Fibonacci Sequence ensemble, it is a composite one where commemoration is only one of many symbolic resonances.

Contemporary musical responses to the Centenary of the First World War

The shift from the individual to the universal, what Butler defines as making 'a tenuous we of us all', in terms of the ability to narrate ourselves not only from the first person alone, is displayed in women's musical responses for the centenary commemoration.[50] The approaches to the composition of these works by Cecilia McDowell, Catherine Kontz and Susan Philipsz, highlight the reworking of established war narratives in music. These are presented as examples of 'sites of memory' in the context of what Nora identifies as 'alienated memory', where collectively we have now become disconnected from any sense of continuity with the past. Thus '[t]he old ideal was to recreate the past, the new ideal is to create a representation of it'.[51]

Cecilia McDowall's work for solo soprano and choir, *Standing as I do Before God* (2014), is an intricate interplay between multiple singing voices.[52] It was commissioned by the Sospiri choir who requested settings of unusual war stories/voices rather than settings of war poetry. It sets Sean Street's poetical response to Edith Cavell's last words before her execution in Brussels on 12 October 1915:

I have seen death so often that it is not strange or fearful to me

Standing as I do in view of God and eternity,

I realize patriotism is not enough.

I must have no hatred or bitterness towards anyone.[53]

With meditative qualities and plainsong soundscapes, in general the soprano soloist vocalises Cavell's words, whereas Street's lines are set for the choir. The soloist and the group alternate to provide a ghostly counterpoint as atmospheric response. However, in the opening bars, it is in fact the choir who sing Cavell's first line, emphasising the 'universal collective' before the soloist reiterates this line and the choir fragments. Musical devices such as the shift chromatically downwards resolving amen-like in bars 14–15, contribute a sense of religious spirituality. Towards the end of the piece, the roles are, again, reversed between the choir and soprano as the soloist almost imperceptibly joins the collective voices on the word 'infinity':

a flame alight in hours

before infinity,

in the presence of death

leaving all enmity

we are air after breath.[54]

Indeed the piece finishes as the soprano soloist (Cavell) sings the last three of Street's final lines and provides a counterpoint where 'leaving all emnity' and 'in view of God' are reiterated, while the choir have transformed into ghostly sound resonance.

Cavell's tragic story remains in the collective public consciousness, partly due to the repercussions of her death, which particularly resulted in the increase of men signing up for active service, and public fundraising for the Cavell Homes for Nurses.[55] The British/American propaganda in the press, at that time, also significantly damaged the German position. Her martyrdom meant that she has come to represent an 'exceptional' version of womanhood and has resulted in the perpetual invoking of her name, thus the mourning process has reoccurred in a Derridian loop.[56] McDowall's approach, however, seems to move beyond the simple reclaiming of a voice by displacing it throughout the ensemble and musically evolving into Street's response. Therefore, the listener is not merely a mourning appendage or a witness to an injustice, but rather a medium through which the process of collective mourning and grief halts.[57] This process has moved beyond the official narrative claimed by the imagined community of the state, which as Anderson explains because there is no natural birth or death of a nation its narrative is structured through deaths: 'exemplary suicides, poignant martyrdoms, assassinations, executions, wars and holocausts.'[58] Yet at this temporal distance the individual is integral to the collective response. Indeed in such cases the time passed is vital to the disruption of the mourning loop, which risks being undertaken too rapidly, as Butler has argued in the context of the 9/11 attacks, 'our fears can give rise to the impulse to resolve it [grief] too quickly, to banish it in the name of an action invested with the power to restore the loss or return the world to former order ... '.[59]

As opposed to the exceptional individual, Catherine Kontz uses family voices as her compositional material for *Papillon* (2014), an a cappella piece for choir, treble and children's choir.[60] The work consists of five excerpts from the Papillon family letters, October 1915 to July 1916, published as *Si Je Reviens Comme Je L'Espère* (If I come back as I hope).[61] The Papillon children: Marthe, Joseph, Lucien and Marcel, write of their war experiences to their parents, receiving replies from their mother Mme Papillon. Collectively, the letters express worry, complaints, continuous waiting for news, conditions at the front and the weather. Therefore, even though they are contemporaneous with Edith Cavell, by contrast they evoke everyday concerns. Kontz presents the family as a site of commemoration, which as Helle Bjorg and Claudia Lenz argue, represents the intersection between public and private memory where 'family memory is deeply inscribed into collective discourses of the past'.[62] This is reflected in the compositional structures of the work where each child's voice is represented by a particular combination of voice types from the choir, whereas Mme Papillon is sung by the full range of singers from the choir, thus, representing the 'whole'. The piece starts with multiple voices singing speech rather than pitched notes, creating the impression of chattering. Out of this collective soundscape emerge individual concerns; however, the counterpoint of voices crossing each other mirror letters moving between family members and highlight the difficulties in communication as well as the strain of no news. The use of whistle noises produced by the singers is also highly evocative of the trains which would have carried both letters and people to their destinations.

Musically the mother's line—unusually for a female voice, at the lowest line of the stave—comprises of all the notes used by her children, whereas their musical palates are limited in pitch. The individual performance parts within the work are constructed with shifting rhythms and interjections of repeated phrases, which means that each character is on a slightly different musical trajectory; however, the mother acts as the unifying force between the individual and the collective. Kontz is on one level commenting on the gendered nature of correspondence; letters are written to the parents, but it is the mother who replies and the mother who is the musical whole. Yet the work can also be read as a dominated site of memory infused with the rituals of family life, but perhaps more explicitly, it taps into Butler's 'we', in a way that could be argued to be more easily accessible to contemporary audiences than narratives of the 'heroic' individual.

War Damaged Musical Instruments (2015–2016) by sound-artist Susan Philipsz was commissioned as part of the 14–18 NOW arts project commemorating the War.[63] Rather than building on the individual voices and experiences to initiate a collective memory, as in the case of McDowell and Kontz, Philipsz takes the well-known sound trigger of the tune of the Last Post, as her starting point to explore how personal fate intertwines with constructed societal narratives of the War. This sound piece uses damaged brass and woodwind musical instruments found in museum collections in the UK and Germany, including a bugle of a fourteen-year-old drummer who was in active service at the Battle of Waterloo. Fourteen sound recordings were made of musicians attempting to play the Last Post on these instruments which, depending on the extent of the damage, range from being recognisable as such to being merely the sounds of the players' breath; however, '[a]ll the recordings have a strong human presence'.[64] These recordings were then played through multiple hanging speakers in the Duveen Galleries at alternating intervals, aurally catching visitors to the museum by surprise. The power of the sounds on the body is indicated in the fact that both the sudden and insistent interjection of brass and the subtle whispering of human breath sounds caused visitors to stop and physically rotate towards the speakers.

The function and meaning of the Last Post has evolved since its eighteenth-century roots. Starting as one of multiple calls in barracks, later it signalled to lost or wounded soldiers on the battlefield that it was safe to return to base, its contemporary function is at military funerals and remembrance ceremonies. In itself it is a site of memory, having been appropriated for state funerals, left- and right-wing political demonstrations, and British colonies' independence ceremonies. In 1921 the cabinet committee's proposed manipulation of the format of the Cenotaph ceremony, which did not include the Last Post, and was meant to be a 'commemoration of a great occasion in national history', was met with a public insistence of a day of mourning, with the Last Post as central.[65] As Alwyn Turner has observed 'it was the bugler with his secular spirituality and despite his military status who seemed better able to articulate the nation's response to war'.[66] Therefore, the echoing, cathedral-like space of the Duveen galleries at the Tate, allows the sound to resonate through the recordings of the instruments as 'indexical traces of the past' and through the listeners' bodies.[67] The acknowledged function of the Last Post in triggering collective memory is instantly questioned and re-formed here by the multiple distortions of the tune. Just like memory itself the recognised aural fragment is fleeting and corrupted. As opposed to the daily performance of the Last Post at the Menin Gate which can be identified as a dominant and 'pure' site of memory in that its only function is commemorative, Philipz's work disrupts this construction and moves towards being a dominated, composite site.

The historical works discussed reflect the composers' personal experience of the cultural impact of the War. As Spain-Dunk's Phantasy was the only piece to have been performed and disseminated through publication during the War, these works are perhaps *potential* sites of memory displaying dominated, private and composite qualities, rather than being part of the collective state narrative. Therefore, the temporality of Owen's and Maddison's works is distinct and perhaps more contemporaneous. Despite the double-bind faced by women in terms of authority to represent war and to identify as composer, in the lead up to and during the War, they were, however, in a position to develop women's music and disrupt the progressively linear, canonical music tradition. The changed authority and professional status of contemporary women composers is reflected in the fact that all three works discussed here were officially commissioned. They function as sites of memory as they contain the will to remember, although it can be argued that they represent more public and pure responses than the historical works, in that their primary function is to commemorate. Therefore, they perhaps occupy a space between dominant sites and dominated sites of memory. For example Philipsz's work is part of the 14–18 project and installed at the Tate Britain; both receive state funding. However, she deliberately subverts the current understanding of *The Last Post*'s role in the war narrative. No longer is the validity of the 'moral witness' status required as part of identity for women composers to write the War, at a point in the grieving process where the collective are alienated from memory. The centenary of the War has spotlighted certain obscure musical works generally and has allowed for anachronistic readings. Here, the analysis of both the historical and contemporary works has highlighted that while only MacDowall's and Kontz's works overtly deal with gendered themes, the creation of these of sites of memory, or indeed *potential* sites are connected. They revise the collective sense of the imagined community of the nation and offer an alternative war narrative through sound by acting as markers for questioning how we collectively remember the plurality of war stories, experiences and responses.

Notes

1. Vanessa Williams (2014) 'Welded in a Single Mass': concert halls during the first world war, *Journal of Musicological Research*, 33, pp. 27–38.
2. Works range from Jonathan Dove's choral work *For the Unknown Soldier* based on nine First World War poems, to BBC Radio 3's extensive commemoration programming to multimedia works commissioned for the 14–18 NOW project including *Dr Blighty* at the 2016 Brighton Festival: see https://www.1418now.org.uk/
3. Works of this nature by women include Liz Lane's *Hall of Memory* (2013) with text by Jennifer Henderson; Emily Hall's *Gastenboek* (2014) based on the comments book from Flanders Fields Museum; Sally Beamish's *Equal Voices* (2014) a setting of Andrew Motion's poem; Rhian Samuel's *A Swift Radiant Morning* (2015) a memorial in words and music of poet Charles Hamilton Sorley, and Rachael Morgan's *Seeking Answers to the Riddle* (2015) an instrumental interpretation of war letters.
4. Pierre Nora (1996) General Introduction: between memory and history, in Pierre Nora (Ed.) *Realms of Memory: Rethinking the French Pasr*, Vol. I (New York: Columbia University Press). For discussion of collective memory and collective remembrance see Jay Winter (2006) *Remembering the War: the Great War between memory and history in the twentieth century* (Newhaven: Yale University Press); Geoffrey Cubitt (2007) *History and Memory* (Manchester: Manchester University Press).

5. Nora, *Realms of Memory*, p. 7.
6. Ibid. p. 19.
7. Benedict Anderson (2006) *Imagined Communities*, Rev. Edn (London: Verso), p. 26.
8. Amanda Harris (2014) The Spectacle of Woman as Creator: representation of women composers in the French, German and English feminist press 1880–1930, *Women's History Review*, 23(1), pp. 18–42.
9. David W. McIvor (2012) Bringing Ourselves to Grief: Judith Butler and the politics of mourning, *Political Theory*, 40(4), pp. 409–436.
10. Tim Cross (1988) *The Lost Voices of World War I* (London: Bloomsbury), p. 3.
11. Williams, 'Welded in a Single Mass'.
12. For information on twentieth-century Phantasies see Laura Seddon (2013) *British Women Composers and Instrumental Music in the Early Twentieth Century* (Farnham: Ashgate).
13. Anderson, *Imagined Communities*, p. 6.
14. Elgar wrote *Carillon* as a contribution to *King Albert's Book* which was published at Christmas 1914 to raise funds for Belgian Refugees in Britain. It contained contributions by leading politicians, writers, poets, artists and composers including Claude Debussy, Ethel Smyth, Liza Lehmann and Camille Saint-Saëns.
15. Williams, 'Welded in a Single Mass'.
16. Winter, *Remembering the* War, p. 5; Cubitt, *History and Memory*, p. 18.
17. Wolfgang Marx (2012) 'Requiem Sempiternam?' Death and the musical requiem in the twentieth century, *Mortality*, 17(2), pp. 119–129; Stefan Schmidl (2015) Music of the Great War: observations in a neglected repertoire, *New Sound*, 44(2), pp. 121–132.
18. Kate Kennedy (2014) A Music of Grief: classical music and the First World War, *International Affairs*, 90(2), pp. 379–395; Jeffrey Wood (2014) The Great War and the Challenge of Memory, *New Sound*, 44(2), pp. 109–120.
19. Winter, *Remembering the War*, p. 239.
20. Ethel Smyth (1933) *Female Pipings in Eden* (London: Peter Davies), p. 12.
21. Membership Lists 1911–1920, SWM Archive, RCM, London.
22. Katherine Eggar (1911) Address at the Inaugural Meeting, 15 July 1911, SWM Archive, RCM, London.
23. Harris, 'The Spectacle of Woman as Creator', p. 20.
24. Ibid. p. 36.
25. Ibid. p. 29.
26. *The Musical Times*, April–August 1915, pp. 866–869.
27. Student Record for Susan Spain-Dunk, Student Entry Records 1902, RAM Archive, London, p. 426.
28. Glenn Watkins (2003) *Proof Through the Night: music and the Great War* (Berkeley: University of California Press).
29. Williams, 'Welded in a Single Mass'.
30. Ernest Newman (September, 1914) The War and the Future of Music, *The Musical Times*, 859, pp. 571–572.
31. See Seddon, *British Women Composers*, pp. 117–118.
32. Katherine Eggar & Marion M. Scott (July 1914) Women's Doings in Chamber Music: women as composers of chamber music third paper, *Chamber Music: a supplement to the music student*, 9, p. 98.
33. Betsi Hodges (2008) *W.W. Cobbett's Phantasy: a legacy of chamber music in the British musical renaissance* (PhD, University of North Carolina), pp. 22, 27.
34. Williams, 'Welded in a Single Mass', p. 38.
35. n.a., 'Germans Regret Rheims; Order to Save Cathedral', *New York Times*, 21 September 1914.
36. Toby Thacker (2004) *British Culture and the First World War: experience, representation and memory* (London: Bloomsbury), p. 48.
37. Susan R. Grayzell (1999) *Women's Identities at War: gender, motherhood, and politics in Britain and France during the First World War* (Chapel Hill: University of North Carolina Press), p. 12.

38. Letter from Morfydd Owen to Kitty Lewis (8 September 1914) in Rhian Davies (1999) *Morfydd Owen (1891–1918): a refined and beautiful talent* (PhD, University of Wales Bangor), p. 177.

39. Alexander Campbell Mackenzie (1927) *A Musician's Narrative* (London: Cassell & Co), p. 247.

40. Kennedy, 'A Music of Grief'.

41. Byron Almén (2008) *A Theory of Musical Narrative* (Bloomington: Indiana University Press), p. 27.

42. Nora, 'General Introduction', p. 14.

43. *Carillon* was performed by the London Symphony Orchestra in 2014 and by the Flanders Symphony Orchestra in 2015.

44. Sophie Fuller (2002) Devoted Attention: looking for lesbian musicians in fin-de-siècle Britain, in Sophie Fuller & Lloyd Whitesell (Eds) *Queer Episodes in Music and Modern Identity* (Urbana: University of Illinois Press), pp. 79–101.

45. Letter from Adela Maddison to Mabel Batten (1914), Cara Lancaster Archive, Lancaster Family Collection, London.

46. B.V. (October 1925) Chamber Music, *The Musical Times*, 66 (992), p. 909.

47. McIvor, 'Bringing Ourselves to Grief'; Judith Butler (2004) *Precarious Life: the powers of mourning and violence* (London: Verso), pp. 29–30.

48. McIvor, 'Bringing Ourselves to Grief', p. 412.

49. Jacques Derrida (1996) By Force of Mourning, *Critical Inquiry*, 22(2), pp. 171–192.

50. Butler, *Precarious Life*, pp. 20, 8.

51. Nora, *Realms of Memory*, p. 12.

52. Cecilia McDowall (2014) *Standing As I Do Before God: a reflection on the execution of Edith Cavell 12 October 1915* (Oxford: Oxford University Press). The first performance of this work was recorded live on 9 November 2014: https://www.youtube.com/watch?v=QkUXdMT1nvk (accessed 19 February 2017).

53. Cecilia McDowall (2014) *Programme Notes* (including Sean Street's text), sent to the author.

54. Ibid.

55. Diana Souhami (2010) *Edith Cavell* (London: Quercus).

56. Derrida, 'By Force of Mourning'.

57. Liz Stanely (2002) Mourning Becomes … : the work of feminism in the spaces between lives lived and lives written, *Women's Studies International Forum*, 25(1), pp. 1–17.

58. Anderson, *Imagined Communities*, p. 206.

59. Butler, *Precarious Life*.

60. Catherine Kontz (2013) *Papillon* (Commissioned by the European Concert House Organisation), copy sent to author.

61. Marthe Papillon, Joseph Papillon, Lucien Papillon & Marcel Papillon (2003) *Si Je Reviens Comme Je l'Espère: letter du front de l'arrière 1914–1918* (Paris: Grasse).

62. Helle Bjorg & Claudia Lenz (2012) Time out for Nation Heroes? Gender as an analytical category in the study of memory cultures, in Eric Langenbacher, Bill Niven & Ruth Wittlinger (Eds) *Dynamics of Memory and Identity in Contemporary Europe* (New York: Berghan), p. 43.

63. For details of Philipz's work at the Tate Britain, London see: http://www.tate.org.uk/whats-on/tate-britain/exhibition/susan-philipsz-war-damaged-musical-instruments (accessed 19 February 2017).

64. Susan Philipz (2015) 'War Damaged Musical Instruments': http://www.tate.org.uk/whats-on/tate-britain/exhibition/susan-philipsz-war-damaged-musical-instruments (accessed 19 February 2017).

65. Alwen Turner (2014) *The Last Post* (London: Autum Press).

66. Ibid. p. 120.

67. Linda Schädler (2015) 'Exhibition essay: Susan Philipsz: war-damaged musical instruments', Tate Britain online curatorial essay, http://www.tate.org.uk/whats-on/tate-britain/exhibition/susan-philipsz-war-damaged-musical-instruments/exhibition-essay (accessed 19 February 2017).

Disclosure statement

No potential conflict of interest was reported by the author.

8 'My Husband is Interested in War Generally'

Gender, family history and the emotional legacies of total war

Lucy Noakes

ABSTRACT

In the autumn of 2014, as Britain embarked on four years of activities to commemorate and mark the centenary of the First World War, the Mass Observation project asked its panellists to reflect on their feelings about the war. Over 180 people responded, writing about their family involvement in the war, about their thoughts and feelings on Remembrance Sunday 2014, and about popular representations of the war in the early twenty-first century. This article examines some of these responses, considering the extent to which gender and age shaped not only the panellists' stated relationship to the centenary of the war, but also the language with which they expressed this relationship. It draws on ideas from the 'emotional turn' in historical studies to argue that older women, who often had a personal memory of the lived legacies of the war, drew on a particularly expressive repertoire to convey both an empathy with the men and women whose lives were shaped by the First World War, and to argue for a particular moral position with regard to warfare. These empathetic responses, which the article argues have much in common with family histories of the war, should be taken seriously by historians who examine the cultural memory of the war and who are often keen to dismiss the widespread sense of the war as a tragic blunder.

Introduction

In the autumn of 2014, as Britain embarked on four years of commemorative activities to mark the centenary of the First World War, the Mass Observation (MO) Project issued a Directive to its respondents, asking them to reflect on their feelings about the war. The Directive was commissioned by the five AHRC World War One Engagement Centres as a means of both capturing the responses of the British people to the centenary, and to provide a snapshot of the cultural memory of the war that was circulating in Britain in late 2014.[1] Among the questions asked were 'do stories about the First World War feature in your family?' 'Have you read any books, or watched any television programmes or films about the war?' and 'Do you observe Remembrance Day?' In addition, respondents were asked to keep a day diary for either Remembrance Sunday, which fell on 9th November, or Armistice Day itself, 11th November 2014.

This article examines some of these responses, considering the ways in which these were shaped by gender and generational position. It focuses upon the responses of women born between the 1920s and the early 1950s. While these women do not constitute a single generation, being aged between ninety-three and sixty at the time of writing, with the majority of those whose responses were analysed being in their seventies and eighties, they can be understood as, in Marianne Hirsch's words, 'the generation after'. By this, Hirsch is referring to a group whose relationship to a past event (in Hirsch's example the Holocaust, here the First World War) is shaped by the impact of this event on those who had first-hand experience, which they then "remember' ... by means of the stories, images and behaviours by which they grew up'. [2] For Hirsch, this 'postmemory' is differentiated from the memories of those with experience of the same past events by its 'imaginative investment', but it shares with them an emotional power, and acts as a means by which emotional connections are made across generations.[3] While none of these women was old enough to have had personal experience of the war years, they were all of an age to have known veterans, to have heard some of their stories, and at times to have had their own early lives shaped by the impact of the war, and the stories that circulated about it. Their experiences also differed widely, of course. As well as the usual differences of class, of occupation, family position and other determining factors, they were divided by history, with the older respondents having experienced the Second World War as adults, while the younger were born in the decade after its end. They were all, however, old enough to have close family members, parents, grandparents, aunts and uncles who had first-hand experience of the First World War and to themselves have formed an impression of the war years which preceded the current cultural memory of the war, which began to emerge in the 1960s and which has been described by Helen McCartney as 'a byword for futility'.[4] They were also all women, a group whose wartime experiences, as this article will go on to demonstrate, have been largely marginal to the wider cultural memory of the war in circulation.

As Hirsch notes, family history, with its ability to reduce distance and abstraction, and its emotional resonance for many, can provide a powerful means for people to engage with the events of the past.[5] Indeed, as much recent work with community groups on the centenary of the First World War has demonstrated, family history has emerged as one of the key ways in which individuals are connecting to commemorative activities.[6] This article examines the interaction between these family histories and the wider, public, memories of the war that have circulated since its conclusion. It considers how these forces may have formed these women's relationships to the war, examining both the appearance of popular narratives of the war in the Directive replies, and the ways in which these were shaped by family history and family and generational position. Firstly though, it considers the ways in which war memories can be understood as gendered.

Gendering War Memories

The transmission of war memories across generations is a subject that has recently been of interest to a number of scholars.[7] Michael Roper's work on the emotional impact and life-long legacies of the First World War on the men who fought in this conflict and their families considers the idea of a male 'war generation' whose emotional, familial and psychic lives were shaped by this defining experience. He has examined this firstly through a careful study of the letters which passed between home front and war front, and later autobiographical retellings of war experiences, and, secondly, through a focus on the stories that veterans' children tell. In both studies, the idea that the war has an afterlife, that it lives on through memory, through culture, through its familial, physical, emotional and economic legacies, is central.[8] In his oral history of the ways that the memory of the First World War influenced male attitudes to military service in the Second World War, Joel Morley considers the ways that young men encountered ideas about what warfare and military service entailed through conversations with older men in their families. In the passing on of versions of their experiences through family stories and conversations, First World War veterans contributed to the 'scripts' from which younger men built their own identities and understood both models of masculinity that were circulating and their own place in their families.[9] These studies illustrate some of the ways that war stories entered into family life, and demonstrate that, counter to the cultural arche-types of the expressive war poet and the silent, traumatised veteran, unable to speak of his experiences and thus unable to heal himself, the majority of men sat somewhere in between: attempting to compose stories about the war that they were comfortable with, and which transmitted particular narratives of service and models of masculine behaviour to the younger men in their families, while perhaps remaining silent about other experi-ences, and amongst other audiences.

However, while these studies explore the ways in which memories and narratives of war are transmitted across generations, they both focus on the ways that these are transmitted by male veterans, and consider subsequent generations through their relationship to these men, to their experiences and memories. The privileging of the narrative of this male veteran over other types of war experience, and other forms of identity that can be seen here is a part of wider patterns in Britain of the cultural memory of the war years. To some extent, academic histories of the war and its multiple legacies are marginal to a widely shared historical understanding of the conflict, which continues largely to focus on the male experience of the Western Front. While there is a large body of research on the gendered history and experience of the First World War, the impact of this work on cultural memory of the conflict has been marginal.[10] While the experiences of the 'home front' in general have been examined in several recent fictionalised represen-tations of the war, the experience of the man on the Western Front has maintained its cen-trality. Thus, even in the television costume dramas of the early twenty-first century, which have traditionally been understood as having a largely female audience, storylines driven by the events of the First World War, exploring their impact on and legacies for, those far away from the front line, the experience of the combatant remains fundamen-tal.[11] As the historian Bart Ziino has argued, 'we remain obsessed with "the soldier's story."'[12] Indeed, representations of women's multiple experiences of the war years, and the wide-ranging and diverse legacies of the war in their lives, remain marginal to British cultural memory of the First World War more broadly, the memoirs of Vera Brit-tain apparently functioning as a satisfactory representation of all female experience.[13] While Penny Summerfield has written perceptively on gendered memories of the Second World War, there has been little consideration of the multiple ways that First World War stories might have shaped the scripts that were available to the daughters and granddaughters of the women who worked in the fields and factories, served in the militaries, nursed the combatants, bought up children, campaigned for peace, or contributed to or worked against total war in numerous ways between 1914 and 1918.[14]

This focus on male stories of war, and their impact on the ideas of masculinity that were available to a younger generation of men, is particularly interesting as women are often the key transmitters of stories within families and across generations.[15] Many of the continuities of family life that our ancestors took for granted have been dissolved by the pressures and possibilities of modernity: families are less likely to share a home across multiple generations and may be spread across the globe. These changes, and the disruption that they can bring not only to family relations but to a stable sense of self, rooted in part in a secure relationship to the past, can help to explain the current popularity of genealogy as a leisure pursuit. Pierre Nora, writing about the history of France, and the ways in which this history fed into and shaped French national identity, identified moments of rupture and rapid social change as points at which history becomes particularly important and visible. As societies change, Nora argued, we become more and more attached to a 'memory' of the past, a memory which gives us a sense of stability and continuity.[16] This desire for a knowable past operates on an individual and familial level, as well as the national level Nora identified. The multiple and rapid changes of recent years can help to account for the current popularity of family history as seen in the media, in local education classes and in the use of online commercial family-history databases such as Ancestry.com.[17] As Anne-Marie Kramer has argued, 'this seemingly unprecedented boom in the family heritage industry' acts not only to build links between the past and the present, but enables individuals to construct subjectivities that position them in relation to this past.[18]

Despite the popularity of family history as a leisure pursuit, as a means of identity formation and as a bounded means of carrying out historical research, academic history has often failed to pay serious attention to this form of historical research and writing.[19] Family history operates in the public sphere as well as the more private and familial; for example, the online projects *Lives of the Great War* and the BBC's *The People's War* both bring together multiple narrative accounts of the First and Second World Wars, often entered onto the websites by the children and grandchildren of veterans, keen to ensure that their familial experience has a place in wider histories of both conflicts.[20] Indeed, the publication of family histories, and of the diaries, letters and autobiographies left by those who experienced both wars, has become a widespread phenomenon in Europe, Australia and the United States.[21] As James Wallis has demonstrated, this family history, which he terms 'grass roots commemorative practice', is impacting on the wider cultural memory of both wars.[22] Memories circulate and are reproduced and reformed within family and kinship networks, entering onto the public stage when they relate to elements of the wider cultural memory in circulation there. These more public representations of the past, which in the case of the First World War largely group around the tragic figure of the male combatant, as well as the legacy of his experiences for those at home, in turn shape the kinds of stories which survive within families. The ongoing attachment to a particular cultural memory of the war, decried by some as a 'Blackadder myth', stands in opposition to the revisionist histories of the late 1990s and early 2000s.[23] This gap, between some academic histories of the war and family histories, still sometimes perceived as 'misty eyed and syrupy', has perhaps contributed to an unwillingness amongst some in the historical profession to engage with family history as a valid form of historical practice.[24] Nonetheless, family history remains a key way in which people engage both with the past more widely, and in particular with the total wars of the twentieth century as moments in which their family experiences enter onto the public stage. As Wallis argues, family history 'will play a fundamental role in promoting public engagement with the First World War over the course of the centenary'.[25] How, then, is family history gendered?

While men may for many years have been the authors of formal family histories, writing autobiographies and family biographies, more informal family traditions have long been collected and passed on by women.[26] Sometimes these have taken a material form—recipes, photo albums, commonplace books, christening robes—and for others they can be found in the family stories that are passed on between generations. While never solely the possession or duty of women, family traditions and histories have nonetheless often been borne by women: usually the primary carers of children, and thus more likely to spend time in the home and with other family members than men, women have traditionally been the keepers and transmitters of culture. As Kate Hodgkin has shown in respect of early-modern Britain, women were 'bearers of significant traditions, keepers of memory within the family for future as well as past generations'.[27] Given this, why has there been so little attention paid to the ways that women tell stories about the First World War? I would suggest that the gendered nature of the dominant cultural memory of the war, a memory in which men serve and suffer in the trenches of the Western Front, while women either wait, and usually grieve, at home, or nurse the injured men, has meant that less attention has been paid to the ways in which women both respond to the memories of the war that circulate on the public stage, and think about, and transmit, family histories of the war years. In the hierarchy that structures the cultural memory of the war, the male combatant, particularly the combatant in the trenches of the Western Front, is privileged over all other figures.

The figure of the sacrificial combatant has been at the heart of commemoration and memorialisation of the war years since its immediate aftermath. While cultural memory is always contested, slippery and mutable, the presence of the soldier as victim is remarkable for its stability. The cenotaph in London's Whitehall, originally erected as a temporary monument to the Empire's war dead in 1919 proved such a potent symbol of loss and bereavement that Lutyen's permanent replacement was swiftly commissioned. By 1920 the cenotaph, and the body of the Unknown Warrior, interned that year at Westminster Abbey, had come to sit at the heart of British commemorative practice which was itself echoed in similar rituals and memorials around the Empire. Although the importance of this figure faded in the 1940s and 1950s, and was being contested in Britain by the late 1930s, the early 1960s saw its definitive re-emergence.[28] Driven by the confluence of the fiftieth anniversary of the war and by the anti-establishment and anti-war movements of the decade, the 1960s saw the rediscovery of the war poets and the growing visibility of Wilfred Owen as the key figure of the war: a soldier poet who mourned the death of young men in industrial warfare and who was to become a sacrificial figure himself, dying just before the Armistice.[29] It is this cultural memory of the war, with its focus on tragedy, doomed youth, mud, the missing and the trenches that has, despite the best efforts of Michael Gove and revisionist historians, continued to resonate in British culture.[30]

It is against this shifting and multi-faceted cultural memory of the war that the respondents to the MO Project Directive of 2014 were writing. With relatively few representations of the multiple female experiences of war circulating on the public stage, it is perhaps not surprising that many of the older women writing for MO, several of whom had first-hand, lived, experience of 'total' war, often focused on the legacies of the male veteran in both their recounting of family histories and in their sense of the ways that the war should be remembered. The next section examines the extent to which this gendered cultural memory interacted with family history and the practice of writing for MO to shape the ways that women of 'the generation after' wrote about the war in their Directive replies.

Gender, Life Writing and Mass Observation

Dorothy Sheridan, who was for many years the archivist at MO, has described writing for the project as a form of life writing, or a 'collective autobiography' which gives us access to some aspects of everyday life in modern Britain. Sheridan writes that, through people's responses to MO Directives:

> We may come to learn about people's hopes and fears, their individual choices in relation to wider social and political change, their rational and unconscious motives for acting, and above all, the meaning and significance which they give to their lives.[31]

If we understand the practice of writing for MO as a form of life writing, then we need to think about the ways in which it differs from, and has similarities to, other forms of life writing and life telling, such as the oral-history interview, the memoir, the formal autobiography and the online blog. As with these other forms of life writing and life telling, Mass Observers choose to produce a sense of self in a public form; unlike memoirs, autobiographies and online blogs however, they respond to specific questions and agendas set by the Directive authors. Like the oral-history interview, MO volunteers are responding to a set of, usually, open-ended questions; unlike the interviewee, however, they write their responses, and can more easily decide whether or not to respond to a particular Directive or to particular questions. They are thus arguably more likely to successfully achieve and maintain a sense of composure in their writings; to craft answers which can act to validate their sense of self and which support a particular point of view or a life narrative. Difficult questions, or Directives, can simply be ignored, as there is no imperative to answer each one.[32]

There is also an inter-subjective dimension to MO writing. While unlike the subjects of oral-history interviewers, the panellists are not engaged in a personal conversation with an investigator, many convey a sense of the audience they believe they are writing for, and whom they are addressing.[33] For example, a retired clergyman began his response by explaining that he would not 'jot down ten words/phrases that conjure up World War One' (the first exercise the respondents were asked to undertake), because 'it seems rather a pointless exercise, and I hope the person sponsoring this exercise takes that comment to heart.'[34] Mass Observers are also motivated by the sense of taking part in a collective project, in contributing to the enhancement of social knowledge.[35] They often present themselves as critics of wider social beliefs and vested interests, giving voice to views that are less often heard, an alternative to 'an increasingly powerful media and state which are perceived as manipulative and failing to represent public opinion fairly'.[36] This sense of providing a critical voice may have led to the wide-ranging criticism of, and scepticism towards, much of the centennial commemorative practice articulated by many of the respondents.[37] The fact that more women than men write for MO today, and that the current panel is weighted towards older authors may well reflect a sense amongst older women that they and their views and values are largely invisible and often under-valued on the wider stage of public debate and commentary in contemporary Britain.

While the MO panel are not a representative sample of the population, the strength of the material they produce for historians lies in the access that it gives us to the constant processes of subjectivity formation.[38] In common with the other, multiple 'technologies of the self' upon which the modern individual can draw, writing for MO can be understood as one way in which subjectivity is both composed and performed. The process of writing for the project can thus be understood as one way of 'writing the self', and in this production of selfhood, of subjectivity, the authors draw upon public accounts of the past, of events and of identities. In this 'cultural circuit' private and public accounts of the past become intermingled and shape one another: public versions of past events reflect more intimately produced stories which enter public discourse; public versions of events shape the more private renderings of one's own life and opinions. Individuals make use of public stories and cultural memories that help them to produce a composed and coherent sense of self.

In this circuit, some versions of the past, and some subjectivities, become more 'speakable' than others, gaining a greater purchase on the public stage, and thus a greater influence over more private accounts. For example, the currently dominant cultural memory of the First World War makes stories of relatives and ancestors who were harmed or traumatised by the war perhaps more visible than stories of those who had a 'good' war, and who benefitted from the shifts and changes that total war bought in its wake.[39] While many of the respondents, across both gender and generation, stated that they participated in the rituals of Remembrance Sunday, and felt them to be important, many others expressed a sense that not only was the First World War a needless loss of life, but that the centenary commemorations were an attempt to manipulate public opinion, to celebrate, rather than to commemorate, Britain's history as a military nation, and by so doing, to ensure support for current and future conflicts. This belief, often expressed as a hostility to the practices of Remembrance Day, is less often articulated in wider public forums, and the opportunity to write for MO may well have given many of the respondents an occasion on which to 'vent' feelings of frustration, anger and cynicism that are difficult to express elsewhere. One woman in her thirties argued that Remembrance Day was 'too militaristic—it seems to glorify war and the soldiers who died' while a woman in her sixties complained that 'the orthodoxy is to be totally involved in remembering total war.'[40] For contributors such as these, writing for this Directive may have both given them an opportunity to express views often silenced elsewhere, and to produce and perform a sense of themselves as critical and reflective citizens.

Women Writing on War

So how did the women examined in this article, born between the 1920s and the early 1950s, write about the First World War in 2014? To what extent were their personal reflections and family histories reflective of the stories and representations of the First World War that circulate today, or that were circulating in earlier periods of these women's lives? The first, and most striking, aspect of almost all of the writing by these women in response to the Directive is the extent to which they chose to write about the male experience of war, and particularly about the soldier on the Western Front, the figure who lies as the heart of the cultural memory of the war in Britain. Indeed, only one woman put her mother's history, rather than that of a male relative, at the heart of her narrative.[41] The prevalence of the soldier-victim in the writings of respondents whose age meant that they did have memories of the direct impact of the war on their families however, suggests that the cultural power of this figure has acted to shape these memories, or the way they are articulated, perhaps making it more difficult for positive wartime experiences to be expressed. The experiences of these soldiers that the respondents focused on largely sat comfortably within the dominant cultural memory of the Western Front as a place of mud, blood, futility and sacrifice. The first exercise that respondents were asked to complete, and which so angered the man quoted above, was a list of ten words or phrases that they associated with the First World War. The list of words that respondents associated with the war were comparable across genders and ages: a seventy-eight-year-old widow's list of 'bloodied, muddied, battlefields, inhumanity, appalling loss of life, lack of diplomacy, cenotaph, unforgotten, lambs to the slaughter, youth, pals, (and) bereaved' was fairly typical, similar for example to the 'death, blood, mud, futility, young men, uniforms, nurse, bandages, gas, (and) trenches' listed by a fifty-five-year-old housewife and the listing of 'mass slaughter, mud, trenches, horses, the cenotaph, Oh! What a Lovely War, Blackadder Goes Forth, war poets' by a seventy-year-old man.[42] These are strikingly similar to the lists produced annually by students at the University of Brighton at the beginning of an optional course on Europe in the First World War, and by students at the University of Exeter taking a similar course.[43] If we understand these lists as an indicator of the cultural memory of the war that the respondents were operating within, it is perhaps not surprising that the stories that were recounted emphasised soldier-victims, and their ongoing legacy within families.

Stories of death and injury were widespread: a seventy-four-year-old retired librarian recalled that her maternal grandfather had two brothers who were gassed, and that her mother-in-law's twenty-one-year-old brother had been killed, while a sixty-eight-year-old widow described her grandfather dying in 1926 aged just forty-one as a result of gas inhalation.[44] Others wrote of an uncle killed at Passchendale, listed as missing, and a grandmother's long-cherished hope that he might return one day, and of uncles who returned, one 'severely shell shocked, the other so damaged you couldn't touch his skin'.[45] Some responses seem to reflect narratives of the First World War that are currently circulating within cultural memory: one woman, aged eighty-four, recounted a friend's memories of the 1914 Christmas Truce in the trenches of the Western Front, commenting that 'this sorry tale made me realise the futility of war.'[46] Another respondent perhaps drew on the popularity of the Michael Morpugo novel *War Horse,* now both a successful film and theatre production, when relating how her grandfather 'spoke of his pain when most of the farm horses were led away'.[47] The First World War's familial and personally felt legacies of death, injury and loss, while also recounted by several of the male respondents, appear to have given many of these older female respondents a means of articulating a relationship to a conflict largely represented as a male experience.

Despite this focus on the traumatic legacies of the Western Front for their families, several women prefaced their comments about trench warfare with a gendered disclaimer: one respondent began a lengthy and informed reply with the comment: 'I won't be able to remember and place in time the names of various battles, so there's no clue there.' Knowledge of military history, strategy and tactics was largely understood as a male preserve, one woman explaining that 'my husband was always interested in the war and he had lots of books about it' while another remarked that 'my husband is interested in war generally ... he also had a bit of a thing about the Battle of Jutland, and I know that's World War One!'[48] While many of the older women discussed in this article actually had a great deal of knowledge about the war, often being widely read and several having visited the battlefields of the Western Front, none claimed a knowledge of military or political history in their reflections on the war years, instead relying upon their knowledge of the war's multiple familial and personal legacies for an authoritative voice.

This gendered division of knowledge was echoed in many of the male responses. Men listed their non-fiction reading on the First World War and drew on their knowledge of the war to criticise dramatic representations for inaccuracy, one man complaining that:

> All sorts of basic mistakes crop up and on every occasion there is a character who was too young to have joined up without the connivance of a recruiting officer, or a youngster who could not take the strain and was shot at dawn because of it. So very, very predictable.[49]

Younger men sometimes supplemented this with a description of their childhood interest in war games and games of strategy, again using their expertise in what appears to be a gendered activity to articulate their views on the war from a particularly authoritative position, a middle-aged IT consultant explaining that 'the reality was that this was a war fought between empires ... it was based on a paradigm of international relations that became outdated.'[50] Another man, after listing the factual books he had read on the war made a plea for more coverage of 'the economic, logistical, medical or technological aspects' and less on the 'blinkered and sentimentalised view'.[51] In this, the responses echoed those of MO authors in the 1980s and 1990s: when asked to write about the Falklands and Gulf Wars, men were able to draw upon a gendered knowledge and military experience in order to speak with a level of authority that was rarely available to the female respondents, even those with lived experience of warfare.[52] It's striking that in the case of the First World War, which none of the respondents had directly experienced, knowledge of military history, tactics and strategy gave some of the men who replied a sense of expertise and a concurrent belief that their views bore more weight than those without such knowledge. These men were able to convey a sense of composure and authority in their responses that was often absent from the replies of those who drew primarily on family histories and popular culture when framing their thoughts about the First World War.

For several of the respondents the First and Second World Wars were interwoven in their sense of the past, and in their own life histories. While some younger respondents began their replies by expressing their confusion between the First and Second World Wars when there were no living relatives who had experienced either conflict, for others the wars were linked by an emotionally charged sense of their impact and legacies.[53] Empathy for the dead and the bereaved of the First World War was articulated through their own experiences of loss in wartime. Questions about the First World War prompted some respondents to reflect on their memories of bereavement in the Second. One woman, who had served in the Women's Auxiliary Air Force during the Second World War, and who attributed her father's disdain for non-combatants in that conflict to his own wartime experience between 1914–1918, recalled the death of her husband's navigator, and 'the shock of his father's visit many years later, when we discussed this boy's death in the war … and the subsequent death of his mother, who died of a "broken heart"'.[54] The woman, born in 1923, who described her grandfather's sadness when the horses were taken from the farm where he worked during the First World War moved in the same sentence to her own visit to the Second World War Commonwealth War Graves Cemetery at Monte Cassino, where she 'walked around, with tears running down, reading the names and ages of the young men'.[55] While these women clearly separated the history of the two wars, the emotional experience and legacy of conflict, understood as one of grief, loss and bereavement for theirs and their parents' generations, was common to both, and, drawing on their personal and generational experiences, questions about the First World War led to reflections on the losses of the Second.[56]

These responses were shaped by what the historian Joy Damousi, writing about the impact of the First World War in Australia, has termed 'the labour of loss'. This, Damousi argues, is both emotional labour, as the bereaved struggle to overcome the shock of untimely death, but also social and cultural labour, as they are expected to perform roles specific to death in war—that of the proud parents, or the brave widow.[57] The reflections on loss articulated here by several of the women demonstrate both the lasting emotional legacies of wartime death, but also the particular role of women as mourners. A ninety-four-year-old woman remembered the shrine to a dead son a neighbour kept in her house while another said she looked 'in absolute horror at any celebrations as I think of all the millions of young men who were killed'.[58] A seventy-eight-year-old widow described the silence on Remembrance Day as 'overwhelming when you consider the grief of the bereaved', and for a woman in her eighties the grief of the bereaved, read through the traditions of Remembrance Sunday, was never ending, as 'not even time makes the mourning any the less.'[59] A sympathetic discussion of the dead and injured combatants was common to many of the respondents, but older women in particular expressed a compassion for not just the young soldiers, but also for their wives and mothers, producing though their writing a subjectivity that was both empathetic and gendered, shaped by an identification with the perceived emotions of the bereaved women.

Female bereavement, as we have seen, was personified both by mothers who had lost sons, and by women who had lost lovers, fiancés and husbands. The idea of a 'lost generation', expressed so powerfully by Vera Brittain, was a gendered narrative in which men died and women were left behind, unable to find a romantic partner from amongst the denuded male population. Reflections on this loss were common: one woman described how 'I often think of the women who never married … and the men who never returned', another recalled an elderly friend of her childhood who had never married after her fiancé was killed in the war, while another remembered 'having lots of aunties as a child as … there was a shortage of marriageable age men'.[60] The only respondent to put a woman at the heart of her family history of the war wrote her mother's history as a combination of romance, early loss, and feminine strength, endurance and bravery. In this response, the First World War forms a backdrop to a home-front focused account of courtship, work patterns, childbirth and death, as her mother's first husband, weakened by his war injures, died in 1918 from the Spanish Flu, aged just twenty-one.[61] This narrative combines romance with a feminist claim to female independence and power, a perspective that runs through many histories of woman and war, but which is absent from the other responses, perhaps a victim of the soldier-victim motif that has become so dominant.

Many of the responses to the Directive by older women express a sense of the necessity of handing down their knowledge of the war and its impact to the younger members of their family. While this was articulated by one man, who termed himself 'the family historian', many of the older women writers had a less formal sense of themselves as bearers of a family history, but instead often wrote about what they perceived as a gulf of knowledge and interest between themselves and their children or grandchildren.[62] In this they have much in common with the female family historians of seventeenth-century England described by Katharine Hodgkin as 'keepers of family memory, transmitting the past through the present for the use of the future'.[63] Like their forebears, several of the women writing in 2014 expressed a sense that it was their duty to ensure that future generations understood both what the war had meant to their family, but also that they passed on a particular, contemporary cultural memory of the war as a time of tragedy, loss and sacrifice. At times, the articulation and use of this sense of the past was dynamically shaped by the exact circumstances of the present: a sixty-year-old retired teacher, who felt her family were unjustly criticising her for feeling sorry for herself when she had a cold, responded by reminding her children 'of those that died at their age on the battlefields 100 years ago, and how lucky they are not to be enduring it'.[64] Another woman, aged seventy-four, explained exactly why she had started to research the lives of her grandfathers who had served in the war: 'I am now the oldest member of my family and I realise that if I don't learn about the past and disseminate this knowledge, it will have gone forever.'[65] This woman expressed a sense of herself as a bridge between the lived family past and its future, transmitting what had once been lived recollection to future generations as a means of ensuring a (gendered) continuity between the family's past, present and future.

Two separate respondents had visited an exhibition on the First World War at Brighton Museum, which used artefacts and family histories to tell the individual wartime stories of a range of people from the city, intercut with reflections from contemporary observers.[66] The exhibition, which was extremely popular, was notable in part for its expectation of an emotional response from visitors; Pachelbel's Canon in G Minor played quietly throughout the galleries, and placed discreetly next to the book for visitor comments at the gallery's exit was a box of paper tissues. The emphasis of the exhibition was on the individual in wartime, and while a range of different experiences were covered, the expectation amongst both curators and most visitors appears to have been that of an empathetic response to the plight of those who were caught up in the cataclysm of war. This was certainly the response of the two respondents. However, they had been accompanied in one case by grown-up children and in another by grandchildren, and while they had found the exhibition moving, their children and grandchildren had been 'underwhelmed', a response that both women understood as shaped by the impact of new media on their attention spans.[67] A sense of 'bearing witness', albeit to events that they had not personally experienced, was important to both of these respondents, one woman writing 'we have to bear witness to the dreadful things that happened in the past, even if it was a totally different age, and tell our children what happened'.[68] It's notable that the sense of the past these women wanted to pass on was not one that particularly engaged with the macro history of the war, with its geo-politics, its causes or the historiographical debates that have raged around this. Instead, they wanted to pass on a sense of the war that drew on emotional responses for its politics, employing an empathy with both the soldier-victim and his loved ones to ensure future generations understood the full cost of war, and would draw on this to place themselves in opposition to more current and contemporary conflicts. 'Lest we forget', in this context, had quite specific meanings, meanings that may not have been recognised by many of those that the centenary commemorations aim to remember.

Conclusions

The older women whose responses to this Directive on the First World War are discussed here largely produced writing which is clearly recognisable as contemporary, as shaped not only by family histories and by the women's life course, but also by the cultural memory of the First World War that has dominated since the 1960s, a shared sense of the past which has at its heart the figure of the soldier-victim. This figure appeared in the majority of the narratives examined here, either as a relative who failed to return from the war, or who did return but injured and damaged, or as a more abstract figure, one of the numerous military victims of warfare to whom the nation gathers to pay tribute every Remembrance Sunday. Compassion and empathy, both for these men and for the women at home, shaped the writings of these women. While these responses were also expressed by younger women and by men, these other groups also wrote about the war in other ways, perhaps focusing on the military or political history of the war, or using the Directive to reflect on what some saw as a manipulation of the past by the current government, keen to ensure support for contemporary conflicts by a continued reverence for the service and sacrifice of combatants of past wars. Older women, while also sometimes expressing a scepticism about remembrance practices, or alternatively articulating why they saw participation in such practices as important, all wrote sympathetically about the plight of both the soldiers and of those who loved them.

While they do not constitute one generation, being born across a period of almost thirty years, there is a commonality in the responses to the First World War produced by the women considered here that bears investigation. The role of women as mourner, as the chief workers in the 'labour of loss', seems to have permeated the responses of women born in the thirty years or so after the First World War. For those who had adult experience of the Second World War, the emotional impact of the two conflicts appears as a legacy of grief, of a bereavement shared across the years. For almost all the women whose writing is examined here, the memories of returned men, or of mothers and grandmothers who had experienced loss as a result of the war, dominated over other war stories that they could, perhaps, have told. In part this was shaped by the dominant, widely shared, cultural memory of the war, and the representations of the conflict that circulate within popular culture, but it was also a gendered response, driven in large part by the perception of women as mourners and as bearers of the family story. The sacrificial mother and the grieving partner were both culturally important figures in the period between the two world wars, and in wartime since.[69] The figure of the sacrificial mother, giving up her sons to the nation, remains important, a repository of not only national grief but also of national steadfastness and determination.[70] Joined by the figure of the bereaved wife, fiancé or lover, the women bereaved by war were a point of identification and empathy for many of the older women writing for MO.

This empathetic position in relation to the war and its impact can be understood as part of the construction of a gendered selfhood. Feminist theorists have long argued that the process of composing subjectivity is gendered, that the construction of a secure feminine selfhood is complicated and made difficult by femininities' relationship to an apparently more secure masculinity, and by the multiple and contradictory discourses of femininity that circulate.[71] While work on masculinity has demonstrated that masculinities are also unstable, multiple and fractured, the centrality of the soldier-victim to contemporary narratives of the First World War acted to place women in relationship to the combatant male.[72] By positioning themselves as sympathetic to the historic victims of warfare, the women writing here were giving voice to a role that has long been filled by women. This position appeared to give many of the women authors a sense of composure: as a gendered means of writing about war which sat comfortably with both current cultural memory of the conflict and a historically recognised female relationship to war, and as a means of writing about family relationships and histories which may have often been difficult to negotiate, the empathetic voice seen here allowed these women to write in ways that they were comfortable with.[73]

These women's relationships to the generation which had experienced the war, their parents and grandparents, can be understood as a form of 'postmemory', as they inherited memories of the war and its impact which they felt important to pass on to younger generations. The centrality of the soldier-victim to the cultural memory of the war encouraged responses which focused on the experience and legacy of dead, injured and traumatised men for their families. In articulating an empathetic relationship to both these men and to those who loved them, the women produced responses to the Directive that were shaped both by their gender, and by the function of family history as a means of bringing together past, present and future generations. Rather than simply transmitting stories of the past, these Directive responses should be understood as dynamic, shaped as much by the subjectivity of the narrator and their relationship to family and to current cultural memories of the war as by the experiences and legacies being recounted. Age, gender and family position thus interacted in these responses to produce a body of writing which was shaped by a desire to pass on an empathetic understanding of the First World War, and its negative impact for those who lived through it, to future generations.

Notes

1. For details of the work of the five Engagement Centres, see http://www.ahrc.ac.uk/research/fundedthemesandprogrammes/worldwaroneanditslegacy/worldwaroneengagementcentres/
2. Marianne Hirsch (2008) The Generation of Postmemory, *Poetics Today*, 29(1), pp. 103–128, here pp. 106–107.
3. Hirsch, 'Generation of Postmemory', p. 109.
4. Helen McCartney (2014) The First World War Soldier and His Contemporary Image in Britain, *International Affairs*, 90(2), pp. 219–315, here p. 219.
5. Hirsch, 'Generation of Postmemory', p. 116.

6. For examples of some of these see the Heritage Lottery Funded projects that the *Gateways to the First World War AHRC Public Engagement Centre* has worked with. http://www.gatewaysfww.org.uk/projects.

7. See, for example, Penny Summerfield (2013) The Generation of Memory: gender and the popular memory of the Second World War in Britain, in Lucy Noakes & Juliette Pattinson (Eds) *British Cultural Memory and the Second World War* (London: Bloomsbury, 2013); Patrick Hayes & Jim Campbell, *Bloody Sunday: trauma, pain and politics* (London: Pluto Press 2005).

8. Michael Roper (2009) *The Secret Battle: emotional survival in the Great War* (Manchester: Manchester University Press); Growing up in the Aftermath: childhood and family relationships between the wars, *Lecture for the British Psychological Society*, 2014. Available online at: https://www.youtube.com/watch?v=FBHNyNsAuI4&list=PLCkLQOAPOtT28X05RoZ8--31ojkigpkAl.

9. Joel Morley (2013) *An Examination of the Influence of the First World War on Attitudes to Service in the Second World War* (Unpublished PhD, Queen Mary and Westfield, University of London).

10. See, for example, Gail Braybon (2012; first published 1981) *Women Workers in the First World War* (London: Croom Helm); Joanna Bourke (1999) *Dismembering the Male: men's bodies, Britain and the Great War* (London: Reaktion Books); Susan R. Grayzel (1999) *Women's Identities at War: gender, motherhood and politics in Britain and France during the First World War* (Chapel Hill: University of North Carolina Press); Nicoletta Gullace (2002) *The Blood of Our Sons: men, women and the renegotiation of British citizenship during the Great War* (Basingstoke: Palgrave Macmillan); Deborah Thom (2000) *Nice Girls and Rude Girls: women workers in the First World War* (London: I.B. Tauris); Janet K. Watson (2004) *Fighting Different Wars: experience, memory and the First World War in Britain* (Cambridge: Cambridge University Press); Angela Wollacott (1994) *On Her Their Lives Depend: munitions workers in the Great War* (Berkeley: University of California Press)

11. See, for example, Series One of the *The Village* (BBC: 2013), which, while focusing entirely on life in a Peak District village during the war, has at its heart the experience of a young soldier who suffers from shell shock and is shot for desertion. In early June 2016 the forty-nine television and radio programmes listed by the BBC on its *World War One* page included five that focused on the home front and twelve that focused on the battlefront. The remainder examined the political and cultural causes and legacies of the war. http://www.bbc.co.uk/programmes/p01nb93y/members.

12. Bart Ziino (2015) Introduction: remembering the First World War today, in Bart Ziino (Ed.) *Remembering the First World War* (Abingdon: Routledge), pp. 1–18, here p. 7.

13. Vera Brittan (1933) *Testament of Youth* (London: Victor Gollancz); Alan Bishop (Ed.) (1981) *Chronicle of Youth: Great War diary 1913–17* (London: Victor Gollancz); BBC Television *Testament of Youth* (1979); Dir. James Kent (2014) *Testament of Youth*.

14. Penny Summerfield (1998) *Reconstructing Women's Wartime Lives: discourse and subjectivity in oral histories of the Second World War* (Manchester: Manchester University Press); The Generation of Memory, *British Cultural Memory and the Second World War*

15. See Daniel Woolf (1997) A Feminine Past? Gender, Genre and Historical Knowledge in England 1500–1800, *American Historical Review*, 102(3), pp. 645–679; Anne Blue Wills (2010) Mourning Becomes Her: women, tradition and memory albums, *Religion and American Culture: A Journal of Interpretation*, 203, pp. 93–121.

16. Pierre Nora (1989) Between Memory and History: les lieux de mémoire, *Representations*, pp. 7–25.

17. Paul Basu (2005) MacPherson Country: genealogical identities, spatial histories and the Scottish diasporic landscape, *Cultural Geographies*, 12(2), pp. 123–150; Anne-Marie Kramer (2011) Mediatizing Memory: history, affect and identity in *Who Do You Think You Are?*, *European Journal of Cultural Studies*, 14(4), pp. 428–445; Ronald Lambert (1996) The Family Historian and Temporal Orientations Towards the Ancestral Past, *Time and*

Society, 5(2), pp. 115–143; Carol Smart (2007) *Personal Life: new directions in sociological thinking* (Cambridge: Polity Press).

18. Anne-Marie Kramer (2011) Kinship, Affinity and Connectedness: exploring the role of genealogy in personal lives, *Sociology* 45(3), pp. 379–395, here p. 380.

19. On this see Anne-Marie Kramer (2011) Mediatizing Memory, *European Journal of Cultural Studies*, 14(4), pp. 428–445. For a recent example of academic history which explicitly engages with family-history research and related methodological issues, see Alison Light (2015) *Common People: the history of an English family* (London: Penguin).

20. https://livesofthefirstworldwar.org/; http://www.bbc.co.uk/history/ww2peopleswar/

21. See Ziino's insightful analysis of this phenomenon. Bart Ziino (2010) 'A Lasting Gift to His Descendants': family memory and the Great War in Australia, *History and Memory*, 22(2), pp. 125–146.

22. James Wallis (2015) Great-Grandfather, What Did *You* Do in the Great War? The Phenomenon of Conducting First World War Family History Research, in Ziino (Ed.), *Remembering the First World War*, pp. 21–38, here p. 21.

23. See Michael Gove, 'Why Does the Left Insist on Belittling True British Heroes?', *Daily Mail*, 2 January 2014. On recent histories of the war, including revisionist histories of both battle front and home front, see Heather Jones (2013) As the Centenary Approaches: the regeneration of First World War historiography, *The Historical Journal*, 56(3), pp. 857–878.

24. Tanya Evans (2011) Secrets and Lies: the radical potential of family history, *History Workshop Journal* 71(1), pp. 49–73 here p. 29.

25. Wallis, 'Great-Grandfather, What Did *You* Do in the Great War?', p. 24.

26. For studies that discuss and utilise male autobiography see, for example, Patrick Joyce (1994) *Democratic Subjects: the self and the social in nineteenth-century England* (Cambridge: Cambridge University Press); David Vincent (1981) *Bread, Knowledge and Freedom: a study of nineteenth-century working class autobiography* (London: Methuen); Julie-Marie Strange (2015) *Fatherhood and the British Working Class, 1865–1914* (Cambridge: Cambridge University Press).

27. Katharine Hodgkin (2013) Women, Memory and Family History in Seventeenth Century England, in Erika Kuijpers, Judith Pollmann, Johannes Muller & Jasper Van Der Stehen (Eds) *Memory Before Modernity: practices of memory in early modern Europe* (Leiden: Brill), pp. 297–313, here p. 312.

28. On Armistice Day between 1919 and 1945 see Adrian Gregory, *The Silence of Memory*; on Mass Observation and Armistice Day between 1937 and 1941 see Lucy Noakes (2015) A Broken Silence? Mass Observation, Armistice Day and Everyday Life in Britain, 1937–1941, *Journal of European Studies*, 45(4), pp. 331–346.

29. For a tracing of the cultural memory of the First World War between the war itself and the early twenty-first century, see Todman, *The Great War* (2005).

30. Michael Gove, *Daily Telegraph*, 3 January 2014.

31. Dorothy Sheridan (1993) Writing to the Archive. Mass-Observation as Autobiography, *Sociology*, 27(1), pp. 21–40, here p. 28.

32. On the issue of composure in oral-history interviews, see Penny Summerfield (2004) Culture and Composure: creating narratives of the gendered self in oral-history interviews, *Cultural and Social History*, 1(1), pp. 65–93.

33. On the ways that respondents write 'to' the archivists, see Sheridan (1993) 'Writing to the Archive'.

34. Mass-Observation Project Directive (henceforth MO), Autumn 2014, Respondent no. B2710.

35. Summerfield, 'The Generation of Memory'.

36. Tony Kushner (2004) *We Europeans? Mass-Observation, 'Race' and British Identity in the Twentieth Century* (Aldershot: Ashgate), p. 256.

37. See, for example, MO, Autumn 2014, Respondent no's A1706, A4127, B42, B1180 and B3227.

38. Of the 198 who responded to this Directive, 199 were women, and 162 lived in England. There are no figures for social class or ethnicity, but of the 162 respondents from England, 143 lived in areas designated as areas with low levels of deprivation (see English

Indices of Deprivation, 2010. https://www.gov.uk/government/statistics/english-indices-of-deprivation-2010). Seventy-nine of the respondents to this Directive, both male and female, were born before 1951.

39. Dan Todman (2008) 'The Ninetieth Anniversary of the Battle of the Somme', in Michael Keren & Holder Herwig (Eds) *War Memory and Popular Culture: essays on modes of remembrance and commemoration* (North Carolina: McFarland).
40. MO, Autumn 2014, Respondent no C3210.
41. MO, Autumn 2014, Respondent no F1373.
42. MO, Autumn 2014, Respondent no's B1771, C3315.
43. Catriona Pennell (2012) Popular History and Myth-Making: the role and responsibility of First World War historians in the centenary commemorations, 2014–18, *Historically Speaking*, 13(5), pp. 11–14, here p. 11.
44. MO, Autumn 2014, Respondent no's H2639, L002
45. MO, Autumn 2014, Respondent no's H2637, B1180.
46. MO, Autumn 2014, Respondent no H260.
47. Michael Morpurgo (1982) *War Horse* (London: Kaye and Ward Ltd); MO, Autumn 2014, Respondent no H266.
48. MO, Autumn 2014, Respondent no's A1706, J1890.
49. MO, Autumn 2014, Respondent no's B2710, B4318.
50. MO, Autumn 2014, Respondent F4873, G1846.
51. MO, Autumn 2014, Respondent G4374.
52. Lucy Noakes (1998) *War and the British: gender, memory and national identity 1939–1991* (London: I.B. Tauris).
53. MO, Autumn 2014, Respondent no B4458.
54. MO, Autumn Directive, Respondent no F1560.
55. MO, Autumn Directive, Respondent no H266.
56. On death, loss and grief in Second World War Britain, see the special edition of *Journal of War and Culture Studies* 'Silenced Mourning' 8(1); Pat Jalland (2012) *Death in War and Peace: a history of loss and grief in England, 1914–1970* (Oxford: Oxford University Press).
57. Joy Damousi (1999) *The Labour of Loss: mourning, memory and wartime bereavement in Australia* (Cambridge: Cambridge University Press).
58. MO, Autumn Directive, Respondent no's E174, F1560.
59. MO, Autumn Directive, Respondent no's B1771, F 310.
60. MO, Autumn 2014 Directive, Respondent no's B1771, H1705, L1991.
61. MO, Autumn 2014 Directive, Respondent no F1373.
62. MO Autumn 2014, Respondent no A4127.
63. Hodgkin, 'Women, Memory and Family History', p. 302.
64. MO, Autumn 2014, Respondent no G1846.
65. MO, Autumn 2014, Respondent no F3641.
66. 'War Stories: voices from the First World War', *Brighton Museum and Art Gallery*, 12 July 2014–1 March 2015. See http://brightonmuseums.org.uk/brighton/about/brighton-museum-past-exhibitions/past-exhibitions-2014/war-stories/
67. MO, Autumn 2014, Respondent no's L1991, L4071.
68. MO, Autumn 2014, Respondent no L4071.
69. For a recent and highly pertinent example of this, see the Armed Forces Memorial at the National Memorial Arboretum, Staffordshire. Dedicated in 2007 and designed to commemorate British Service personnel killed on active service since 1945 it contains a bronze sculpture of a dead soldier, carried on a bier by his comrades and watched by a grieving woman and distraught child.
70. Susan R. Grayzel (1999) *Women's Identities at War: gender, motherhood, and politics in Britain and France during the First World War* (Chapel Hill, N.C.: Chapel Hill Press)
71. See, for example, Bronwyn Davies (1992) 'Women's Subjectivity and Feminist Stories', in Carolyn Ellis & Michael Flaherty (Eds) *Investigating Subjectivity: research on lived experience* (London: Sage).

72. Raewyn Connell (1995) *Masculinities* (Berkeley and Los Angeles: University of California Press).

73. On composure as a concept, see Graham Dawson (1994) *Soldier Heroes: British adventure, empire and the imagining of masculinities* (London: Routledge).

Acknowledgement

Thanks also to Jessica Scantlebury for the figures cited in note 58 and to Penny Summerfield, Michael Roper and the anonymous readers of this article for their helpful and constructive comments on this research.

Disclosure statement

No potential conflict of interest was reported by the author.

Funding

The author wishes to thank the Trustees of the Mass Observation Archive (University of Sussex) for permission to quote from the Archive, and the Arts and Humanities Research Council First World War Engagement Centres for funding the Directive.

9   *What the Women Did*
Remembering or reducing women of the First World War on the contemporary British stage

Amanda Phipps

ABSTRACT
This article examines the role of women in theatre productions performed at the beginning of the centenary. The numerous plays produced in response to the start of the centenary often focused on a dominant narrative of the First World War in which soldiers at the Western Front gained the lion's share of attention. It is against this theatrical backdrop that a study takes place of *What the Women Did*, a trio of wartime plays revived by Two's Company at the Southwark Playhouse in 2014. This fringe theatre brought women's stories to life by revealing their failings, suffering and ambivalence towards men. *What the Women Did* provides a fruitful case study to explore why complex female experiences during the war struggled to reach modern audiences. This article will ultimately demonstrate the competitive and commoditised nature of remembrance that dictates which stories are kept alive in the twenty-first century.

Contemporary collective memory of the First World War is based around an image of trenches filled with blood, mud, rats and, most importantly, men.[1] This impression depicts the key theme of tragedy which has come to be heavily associated with the conflict, and specifically the trenches.[2] As Janet Watson notes, the focus on 'gruesome bloodshed' in the trenches has meant 'valid voices' about the war 'could only belong to those men who had shared this "experience"'.[3] The dominance of trench warfare has meant many other experiences, stories and opinions have not received equal public attention. In particular women have suffered from the dominating presence of soldiers in the trenches. The following discussion will examine the position of women in performances of the conflict at the beginning of the centenary. Such theatrical representations provide a method of documenting women's positions in contemporary collective memory, because as Susan Bennett states 'theatre-going can be a significant measure of what culture affords to its participants and what theatre itself contributes to cultural experience and expression'.[4] Consequently theatrical productions during 2014 and 2015 will be used as a means of charting the stories of men and women viewed as important to re-live and recreate for audiences one hundred years after the conflict began. In particular a production at the Southwark Playhouse entitled *What the Women Did* will be explored for its alternative approach

to women during the war. It will be argued that whilst there was an overwhelming repetition of the soldier's experience on British stages, there were some performances
which showed the multiple roles and positions women found themselves in during the
First World War.

There are a number of reasons as to why a dominant narrative about the war has
formed around tragedy and the trenches. Brian Bond believes that in the 1960s there
was a fundamental shift in perceptions of the war to a 'pointless waste of young lives'
due to events and concerns in that 'turbulent decade'.[5] In the second half of the twentieth
century British society was living through the Cold War with its threat of nuclear annihilation and was also witnessing America's conduct in the Vietnam War. The result was mass
outrage in Britain with 25,000 anti-war protestors gathering in Grosvenor Square on just
one occasion in 1968.[6] Tony Howard and John Stokes claim 'Vietnam transformed' how
many British people 'regarded wars past and present'.[7] For example, reappraisal of class
discrimination and individuals' rights during the 1960s made class-based ranking of soldiers during the First World War appear retrospectively unjust.[8] Dan Todman also notes
that the passing away of veterans and survivors in the 1960s and 1970s meant a 'powerful
limiting factor' to a 'violently critical assessment' of the conflict had been removed as it
would not be personally offensive to survivors.[9] Consequently many scholarly and
popular works took an ambivalent attitude to the conflict. Popular history books on the
First World War were published such as Alan Clark's *The Donkeys* in 1961 and A. J. P.
Taylor's *The First World War: an illustrated history* in 1963. These books heavily criticised
upper-class generals for avoiding the trenches and blamed their incompetence for the
heavy number of causalities.[10] Such stereotypes were reinforced by popular representations like the 1963 play *Oh What a Lovely War* which achieved significant recognition
for its scathing depiction of the war as pointlessly begun and disastrously led.[11] From this
perspective current events restricted alternative approaches to remembering the war,
changing the lens through which the past could be perceived.

In this dominant narrative of the war, women remained secondary to the main protagonist of the soldier. Christa Hämmerle et al. explain that 'the total war of 1914–18 led to
extensive support by women not only at the so-called "home front" —which was mainly
conceived as a woman's sphere—but also in the battle zones'. Yet, despite growing scholarly investigation of female roles in the conflict by gender historians, 'mainstream history
of the First World all too often still ignores a gender perspective', because 'the study of war
easily excludes women since any participation by them is "insignificant"' in comparison to
fighting men.[12] This is demonstrated by a case study conducted by the author at a school
in the London Borough of Southwark from 2014 to 2015. Here Year 9 pupils were learning
about the First World War as part of their history education.[13] In one of the last lessons of
the module when the class was making posters summarising what they had learnt about
the conflict, a pupil turned to his teacher and asked 'what were women doing during the
war?' It was then that the rather flustered teacher realised she had managed to go through
several lessons on the conflict describing the reasons for the outbreak of war, conditions of
the trenches and popular representations such as Wilfred Owen's poetry, without men-
tioning a single woman.[14] This anecdote is not shared to criticise the teacher, but
instead to highlight how a dominant narrative of the war has become engrained with
key moments, themes and attitudes needing to be covered. In this narrative it appears

that women can sometimes be diminished or become side-characters because of the need to communicate the horror of the soldier's trench experience.

Arguably, the centenary offered a unique period of time to broaden collective memory on the conflict. As Catriona Pennell notes the centenary offered an 'once-in-a-lifetime opportunity' to take advantage of rejuvenated interest in the First World War, 'act[ing] as a canvas to explore fictional/semi-fictional stories for entertainment and educational purposes'.[15] Indeed, the beginning of the centenary saw a burst of activity on the conflict and in particular a number of cultural outputs being utilised to commemorate the war.[16] Then Prime Minister David Cameron claimed the government 'stand ready to incorporate more ideas' and through the Heritage Lottery Fund and arts programme 14–18 NOW promoted commemorative activities and representations that were 'opening up new perspectives on the present as well as the past'.[17] Several cultural outputs did incorporate the role of women. The TV production *The Crimson Field* aired in 2014 and portrayed the lives of nurses stationed in France.[18] The Imperial War Museum incorporated women into their First World War exhibition through Home Front displays.[19] The Heritage Lottery Fund also provided financial support to local and community projects such as the Florence Nightingale Museum's display of *Hospital under Canvas* paintings and *Gas Girls*, a series of cultural outputs on Bristol's mustard gas factory workers.[20] Nevertheless, as Ana Carden-Coyne bemoaned, the majority of cultural outputs still suggested that the conflict was 'very much a white man's war'.[21] Consequently, it is questionable if the cultural outputs which did focus on women filtered through or chipped away at the dominance of the soldier's experience. For example, in ten schools observed during 2014 and 2015 only one added in the female experience through commemorative centenary events.[22] Whilst this is clearly not representative of all remembrance and teaching across Britain, it gives an indication of how much people were being engaged about the roles of women at the beginning of the centenary.

One genre of cultural outputs which deserves exploration due to its response to the beginning of the centenary is the world of theatre in which productions on the conflict were revived and created to meet popular demand. It is therefore interesting to explore whether in this theatrical realm of representation the pupil's desire for more information about women's experiences would have been met. The answer is not particularly positive. At the beginning of the centenary popular plays trying to attract schools such as *War Horse* and *Regeneration* had a male-centric cast whose stories revolved around soldiers' experiences at the Western Front.[23] There were also revivals of plays such as *Journey's End*, which famously includes no female characters, and *Oh What a Lovely War* which heavily focuses on the plight of the working-class private.[24] Plays made specifically for school audiences continued this trend, for instance *The Muddy Choir* was also a trench-specific all-male cast which was fully booked for its schools' tour.[25] Thus, the hive of representations which sprung up around the centenary should not be seen as creating a swarm of diverse productions around the First World War because the image of the soldier in France continued to loom large.

Focus on the soldier figure in such theatrical works also reduced the array of male experiences from the First World War which were being represented. Soldiers on the Western Front gained the lion's share of attention through representations of the horrific conditions and events of this war zone. Plays such as *Journey's End* and *War Horse* remain within the recognisable narrative of male suffering and heroism in the trenches.

Characters in these plays seem to represent the 'everyman' of the soldier fighting during the conflict, the repetition of events, soldier's experiences and tragedy creates an all-consuming picture of what it must have been like to serve. Even some public commentators were against such a dominant narrative. Columnist Simon Jenkins claimed in the *Guardian* that the centenary had led to a 'media theme park' of 'Great War plays' which presented 'The repetition of virtually identical "stories from the trenches" becom[ing] banal, a nightly pornography of violence'.[26] Thus whilst women may have been sidelined, the male-dominated stage did not necessarily result in greater understanding of experiences during the conflict for all men. For example, there was only a smattering of productions on the global aspects of the conflict or the role of Indian and African soldiers in the British Empire.[27] Instead the focus on Western Front soldiers in these plays meant men could often lose their sense of individual identity as they merged into one overall image of the pitiful soldier.

The lack of diversity in First World War plays during the beginning of the centenary is even more pronounced when it comes to examining the representation of women. Women did have the opportunity to walk the boards during some First World War productions. There were plays such as the Royal Shakespeare Company's *The Christmas Truce* and *Doctor Scroggy's War* at Shakespeare's Globe which included female counterparts.[28] Women made it onto the stage as nurses in both these productions, their stories running parallel to the (still dominant) narrative of men at the Western Front. Indeed, *The Christmas Truce* received mixed feedback with reviewers picking out this weakness. The *Guardian*'s reviewer Michael Billington saw aspects of the nurses' story as having 'an air of padding' and Stephen Collins from British Theatre scathingly claimed the women's 'scenes were quite dreadfully written, melodramatic and unbelievable' with the production presenting 'a facile, shabby conglomeration of stock situations and characters'.[29] It seems that for Billington and Collins the narrative of the nurses fell back on female stereotypes and presented women in the narrow light of overly-emotional supporters of the fighting men. As historian Marc Calvini-Lefebvre has noted, this situation is worrying because 'the marginal position of women's history' appears 'a reflection of women's marginal position in the societies of the past'.[30] Thus, even when women were incorporated into big-budget productions the results were not always deemed positive or enlightening. It is needless to say that audience members who viewed these productions would not have necessarily gained new insight into the multiple and essential roles of women during the conflict.

It is quite possible at this point to give credence to former Education Secretary and MP Michael Gove's statement that there was a 'fictional prism' surrounding the war which limited pupils' knowledge.[31] Arguably the image of the male soldier, limited in itself, was at the forefront of portrayals of the First World War meaning that women often failed to receive thorough and varied attention. If the pupil from Southwark was to have attended any of the above popular theatrical representations it is unlikely that their interest would have been satisfied. However, whilst big-budget productions often failed to stray from the dominant narrative, alternative stories were available at the beginning of the centenary for those who were willing and able to look beyond mainstream theatre. In smaller establishments and amateur theatres women seemed to fare much better. There are examples such as *Out of the Cage* at Park Theatre and *Flowers of the Forest* at Jermyn Street Theatre which provided gritty portrayals of the female sex. *Out of the Cage* explored the attempts of a group of munition workers to rebel against their treatment and pay, showing the impact such work had on their health and home lives.[32] *Flowers of the Forest* charted the impact that the war continued to have on a woman's life long after the fighting ceased, demonstrating the long-term mental damage that could be done to those 'left behind'.[33] These relatively small theatres offered audiences an alternative to the trench narrative, showing the suffering that took place on the Home Front on a case by case basis.

The remainder of this article will look at one fringe theatre and a performance company which felt the female experience warranted a production of three short plays. The South-wark Playhouse was founded in 1993 in a disused workshop in a relatively 'neglected' part of the Borough and has served the local community ever since as a studio theatre for 'high quality work by new and emerging theatre practitioners'.[34] Fitting with the almost una-voidable trend in 2014 of presenting some form of response to the centenary, Southwark Playhouse billed two productions, an adaptation of the anti-war novel *Johnny Got His Gun*, which looked at the psychological impact on a severally wounded soldier, and *What the Women Did*.[35] The latter was a trio of plays written and performed during and shortly after the war and revived by Two's Company between 22 January and 15 February 2014. The opening piece was Gwen John's *Luck of War*, a play about a woman who had been informed that her husband was missing presumed dead in battle and is on the cusp of starting a new life with another man. It is at this moment that her husband unex-pectedly returns from being hospitalised and she must cope with the domestic fallout. Second was *Handmaidens of Death* scripted by Herbert Tremaine (the pseudonym of the female writer Maude Deuchar) which threw light on a group of munition workers from different social spheres who all long for male company and struggle to see that their concerns and desires are the same although their social backgrounds are different. Finally J. M. Barrie's *The Old Lady Shows Her Medals* looks at a charlady's desire to have a son in the war to be proud of and the need to have a relative fighting to be able to socially comment on the conflict. When she fabricates the existence of a son, a Scotsman by the very same name enters her life and they decide to continue the illusion of mother and son until his death at the Front. Whilst *Johnny Got His Gun* adhered to the soldier-centric focus of much theatre (although admittedly offering a unique angle on mental suf-fering), it is *What the Women Did* which offers a departure from the dominant narrative and therefore deserves particular attention.

In many ways the triple bill and Two's Company's intention in mounting the pro-duction follows themes in contemporary collective memory of the First World War and recent plays on the topic. For example, the theatre company began specialising in reviving First World War plays in response to the U.S. and U.K.'s invasion of Iraq in 2003. The Company explained that in First World War plays 'We felt that this cry of pain and rage … expressed better than anything the folly of starting another war'.[36] It was therefore a desire to focus on the futility of war which led the company to begin running seasons of First World War plays as part of a 'Forgotten Voices' series. In this way a triple bill of plays about women suffering during the war still fitted neatly into their overall agenda and maintained the bleak perspective associated with past and present conflicts. These plays were picked for their examination of how the war had damaged lives, especially as there were an abundance of plays written during the period that would have offered a far more patriotic view.[37] Here past plays were chosen to serve modern purposes and fit within modern understandings of warfare. Whilst the scripts may have departed from the trenches, they cannot be seen as completely diverting from collective memory of the conflict in the twenty-first century. Tragedy was still present in the production, it was the choice of cast that offered a new intrigue for the audience.

Complex female protagonists did allow *What the Women Did* to explore the war's bleakness in a different and nuanced fashion. Karen Hunt has highlighted that 'when we visualise women on the First World War Home Front we tend to think of women munition workers'. This suggests that representing munition workers is still a selective and familiar trope of collective memory. However, Hunt believes they are popularly 'remembered as young, energetic and patriotically "doing their bit"'.[38] In *Handmaidens of Death* it is the complex moral position of the munition workers which stands out. In this play the women decide to include love messages for 'Fritz' in the shells they are making at the munition factory. Then one night when the women stand talking, laughing and arguing in the street they are propositioned by ghostly German soldiers. These ghostly figures have come to answer the love letters they received when being torn apart by shells that the women had made. In this case women, who bemoaned the lack of men available to date, are confronted with men, desiring them, but also destroyed by them. Here, the audience of the Southwark Playhouse could have felt torn between sympathy for these German soldiers and fear for the women being advanced upon by deathly figures on a darkened and smoke-filled stage. These women were not being represented as two-dimensional angels in uniforms or dutiful women at home. They were made real by their failings, by their cruelness to men who were dying gruesome deaths and being shocked by the repercussions of their actions. Women were not simply seen as staying behind at the Home Front, but were held responsible for their share in the bloodshed. The juxtaposition of shell creator and shell receiver traced a line which showed the responsibility of munition workers in the national machine of death. Yet, the natural reaction was to also fear for these women's safety in such a frightening confrontation. This moral conundrum asked spectators to see the war as utterly tragic, but to also take a more nuanced approach to issues of responsibility and morality. There was no clear divide between characters who were right, moral and likable and those who were the enemies of the piece. Instead in *Handmaidens of Death* the ghostly vision brought a sobering reality to the part everyone played in the conflict.

The realness associated with the characters and an avoidance of resorting to stock figures allowed *What the Women Did* to break free from stereotypes and create realistic female characters. They had faults, moral dilemmas, fears and concerns which were annoying and unglamorous. For example, *Luck of War*, the first of the three plays, showed Ann starting a new life with a slightly boring man who nevertheless could provide for her children. It is at this moment her husband, who up until then had been 'missing in action presumed dead' for some time, returns from the Western Front. He is uncouth and demanding, and he has an injury which suggests that Ann will have to take significant care of him. In *Luck of War* it is men who are assessed for what they can offer to a woman's life and the supporting role that Ann requires. Her new partner would be a much more desirable husband for producing a calm family environment. Yet, eventually social pressure, her children's reputation and the unwillingness of her new partner to come between a legal marriage means Ann accepts that her old life must resume. The realism of the character means she does not do so as a doting wife.

She visibly shows her dismay at this change in affairs as she continuously argues with her husband. It is the pragmatic nature of Ann which is striking; this is not about love as it is in *Doctor Scroggy's War* or *The Christmas Truce* where nurse and soldier are neatly partnered up for romance. It is about the reality of how to keep her house functioning. It is logic and money and the law, but she is not going to pretend to be happy about it. This allows true empathy to be created for Ann, as the complexity of the situation she finds herself in seems painfully unfair. It is not difficult to imagine that one's own reaction would be the bitterness Ann displays at having both her old and new life destroyed by the war and dictated by men.

Perhaps more so than the two other pieces, *The Old Lady Shows Her Medals* engages with the choke-hold that the soldier and the trenches have on the First World War from a female perspective. This play examines the inability of an older lady to have a voice in society without showing she has contributed to the war in the manner women were expected to which was by providing men to fight.[39] Consequently, in order to have any 'right' to discuss the war that is waging in her country she invents a son who is away fighting. Unbeknownst to her a man exists with exactly the name she has invented in the regiment she claimed he belonged to. After the soldier seeks the charlady out to confront her about lying, both decide to accept the fictionalised relationship in order to create the sense of family they are missing. The charlady can now show off her 'son' to other mothers and they keep each other company through letters until she receives news of his death. Humour punctuates the play throughout and makes the sadness of the soldier's passing all the more poignant. Yet the audience simultaneously feels the loss of the soldier and also the loss of a companion for the woman. The death is not represented on stage, only the impact on the charlady is in plain view for the audience. He had given validity to her voice during a war that threatened to exclude her and had given her company when it had been scarce. In showing this loneliness the play emphasised how dependent women were on their male counterparts, not just for income and love, but for any social authority in the war. Again past and present seemed to collapse, the silencing of the old lady during the war having uncomfortable echoes of how such stories have been silenced by the passing of time and the continued dominance of the soldier.

It is clear therefore that these plays discuss aspects of wartime life that go beyond the stereotypical images of nurse, doting wife or munition worker. The cutting edge nature of the plays' representations meant that they were controversial even when they were written. Sos Eltis has noted that it is 'unsurprising' that *Handmaidens of Death* was never actually performed until 2012 'given that Deuchar's drama of sexually frustrated and resentful munition workers centres on all the problems which others sought to erase' during the war.[40] Similarly, *Luck of War* was only performed by the Pioneer Players in 1917, a small theatre group that specialised in 'controversial wartime plays' and 'provided a link between the theatre of women's suffrage and the theatres of the Left'.[41] Indeed, it was due to the fact that the Pioneer Players were a subscription drama society that they avoided the Lord Chamberlain's licencing regulations which would have likely prevented performances of *Luck of War*. Andrew Maunder notes that as it was critics complained in 1917 of the play presenting a 'sexually immoral' character in Ann.[42] When *The Old Lady Shows Her Medals* was revived in November 1917 (seven months after its first airing) the script was changed so that the soldier did not die. This was 'applauded' by critics at the time, because as Eltis notes it removed 'any uncomfortable association between men's sacrifice and women's enhanced status and pleasurable pride'.[43] Thus the Southwark Play-house in *What the Women Did* combined three plays that had been deemed controversial and unique when they were first written.

Arguably, these nuanced and complex depictions of women in war have not become mainstream even in the twenty-first century. In 2014 the plays' unusual perspectives were regularly commented on in reviews of *What the Women Did*. For example the *Guardian* reviewer Michael Billington stated that the problem of women wishing to re-marry when their husbands had only been declared 'missing' at the Front was an aspect of the war which 'must have occurred more frequently', yet it is rarely mentioned in remembrance. Billington also noted that 'what came across most strongly' in *Handmaidens of Death* 'is something rarely touched on: the sexual ache of the wartime young.'[44] Billington adopts a much more sympathetic approach to women's concerns then critics did in 1917. It seems the focus on the practical repercussions and emotional fallout for those back home gained the reviewer's attention. *The Telegraph*'s reviewer Jane Shilling also praised the plays for 'the willingness of these dramas to explore the hidden stories of wartime'.[45] This could suggest that audiences, at least those regularly exposed to theatre on the First World War, were looking for diversity. Calling the plays 'hidden stories' is interesting considering they are revivals which were controversial when first performed. It suggests in this instance that, rather than Bond's and Todman's ideas about the honing and restricting of remembrance throughout the twentieth and twenty-first centuries, women have remained consistently on the fringe of representations of the war. Initially they were deemed controversial and unpatriotic, whilst more recently such portrayals failed to fit within the dominant narrative of the trenches meaning they have remained relatively 'hidden'. The dominant narrative of the war has become so engrained, that an examination of moral and psychological complexities in women and the diverse experiences they had during the conflict took these contemporary reviewers by surprise.

However, there are examples in other reviews of *What the Women Did* which suggest that stereotypical portrayals of the First World War onstage had become so encompassing that critics struggled to engage with plays that avoided this type of representation. For example, the *Express* began its review by outlining to readers that the war and 'its unspeakable horrors left no family untouched as it rampaged across Europe sucking a generation of young men down into its stinking trenches'.[46] Although there is not a trench in sight in *What the Women Did* it seems that reviewer Caroline Jowett struggled to discuss the conflict outside of this imagery. For the *Express* it seems that *What the Women Did* needed to be seen through the lens of mud, blood and horror in order for a discussion of the women at the Home Front to take place. Similarly Daisy Bowie-Sell, the reviewer for *Time Out*, states that 'Bombs, guns and trenches are all very well, but what about the perils of tea, cake and gossip?'[47] Whilst the review goes on to discuss the performance of the plays seriously, from the outset this comparison suggests that domestic concerns and the role of women are humorously insignificant in comparison to what readers would commonly associate with the conflict. These reviews perhaps demonstrate why theatre companies often stuck to the tried and tested subject of the Western Front in their productions. The soldier and the trench were expected, and if not present they were often interjected into a discussion of the First World War.

This can create a rather bleak image in which plays such as *What the Women Did* are seen as fighting against an overwhelming force which positions the trench narrative above all others. In addition, the play's position in a fringe theatre meant it would never have reached the audience numbers of plays such as *War Horse* and *Journey's End*. And what about the pupil who asked 'what were the women doing during the war?' Despite his school being located within the same Borough as the Southwark Playhouse, he did not have the opportunity to undertake a field trip that so fittingly addressed his curiosity. In 2014 theatre trips had a fragile standing in many secondary schools and correspondence with numerous schools suggested that mainstream theatre productions were predominantly used as their large scale publicity meant busy teachers were more aware of these performances.[48] One teacher noted that 'I would love to take our students to see a play, but unfortunately we only know about *War Horse* and found it impossible to get tickets'.[49] Considering the pressure that schools are under this situation is understandable, especially as the popularity of shows offered a level of quality control, ensuring the school's money was being well spent. In light of the competition theatre productions on the First World War had at the beginning of the centenary, it is difficult not to view *What the Women Did* as a rather little splash in a very big ocean.

Nevertheless, this problem may also be one of the main reasons that the Southwark Playhouse felt able to stray further from the dominant narrative adhered to by the majority of mainstream theatre. Smaller institutions like the Park Theatre and Jermyn Street Theatre were better able to take this step away from popular portrayals of the war because of their size and mandate. After all it is likely that these 'neighbourhood theatre[s]' which focus on 'emerging talent' have audiences with very different expectations to that of the National Theatre or the Royal Shakespeare Company.[50] The more mainstream audience of larger productions create a supply and demand cycle which dictates the plots that can be covered. Different expectations of theatrical establishments allow for different stories to be told. The dominance of trench warfare in collective memory means it was likely that audiences would expect such a focus when visiting the theatre for a night of First World War commemoration. Unless attending the theatre for an 'alternative' or 'off West-End' style of production, why would an audience member expect an alternative approach to the First World War? Thus, by being a fringe theatre, places such as the Southwark Playhouse fulfilled their purpose by looking at stories on the fringe of popular knowledge and understanding. This alone ensured that the 'hidden stories' did not completely disappear from collective memory.

Arguably, the beginning of the centenary created greater opportunities to discuss the war and this in itself should be viewed positively. Several historians criticised cultural responses to the centenary as 'perilously anachronistic', 'swamped by a tsunami of clichés' and 'a betrayal of the memory of the men and women of 1914–18'.[51] Whilst examples can easily be found to support each one of these statements, the beginning of the centenary should not be completely seen as an 'opportunity [that] has been missed'.[52] Without this national momentum plays such as *What the Women Did* may not have been staged even in fringe theatres meaning there is scope to be 'cautiously optimistic' that continued interest during the centenary will lead to continuous discussion and reflection on what has become the dominant narrative of the war.[53] Southwark Playhouse did not simply commemorate the First World War, but placed women as the protagonists in war stories. This is why it is important to pay attention to those representations which attempt to offer something different to the norm. It may be naïve to assume that the dominant narrative will be completely recast as a result, but perhaps a level of plurality and nuance could be achieved. The pupil's question could hopefully become 'what *else* did men and women do during the war?'

Notes

1. The term collective memory has wide ranging applications and connotations within scholarship. Indeed, scholars have tried to make the terminology more specific by suggesting other phrases are more pertinent such as 'cultural memory', 'popular memory' or 'historical remembrance'. In the following article Wulf Kansteiner's definition will be followed in which collective memory is understood as 'shared communications about the meaning of the past that are anchored in the life-worlds of individuals who partake in the communal life of the respective collective'. This definition suggests the use of collective memory includes a vast array of groups from families to national consortiums and takes into consideration numerous methods and means of 'communication': Wulf Kansteiner (2002) Finding Meaning in Memory: a methodological critique of collective memory studies, *History and Theory*, 41(2), pp. 188–189. For further discussion of collective memory in its various forms see for example: Mary Fulbrook (2014) History Writing and 'Collective Memory', in Stefan Berger & Bill Niven (Eds) *Writing the History of Memory* (London: Bloomsbury), pp. 65–88; Jay Winter (2006) *Remembering War: the Great War between memory and history in the twentieth century* (New Haven: Yale University Press); Lucy Noakes (1998) *War and the British: gender, memory and national identity, 1939–1991* (London: I.B. Tauris).
2. Rosa Maria Bracco (1993) *Merchants of Hope: British middlebrow writers and the First World War, 1919–1939* (Oxford: Berg), p. 1; Gary Sheffield (2002) *Forgotten Victory: the First World War: myths and realities* (London: Review), p. 3; Gary Sheffield (1996) 'Oh! What a Futile War': representations of the Western Front in modern British media and popular culture, in Ian Stewart & Susan Carruthers (Eds) *War, Culture and the Media: representations of the military in 20th-century Britain* (Madison: Fairleigh Dickinson University Press), p. 55.
3. Janet Watson (2004) *Fighting Different Wars: experience, memory, and the First World War in Britain* (Cambridge: Cambridge University Press), p. 306.
4. Susan Bennett (1997) *Theatre Audiences: a theory of production and reception*, 2nd Edn (London: Routledge), p. vii.
5. Brian Bond (2002) *The Unquiet Western Front: Britain's role in literature and history* (Cambridge: Cambridge University Press), p. 51.
6. Arthur Marwick (1998) *The Sixties: cultural revolution in Britain, France, Italy, and the United States, c.1958–c.1974* (Oxford: Oxford University Press), p. 635.
7. Tony Howard & John Stokes (1996) Introduction, in Tony Howard & John Stokes (Eds) *Acts of War: the representation of military conflict on the British stage and television since 1945* (Aldershot: Scholar Press), p. 21.
8. Bond, *The Unquiet Western Front*, p. 54.
9. Dan Todman (2005) *The Great War: myth and memory* (London: Hambledon & London), p. 224.
10. Alan Clark (1961) *The Donkeys* (London: Hutchinson), p. 183; A. J. P. Taylor (1963) *The First World War: an illustrated history* (London: Hamish Hamilton), p. 148. Academic history on the First World War underwent revision in the 1990s. This has led scholars such as Gary Sheffield to reach the conclusion that the war should not be viewed as futile as the 'army won the greatest series of victories in British military history' against a Germany which was 'a brutal, militarist, expansionist state'. However, revisionist historians, such as Ian Beckett, have bemoaned the fact that this academic perspective has not seeped through into collective memory: Sheffield, *Forgotten Victory*, p. xvii; Gary Sheffield (2014) The Centenary of the First World War: an unpopular view, *Historian*, 122, p. 23; Ian Beckett (1997) The Military Historian and the Popular Image of the Western Front, 1914–1918, *The Historian*, 53, pp. 11–14.

11. *Oh What a Lovely War*, dir. Joan Littlewood (Theatre Workshop, 1963). The success of *Oh What a Lovely War* is demonstrated by it winning the Evening Standard Drama Award, sharing the Théâtre des Nations prize with Peter Brook's *King Lear* and being turned into a film by Sir Richard Attenborough in 1969: Nadine Holdsworth (2011) *Joan Littlewood's Theatre* (Cambridge: Cambridge University Press), p. 24. *Oh! What a Lovely War*, dir. Richard Attenborough (Accord Productions, 1969).

12. Christa Hämmerle, Oswald Überegger & Birgitta Bader-Zaar (2014) Introduction: women's and gender history of the First World War, in Christa Hämmerle, Oswald Überegger & Birgitta Bader-Zaar (Eds) *Gender and the First World War* (Basingstoke: Palgrave Macmillan), p. 1; Susan R. Grayzel (2002) *Women and the First World War* (Oxon: Routledge), p. 4.

13. This builds upon research conducted as part of the author Amanda Phipps's PhD thesis 'Learning through Performance: Theatre, Education and the First World War at the Beginning of the Centenary Moment' (2017). The author's research examines how pupils in Britain learnt about the First World War through performance at the beginning of the centenary. Consequently, schools in different geographical locations were consulted, with observations and interviews being conducted with pupils and teachers about the conflict and cultural outputs. This research found that the role of women was often understudied, giving way to the main curriculum focus of trench warfare.

14. Author's observation of a Southwark school's Year 9 history lesson, 8 January 2015. See Phipps, 'Learning through Performance'.

15. Catriona Pennell (2012) Popular History and Myth-Making: the role and responsibility of First World War historians in the centenary commemorations, 2014–2018, *Historically Speaking*, 13(5), p. 14; Catriona Pennell (2014) On the Frontlines of Teaching the History of the First World War, *Teaching History*, 155, p. 38.

16. See for example *14–18 Now: WW1 centenary art commissions* (2014) <http://www.1418now. org.uk/> accessed 5 January 2015.

17. David Cameron (2012) Speech at Imperial War Museum on First World War Centenary Plans, 11 October 2012, *Gov.uk* <https://www.gov.uk/government/speeches/speech-at-imperial-war-museum-on-first-world-war-centenary-plans> accessed 24 June 2014; 14–18 NOW (2014) About Us, *14–18 NOW* <https://www.1418now.org.uk/about/> accessed 21 March 2015.

18. Interestingly, *The Crimson Field*'s writer had prepared four series of the drama (one for each year of the centenary), but the show was cancelled after just one series. The B.B.C. said space needed to be made for other programmes: Ben Dowell, 'BBC1 axes First World War drama The Crimson Field', *RadioTimes*, 10 June 2014 <http://www.radiotimes.com/news/2014-06-10/bbc1-axes-first-world-war-drama-the-crimson-field> accessed 17 May 2016.

19. Women are covered in the 'Life at Home' section of the exhibition; the Imperial War Museum's website explains that the gallery would help visitors 'uncover the contribution women made in factories, hospitals and elsewhere to keep the troops fed and fighting': Imperial War Museum London, 'Exhibition: First World War Galleries', *Imperial War Museums* <http://www.iwm.org.uk/exhibitions/iwm-london/first-world-war-galleries> accessed 18 May 2016.

20. Heritage Lottery Fund (2013) Hospital under Canvas: Millicent Sutherland's ambulance in the Great War, *Heritage Lottery Fund* <https://www.hlf.org.uk/our-projects/hospital-under-canvas-millicent-sutherlands-ambulance-great-war> accessed 8 July 2016; Heritage Lottery Fund (2013) Gas Girls: women workers in Avonmouth WW1 mustard gas factories: community theatre, film, booklet, exhibition <https://www.hlf.org.uk/our-projects/gas-girls-women-workers-avonmouth-ww1-mustard-gas-factories-community-theatre-film> accessed 13 December 2015.

21. Ana Carden-Coyne (2015) Masculinity and the Wounds of the First World War: a centenary reflection, *Revue Française de Civilisation Britannique*, 20(1), pp. 5–6.

22. Phipps, 'Learning through Performance'.

23. *War Horse*, dir. Marianne Elliott & Tom Morris (National Theatre, 2007). National Theatre War Horse (2014) Learning, *National Theatre War Horse* <http://www.warhorseonstage.

com/learning/> accessed 10 November 2014; *Regeneration*, dir. Simon Godwin (Royal & Derngate and Touring Consortium Theatre Company, 2014); Royal & Derngate Northampton Regeneration (2014) Resources, *Royal and Derngate* <http://www.royalandderngate.co.uk/Productions/201314/105105/Regeneration> accessed 1 September 2014.

24. *Journey's End*, dir. David Grindley (Lee Menzies, 2011); *Oh What a Lovely War*, dir. Terry Johnson (Theatre Royal Stratford East, 2014).

25. *The Muddy Choir*, dir. Natalie Wilson (Theatre Centre, 2014).

26. Simon Jenkins, '1914: The Great War has become a nightly pornography of violence', *Guardian*, 4 August 2014 <http://www.theguardian.com/commentisfree/2014/aug/04/1914-first-world-war-pornography-violence-centenary-military-propaganda> accessed 29 September 2014.

27. Carden-Coyne, 'Masculinity and the Wounds', p. 6. Notable performances which showed alternative narratives of the war in 2014 and 2015 were *Sepoy's Salute* by Big Brum Theatre in Education Company and school performances led by Trench Brothers. Big Brum and Trench Brothers are relatively small education performance companies. This suggests that similarly to female-focused productions, representations of non-British soldiers in the war may appear more regularly in alternative and fringe theatres and require further scholarly exploration. *Sepoy's Salute*, dir. Big Brum (Big Brum, 2015); Trench Brothers (2015) Performance, *HMDT Music* <http://www.hmdt.org.uk/hmdtmusic/trenchbrothers/> accessed 8 September 2015.

28. *The Christmas Truce*, dir. Erica Whyman (Royal Shakespeare Company, 2014); *Doctor Scroggy's War*, dir. John Dove (Shakespeare's Globe, 2014).

29. Michael Billington, 'The Christmas Truce Review: uneasy family show about the tragic war', *Guardian*, 10 December 2014 <http://www.theguardian.com/stage/2014/dec/10/the-christmas-truce-review> accessed 7 January 2016; Stephen Collins, 'Review: the Christmas Truce, RSC', *BritishTheatre.com*, 2 February 2015 <http://britishtheatre.com/review-the-christmas-truce-rsc-2stars/> accessed 7 January 2016.

30. Marc Calvini-Lefebvre (2015) The Great War in the History of British Feminism: debates and controversies, 1914 to the present, *Revue Française de Civilisation Britannique*, 20(1), p. 6.

31. Michael Gove, 'Why Does the Left Insist on Belittling True British Heroes?', *Daily Mail*, 2 January 2014 <http://www.dailymail.co.uk/debate/article-2532930> accessed 24 June 2014.

32. *Out of the Cage*, dir. Alex McSweeney (Fine Line in association with Robyn Keynes, 2015).

33. *Flowers of the Forest*, dir. Anthony Biggs (Jermyn Street Theatre, 2014).

34. Southwark Playhouse Theatre Company, 'History', *Southwark Playhouse Theatre Company* <http://southwarkplayhouse.co.uk/about/history/> accessed 4 February 2016.

35. *Johnny Got His Gun*, dir. David Mercatali (Metal Rabbit, 2014); *What the Women Did*, dir. Tricia Thorns (Two's Company, 2014).

36. Two's Company (2014) Forgotten Voices from the Great War: *What the Women Did*, a triple bill of plays about the First World War (*What the Women Did* Southwark Playhouse Programme).

37. For an overview of plays scripted and performed during the First World War see: Hienz Kosok (2007) *The Theatre of War: the First World War in British and Irish drama* (Basingstoke: Palgrave Macmillan); Gordon Williams (2003) *British Theatre in the Great War: a revaluation* (London: Continuum).

38. Karen Hunt (2014) A Heroine at Home: the housewife on the First World War home front, in Maggie Andrews & Janis Lomas (Eds) *The Home Front in Britain: images, myths and forgotten experiences since 1914* (Basingstoke: Palgrave Macmillan), p. 73.

39. Maggie Andrews has stated that 'during the conflict, the home and women's associated domestic and emotional responsibilities for nurturing and supporting men were sustained, reworked, stretched and developed in Britain': Maggie Andrews with thanks to Layla Byron (2014) Ideas and Ideals of Domesticity and Home in the First World War, in Andrews & Lomas, *The Home Front in Britain*, p. 6.

40. Sos Eltis (2015) From Sex-war to Factory Floor: theatrical depictions of women's work during the First World War, in Andrew Maunder (Ed) *British Theatre and the Great War, 1914–1919* (Basingstoke: Palgrave Macmillan), pp. 116–117.

41. Katherine Cockin (2015) Edith Craig and the Pioneer Players: London's international art theatre in a 'khaki-clad and khaki-minded world', in Maunder, *British Theatre and the Great War*, pp. 121, 122.
42. Andrew Maunder (2015) Introduction: rediscovering First World War theatre, in Maunder, *British Theatre and the Great War*, p. 19.
43. Eltis, 'From Sex-war to Factory Floor', p. 114.
44. Michael Billington, 'What the Women Did: Review', *Guardian*, 26 January 2014 <http://www.theguardian.com/stage/2014/jan/26/what-women-did-review> accessed 4 February 2016.
45. Jane Shilling, 'What the Women Did, Southwark Playhouse, Review', *Telegraph*, 26 January 2016 <http://www.telegraph.co.uk/culture/theatre/theatre-reviews/10597757/What-the-Women-Did-Southwark-Playhouse-review.html> accessed 4 February 2016.
46. Caroline Jowett, 'What the Women Did Review: a poignant look at the impact of First World War', *Express*, 29 January 2014 <http://www.express.co.uk/entertainment/theatre/456803/What-The-Women-Did-review-A-poignant-look-at-the-impact-of-First-World-War> accessed 4 February 2016.
47. Daisy Bowie-Sell, 'What the Women Did', *Time Out*, 10 December 2013 <http://www.timeout.com/london/theatre/what-the-women-did> accessed 4 February 2016.
48. Phipps, 'Learning through Performance'.
49. Author's email correspondence with history teacher from Richmond (30 January 2015).
50. Park Theatre, 'About Us', *Park Theatre* <https://www.parktheatre.co.uk/about-us> accessed 5 February 2016.
51. Paul Lay, 'Let's Get Serious about the First World War', *History Today* blog post, 29 April 2014 <www.historytoday.com/blog/2014/04/lets-get-serious-about-first-world-war> accessed 8 March 2016; Jonathan Boff, 'Ready to be Dazzled?', *Jonathan Boff: Thoughts on the First World War* blog post, 29 March 2014 <https://jonathanboff.wordpress.com/2014/03/29/ready-to-be-dazzled/> accessed 8 March 2016; Gary Sheffield, 'Put that Light out, Napoleon!', *Gary Sheffield: Military Historian* blog post, 2 April 2014 <http://www.garysheffield-historian.com/?page_id=12> accessed 8 March 2016.
52. Boff, 'Ready to be Dazzled?'
53. Pennell, 'Popular History and Myth-Making', p. 13.

Disclosure statement

No potential conflict of interest was reported by the author.

Index

Note: Figures are indicated by *italic* text.